BETWEEN
FRIENDS

BETWEEN FRIENDS

Edited by
Mickey Pearlman

HOUGHTON MIFFLIN COMPANY

BOSTON   NEW YORK

1994

ACKNOWLEDGMENTS

I would like to reiterate here the continuing importance to me of those friends previously named in the acknowledgments of other books, and to express my gratitude to some heretofore unheralded: my lawyer, Lois Lipton; Michael Schorndorf; Joann Weber; Edie Salk; Frieda Aranoff; Carl Parisi; and Toby Weingarten. I want especially to thank Alan Andres, my editor, who realized early that "we may be entering a time in which the importance of seemingly modest virtues like friendship and honesty will be emphasized and valued in ways we have otherwise neglected."

CONTENTS

Introduction MICKEY PEARLMAN xiii

The Valley of Lost Things MARGOT LIVESEY 1

Nones MICHELLE CLIFF 15

Cathy, Now and Then JILL MCCORKLE 28

Can Writers Have Friends? JANE SMILEY 44

*Best Friend, My Wellspring
in the Wilderness!* CAROLYN SEE 56

The Ginger Dreams ANGELA DAVIS-GARDNER 74

Road Trip: The Real Thing JAYNE ANNE PHILLIPS 85

Where People Know Me SYLVIA WATANABE 94

The Ties that Wound WENDY WASSERSTEIN 109

GirlGirlGirl CONNIE PORTER 114

An Unsolved Mystery JOYCE CAROL OATES 125

Understanding Julien SHIRLEY ABBOTT 129

A Friend in Man MEG PEI 149

The Village Watchman TERRY TEMPEST WILLIAMS 162

Stripes MELINDA WORTH POPHAM 171

Friendship's Gift CHRISTINE O'HAGAN 185

The Friendship Tarot NANCY WILLARD 195

Shall We Dance?
Confessions of a Fag Hag PHYLLIS ROSE 204

Old Friends Are Best JANETTE TURNER HOSPITAL 214

Ringing the Net SUSAN KENNEY 236

Biographical Notes 245

INTRODUCTION

ALTHOUGH I DO HAVE several rusting whisks in my kitchen (along with the obligatory *bain-marie* and assorted ramekins and *timbales*), on the subject of French cooking I know *rien*, and I probably couldn't tell a successful *soufflé glacé* from a failed *Bûche de Noël*. So it has always struck me as surprising that I count Julia Child as my hero — not, I should add, for her usually complicated recipes. It's her simple credo that I like: "Life, itself, is the proper binge."

No doubt Ms. Child was thinking about more than *bon appetit* here: she was encouraging all of us, not just the Cuisinart crew, to leave the kitchen and concentrate instead on the meal, and to take along with us as co-diners those people we call friends. They, I am sure she would agree, have more to do with real nourishment than even the most *superlatif* of Julia's culinary creations.

For writers, of course, her recipe has special resonance since "the proper binge" is, in fact, itself the food of literature. The ingredients of the text are simply observed experience, memory, character, and plot, and the vicissitudes and exaltations of quotidian experience. And since a binge yields no plot at all without binge partners — as a story falls flat without characters — friends and the subject of friendship are the writer's batter and *roux*.

. . . .

Of course there is a downside to this as well. As Jane Smiley points out in "Can Writers Have Friends?", she "never met anyone who was depicted in a story or an essay who wasn't at least somewhat disturbed by the experience . . . Maybe the real question is, why do writers always end up writing about their friends, and since they do, is it actually possible for them to have friends?"

In spite of Smiley's hesitation, what becomes clear in *Between Friends* is that being a writer and the idea of friendship are linked in the writer's mind, probably, as Angela Davis-Gardner suggests, because "honesty in friendship and in writing are related." Whatever differences exist among the writers represented here — who come from various ethnic and racial groups, and with different political agendas and geographical sympathies — that connection recurs repeatedly. The result is that many of the essays are as much about the experience of being a writer as they are about friendship.

Like many writers, those represented here live for the most part in self-imposed isolation, sometimes actual and sometimes emotional, with a created space between themselves and the imagined and real experiences they are transforming into prose. In fact, the decision to write (in spite of jobs, husbands, lovers, kids) is itself a divergence from so-called "real life," as readers envision it, since real life is largely dependent on daily shared experience and on participation outweighing observation. One could even speculate that most writers — who spend many of their days in front of computers in otherwise unoccupied rooms — neither seek nor tolerate the kind of everyday contact on which most friendships rely. Instead a writer's friends are often those people who allow her the freedom to escape for long periods from exactly those aspects of real life about which she is writing. Writers and their friends become participants in a do-not-disturb contract that can seem invisible to the observer. The result of this often unspoken noninvasion pact is that when writers begin to write essays about friendship, what emerges is less about office politics, shared shopping trips, and car pools, and more about an abstract concept that is nurtured by memory, exists in recollection, and invokes the past.

It seems almost simplistic to say that the very choice to allow yourself to *be* a writer (since most writers believe that you can only become a better one), grows somehow from the ineradicable detritus of remembered pain. As Angela Davis-Gardner reminds us, the writer Jean Rhys said that "writing is consolation therapy," or the need, as Michelle Cliff remarks, "to explain myself to myself." This may illuminate why writers become connected to the friend-as-affirmer, often another writer, who allays the anxiety about bad reviews, poor sales, or the worry about whether the work is any good and if someone will actually read it. Unlike the connections in most friendships, many of these are long-distance relationships since writers live everywhere. In fact, all of us could have easily written essays on mail (including E) and phone friendships. The baby Bells, now gargantuan mothers, love every one of us.

Consolation does not take the issue far enough, however. After reading many of the essays in *Between Friends,* one can hardly escape the conclusion that most of these essays are wrapped around the reality of pain and loss, the need for refuge, and the reality of loneliness. The idea of difference, of the writer's usually skewed angle of vision on the world, reverberates in each essay; Jayne Anne Phillips's *Thelma and Louise* trip, for instance, depends as much on her shared feelings of suffocating motherhood as it does on adventure; Jill McCorkle's funny reminiscences of Cathy, her friend since childhood, evolve from that time when divergence spelled disaster; and Melinda Worth Popham's remembrance of times past, triggered by her thirtieth high school reunion, catalogs some unresolved dreams. Remembered pain surfaces in a particularly powerful way in Angela Davis-Gardner's story of Ginger, "a powerful specter of a not-friend" who was the "sun around which the inner circle revolved" — a circle from which Davis-Gardner was pointedly excluded.

Many of these essays depend not only on the reconfigured past but, in spite of a fictionalized and sometimes amazing grace, on what was lost and has not been found. Oates's "An Unsolved Mystery" is a case in point — a journey back almost forty years to the suicide of her childhood friend in May of their freshman year in college. Although as editor I did not anticipate *this* response to *this* subject, as Oates's title suggests, the memory of a friendship lingers long after the friend has died. Oates writes: "Many years after my friend Barbara's death, I still think of her with a stir of hope and dread. As if she hasn't died yet. As if there might be something I could do to prevent her dying."

What was lost reverberates too in Margot Livesey's account of her almost insufferably lonely Scottish childhood in a place she calls the Valley of Lost Things, and of the impact of that solitude on her life today. She has discovered that friends offer "that greatest of luxuries . . . the possibility of a life beyond my own." After a childhood almost devoid of friends of either gender, she realizes now that "women friends do play a role in the plot of my life; even more, they are part of the deeper theme."

Shirley Abbott also writes about loss; in "Understanding Julien" she acknowledges the impact of a friend who has simply disappeared: "Bill James, where are you? Phone home." Like the Barbara of Oates's piece, he is very much a presence in Abbott's mind. She writes, "Perhaps I'd never have become a writer without him — for he assured me that I could write . . . [and] when Bill James said I was a writer, it was different from when my father or my English teacher said it."

Several of the writers do recount the childhood friends who have not been lost, their "wellsprings in the wilderness," as Carolyn See calls them. And, to my surprise, Michelle Cliff was one among several contributors who wrote about lasting friendships with family members. This was a connection I did not expect when *Between Friends* was formulated, since in my mind, at least, family and friends were combinable but distinct, like a warmed croissant and a *café crème.*

This idea of family-as-friend also reverberates in Meg Pei's piece about her father, and again when Sylvia Watanabe writes about her mother and her 108-year-old Big Grandma. With great affection Watanabe quotes her mother, who explained, "'Your grandmother and I were never friends . . . it would never have occurred to us to be friends. That wasn't how it was.' . . . She explains that children were bound to their parents by duty and gratitude. Then she smiles. 'Isn't t a pity that all that's changed?'" Both Cliff and Watanabe describe exactly a generational space that often allows an older relative to befriend a younger member of the family with ease and a certain kind of freedom.

There are also several essays whose emotional genesis grows from a sense of place. Connie Porter writes about growing up in the projects near Buffalo, New York, and about both white and black friends, when they were girls together. Janette Turner Hospital remembers her childhood rival in Brisbane, Australia, who is now a physicist on the verge of a Nobel. She celebrates the old friendships that "are part of muscle and blood . . . of a different order altogether . . . tattoos are easier to erase than the grooves these leave in a life." While not denigrating newer friendships, Hospital says that she and her friend "have intimate knowledge of each other's vulnerabilities, so there is never any pretense, any façade, any face-saving, any need for it." Christine O'Hagan's understanding of friendship also grows from her childhood, this time in an Irish-American neighborhood in Queens, New York. O'Hagan writes of her character in *Benediction at the Savoia*, Delia Delaney, modeled on one of her mother's friends. She writes, too, about her friendship with her own characters: "At least, I thought bitterly, at least you'd think they'd have the decency to write and let me know how they are."

All of these ideas — family, place, loss, consolation, and pain — commingle finally in Susan Kenney's essay, which closes the collection, about the friends who were so supportive during her husband's long battle with cancer. They came often, "in ripples, in waves, a creative tide of helping hands and hearts . . . caring for us and about us."

In a letter from Shirley Abbott about the writing of her essay, she said that she had to "dig new wells for this one." Regarding friendship evoked from all of us previously untapped and unexpected stories, but also energized the deeper and sometimes disturbing memories that accompany our developed facility with description, plot, and character. Editing this collection has reminded me again of Shakespeare's admonition that the past is prologue, and that thinking about our friends and our friendships forces an encounter with the ongoing evolution of one's life.

Itself, as Julia said, the proper binge.

MICKEY PEARLMAN

BETWEEN
FRIENDS

𝔁 𝔁 𝔁 𝔁 𝔁 𝔁 𝔁 𝔁 𝔁 𝔁 𝔁 𝔁 𝔁

The Valley of Lost Things

IN THE FIFTEENTH-CENTURY Italian epic poem *Orlando Furioso*, the hero, Orlando, goes mad. His friend, Ariosto, makes one of the first space voyages recorded in literature. He travels to the moon and there he makes his way to the Valley of Lost Things. After some searching he finds Orlando's missing wits. He brings them back to earth and returns them to Orlando whose sanity is thus restored. Neither of them seems to feel that Ariosto's journey is excessive.

This image of friendship between men is one of many in literature: David and Jonathan, Achilles and Patroclus, Tom Sawyer and Huck Finn. The names come down to us irrevocably linked. But what of friendship between women? Of course there are women friends, often cast in a familial relationship like Jane Austen's sisters, but even now, after nearly a century of votes for women, a novel like E. M. Forster's *Howards End*, in which a friendship between two women is crucial to the plot, is unusual.

It shames me to admit that this trend is mirrored in my own small body of work. In only one or two of my stories is friendship between women the central issue. Mostly my characters, men and women, struggle with familial or romantic problems. A short biographical note might suggest that this is true in my own life, too. The major turning points have been about romance and work. The former brought me from Scotland to North America; the latter keeps me here. But the note would be both accurate and misleading. I think of what I say to my writing students about plot and theme: the outward shape of events and the inner meaning. My women friends do play a role in the plot of my life; even more, they are part of the deeper theme.

My earliest coherent memory is of kneeling beside my friend Sally, making mud pies. I remember the texture of the mud — lumpy, a little gritty, just right to squeeze into shape — and that the sun was shining, but this was in Scotland so I doubt if the day was warm. We had rolled up our sleeves and were working with serious busyness. Later I remember the row that greeted me when I returned home. But probably I was scolded less severely than Sally who was a year older and ought to know better.

I said above that there was a lack of models for women's friendship in literature. If one broadens the arena to include children's books, however, then the situation improves dramatically. The heroines of *Anne of Green Gables, What Katy Did,* and *Little Women* know all about being friends. There are even encouraging and wonderful examples of friendship between boys and girls such as *The Secret Garden* or *The Princess and Curdie.* Sally and I were both ardent readers and with the help of these books, we transformed our daily tasks — building huts and bridges, climbing trees, fishing, teasing the bull, searching for tadpoles — into heroic activities.

Even more immediate models for our friendship were offered in weekly comics. I subscribed to *Bunty,* Sally to *Princess.* Both publications were filled with stories about groups of friends — girls who joined circuses, schooled horses, took over the family business during an emergency. When I last looked on the newsstand a couple of years ago, my favorite serial, "The Four Marys," was still running. The Marys attended a school called St. Bea's and together triumphed over many adversities. Although their hairstyles had changed and they now said "cool" instead of "golly," the girls looked and sounded remarkably as they had thirty years ago.

Part of the attraction of the four Marys was that they occupied a world so different from mine. Sally and I were in a severe minority, both as children and as girls. Our fathers taught at a boys' public school on the edge of the Scottish Highlands. The school was in the valley of Glenalmond, ten miles from the nearest town. The vast majority of the teachers, all men, were in the bachelor tradition and besides myself, Sally, and her three siblings, there were few other children, and those not quite the right age. Of course Sally and I could not attend the boys' school, but made the daily journey over the hills to the town of Crieff and Morrison's Academy for Girls. We both soon had groups of friends, but only within the playground. Going to someone's house after school, for example, was impossible. The shadow of petrol rationing hung over our childhoods and people did not drive ten miles casually, especially on the winding roads.

At that time I did not mind or even notice our isolation. My childhood was governed by my parents, but everything that sustained me came from Sally's family. They lived a few hundred yards away and I ran in and out of their house all day long, unthinkingly, until at the age of eight I left the valley. My father took a new job, at a boys' prep school near a small village in the Borders of Scotland. I attended a private girls' school called Craigmount. Although I was upset to leave Glenalmond I was also excited about our move. It made me feel different and important. On my last day at Morrison's Academy my form mistress, Miss Cameron, a tiny spherical woman who looked as if she had been dipped in powder like a donut, presented me with a copy of *Robinson Crusoe*. In the back of the car going south I read it intermittently and daydreamed about startling achievements and popularity.

Neither occurred. Craigmount was a boarding school and I was among a handful of day pupils. Placed in a class of girls three or four years older than myself, I was a miserable out-cast. The biggest problem was sex. By the time I first met them most of my classmates were acquainted with puberty. They had breasts and periods, wore bras, used deodorants — matters of which I knew nothing. These were subjects of conversation and teasing. Soon after I arrived I remember at the end of lunch being called into the classroom. A mob of girls was holding a girl called Helen. She was quite plump with beautiful, thick, red-gold hair worn in pigtails. They had removed her cardigan, tie, shirt and vest.

"Come here," they said. "This is a bra." And then, with appropriate gestures, "This is what's under it."

I remember the astonishing whiteness of her skin, the pinkness of her nipple. I backed away but did not dare to leave the room. What was truly baffling was that Helen did not seem afraid, and later in geography, the first class after lunch, was cheerful and talkative. I stared at her in amazement.

For the next four years I hid from my classmates. Once, in a moment of particular desperation, I dropped a heavy radiator on my foot in order to avoid being cornered by them. I succeeded in breaking a small bone which saved me for a fortnight. Then I went back to skulking in the library.

At Glenalmond I had taken my parents for granted. In our new home I began to realize how different they were from other parents. For one thing, they were elderly; my father had married for the first time at fifty and after my mother's early death had remarried a woman close to his own age. For another, they had no friends. This had been true all along, but at Glenalmond I had failed to notice. It did not occur to me as odd that I went daily to Sally's house and that they never crossed the threshold. When my father came to collect me, he sat outside in his car, hooting the horn until I emerged. At the time of our move to the village my stepmother purchased the ugliest sofa I had ever seen, a suety-brown object from which even the walls of our living room seemed to retreat. When I think of my parents, I see them side by side on this sofa. deep in a crossword puzzle or a television program. There was no room for anyone else.

My parents did not simply not help me to make friends. They actively raised obstacles. Inviting anyone to our house was too much trouble. Once I had cleaned my room, done the shopping, cut the lawn, and washed the car, I was expected to entertain myself. They never seemed to notice my loneliness. Now I watch with pleasure, and some amazement, the lengths to which my friends go to accommodate their children — the endless rounds of visits, games, music lessons — all as if such things were perfectly natural.

My nearest approximations to friendship were the Miller sisters who lived at 14 Riverside Drive; I lived at number 8. There were three of them, one older, one younger, and one around my age — pretty, musical girls. They also attended Craigmount and on them the dark green uniform looked pleasing, even elegant; mine had been purchased, like most of my clothes, with the notion that I would grow into it. In the mornings I would watch the sisters playing the piano and doing each other's hair as I waited for them to come out and walk with me to the school bus. Especially in cold weather, when my breath puffed like a dragon's and my knees turned blue, their living room glowed with Dickensian warmth.

I had been in the village for a couple of years when the Millers invited me to join the Lily of the Valley Club. I was thrilled. I remember writing to Sally about it with glee. The girls in *Bunty* were always founding secret societies and clubs. We met on Saturday afternoons and sang our club song and set ourselves various tasks — mostly raising funds for the club, which we spent on cupcakes and special notebooks. Once we made an outing to one of the many abbeys in that part of Scotland, Melrose perhaps, or Jedburgh.

What I remember most vividly about those afternoons is sitting at their dining room table, feeling part of the scene I had watched so often through the window, and how lively their house seemed, full of plants and music and piles of clothes waiting to be ironed. Our house was always orderly and quiet. Now I realize that the Millers too must have been in straitened circumstances. That I was the fourth member of the club was a bad sign. And although their house seemed full of life, it was only the three sisters and their mother. No visitors there either. My parents murmured that Mrs. Miller was divorced, but neither she nor her daughters ever alluded to this.

After the initial excitement it was clear that the club was not going to change my life. At the end of our meetings Mrs. Miller would usher me, firmly, out of the house. With my enormous, transparent needs I must have been a threatening guest. Sometimes nowadays on a bus or train I will begin talking to a fellow passenger. At first the conversation proceeds along normal lines; the scenery, how late we are. Then, often quite abruptly, more intimate topics will be touched on: families, jobs, difficult history. My fellow passenger leans toward me. As I edge away, I think of my childhood self.

Besides the three sisters, other possibilities for friendship in the village were as limited as they had been at Glenalmond. Several score of children attended the village school but I might more easily have walked on water than become friends with them. The reason was simple: I was middle-class and they were lower-class. My stepmother dismissed them as "common," a word she also used in correcting me. "Don't be common," she would scold if she caught me eating with just a fork, or saying "pardon." For a few weeks some of the village boys waited to throw stones at me as I went to buy the newspaper. Unlike my tortures at Craigmount, I felt perfectly free to report this to my parents. They took the matter up with the headmaster of the school and the stoning stopped. I did not regard it as any kind of loss.

This period of desolation which lasted from the age of eight to the age of twelve seemed endless and, in the midst of my loneliness, I turned to animals. At home, the family dog was a crucial ally. Typical of our failed middle-class aspirations, Speckie was a pedigree dog — a border terrier — but a runt. She was snaggle-toothed, had uneven ears and a crooked tail, and she smiled often with great sweetness. She performed for me the immense favor of eating the meat I loathed which appeared on my plate every night. In return I abused her horribly. I remember a prolonged attempt to teach her to ride my bicycle and another, equally disastrous, to persuade her to jump through a hoop. One summer afternoon I came home from the swimming pool and my parents announced that she had been put to sleep. A month later they acquired a new dog, a small black and white terrier who was their ally, not mine. My stepmother named him, for no obvious reason, Bran. Periodically he tried to bite me.

My other animal friends lived at Chrissie's farm. I discovered the farm on the outskirts of the village during my first days of exploring and loitered around until Chrissie, out of the goodness of her heart, invited me in. For the four years we lived in the village, scarcely a day passed without my going to help her feed the hens and take care of the animals. I befriended the Muscovy duck, a horse called Ginger, a succession of cats, and a pet calf, whom I called Cornelius after the centurion in the Bible. He had wonderful dark eyes with immense sweeping eyelashes and sometimes, when I was leaving him, he cried. Or so I described the watering of his eyes. I cannot recall what became of him; I fear the worst.

These friendships led to an annual struggle with my parents. I had read somewhere that at midnight on Christmas Eve animals had the power of human speech. Every year I argued passionately against bedtime not because I wanted to see the arrival of Father Christmas — my parents made little effort to support that mythology — but because I wanted to participate in the conversation. Alas, by the time I was allowed to stay up late, my faith had weakened and the animals I addressed yawned, or stared in disappointment at my empty hands.

Although Chrissie's animals were my friends, she herself was not. For one thing she was a grownup. For another, as my use of her Christian name signaled, she was lower class. Throughout my childhood, a number of adults who could be described in this way took pity on me — Chrissie, a woman who cleaned our house, a man who ran the local putting green. My parents viewed such kindness as a matter of *droit de seigneur* and their admonitions to me not to be a nuisance were perfunctory. As far as I know they never met Chrissie. She often sent them presents of hen or duck eggs, and in the spring large bunches of the fragrant purple lilacs which grew beside the farmyard gate. They sent back thanks.

When I was twelve Craigmount closed down. The day this was announced in school assembly remains one of the great radiant moments in my life. There was nowhere else to go to school — the village school was out of the question — and my parents dispatched me to live with Sally's family. There followed a halcyon period. I had little to do with my parents, save a weekly letter. Long-distance phone calls were for emergencies. I returned to Morrison's Academy for Girls. After the dreadful failure of Craigmount I was determined to do better. I was loud, brash, pushy; I pretended to know about sex. I remember being quick to judge a clever girl called Margaret, very good at maths, but with greasy hair. With these credentials I was far from popular, but I escaped ostracism. Again, Sally was my main friend and even after my parents followed me north, I went to her house every weekend.

At university for the first time it was possible for me to get to know people irrespective of my parents' support or the lack thereof. And I did make friends. How crucial that verb seems — to make a friend, to make a story. In doing so I began to discern the possibilities of friendship, although not yet the true dimensions. Friendship still seemed shadowy and pale compared to romance. Like my peers, I was in the grip of what the writer Frank Conroy calls "the emergency of the self."

The year after I finished university I returned to the village. I found the school I hated in ruins. I climbed in a broken window and walked through the rooms, those I had been forbidden to enter and those I had been forced to. In many of them the ceilings had collapsed and flocks of sparrows rose from amongst the rubble. I felt I had got my revenge at last, but uselessly. As for the farm, like the four Marys, after my long absence it looked much the same. I was too shy, too stupid, to go in search of Chrissie.

Years ago, when I read *Bunty* regularly, I failed to notice that a surprisingly large number of the stories were about "orphans." These plucky girls wrestled with difficult stepparents and malicious stepsiblings but were always, finally, triumphantly united with their real parents. The profusion of such stories, three or four per issue, seems to offer clear support for the phenomenon discussed by Freud in his essay "Family Romances." Many children, he claims, pass through a stage in which they imagine that the tediously ordinary people with whom they live are only pretending to be their parents. Their real parents are elsewhere and wonderful.

I do not remember doing this; maybe a happy childhood is a prerequisite for such fantasies. But I did daydream, passionately, about the death of my parents as the only way I would be permitted to join the utopian world of Sally's family. Each time I heard my father hooting his horn outside, I felt that I was being forced to leave a warm, brightly lit party for somewhere cold and bleak. For the last five years of my childhood I went back and forth between my parents, now living in a grim farmhouse, and this other family.

By the time my father did die I was twenty-two and already living away from home. His death and that of my stepmother a few years later had little practical effect on my life. They left neither money nor debts. But in some profound and subtle way, everything changed.

I awoke to the fact that I had no living relatives. I cannot describe what this is like. I used to think it was analogous to being colorblind or tone deaf, an absence of something that most people could happily take for granted. Recently I have felt that a more accurate analogy would suggest something added, not subtracted: perhaps, although this sounds more pretentious than I mean, a little like Cassandra, cursed with an extra dimension of knowledge. This feeling may be quite common or somewhat unusual. I do not know for I have no one with whom I can compare notes. I do meet, alas with increasing frequency, people who have lost their parents, but always there is a sibling or a child. I think often of Oscar Wilde's remark: to lose one parent . . . may be regarded as a misfortune; to lose both looks like carelessness.

And not only parents. When I was seventeen I met someone, a man, who went to the Valley of Lost Things on my behalf — a journey that can never be repaid. He went in search not merely of my missing wits but of my missing self, a self I had not merely lost but never had until he recognized me and stretched out his hand. His journey was one of inspired imagination. It led on my part to a more mundane kind of travel. He lived in North America and I started coming here to see him. I came at first casually, eagerly, having no idea what I was doing. One day in my late twenties I realized that I had made myself into an exile, that I was living between two countries and two cultures, and that I would be hard-pressed now to make my home entirely in either. Unwittingly, it seems, I had recreated in my adult life an image of my childhood, replacing the short distance between Sally's home and my parents' with several thousand miles of ocean.

As if this fragmentation were not enough, I began to earn my living by teaching writing in universities. Simply answering an advertisement I discovered could take me from Boston to the midwest. At the moment I am fortunate enough to have wonderful students and colleagues but I seldom see the people I feel close to in either Britain or America. My daily life is almost as solitary as in the days when I went to Chrissie's farm and in this solitude I appreciate my friends and their absolute and irreplaceable importance in my life. They have become both the curators of my past and the guardians of my future.

One of the main tasks these adult friends faced was to enlarge my narrow idea of conversation. Until the age of twelve conversation played a small part in my life. My parents claimed frequently that a good child should be seen and not heard, and they gave me ample opportunity to practice this. I never, for example, ate supper with them. They had a glass of sherry together on the suety-brown sofa while I sat alone at the kitchen table. With luck I would have smuggled in the dog and a book. This arrangement, which strikes people here as cruel and unusual, seemed to me perfectly natural. Sally and her siblings also ate by themselves in the nursery. When I stayed with them, we read and played racing demon. Occasionally an adult head appeared round the door to tell us to keep the noise down.

Soon after I came to live with them, however, her parents decreed that Sally, her older brother, and I should join them for dinner in the dining room. It was an important step on our journey to adulthood. At family meals the large square table was covered with a tablecloth. Now the dark wood was revealed. We had placemats and coasters for our glasses. The elegance was pleasing but intimidating. Even more intimidating was the business of conversation. After several meals during which I exemplified my parents' dictum, Sally's mother took me to task. My silence was rude, she explained. I must talk to the person on my left, or at the very least encourage them to talk. I nodded, too stunned to answer.

Of course the mere fact of conversing was not enough: choice of topic was vital. Talking about the self especially one's health, did not count as conversation. Nor did gossip. World or local events, a book, an encounter with a farmer, a new theory about Ossian's grave — these were appropriate subjects. Details of some personal misfortune, like a flat tire, were acceptable, but only if converted into an amusing anecdote. Perhaps the stereotype of the British person talking incessantly about the weather stems from this iron rule. In a culture where the question "How are you?" can never be answered truthfully, a fallback position is essential. Sally's parents were both wonderful conversationalists who made these rules seem as natural as breathing. Nowadays, as I struggle with my taciturn characters, I often recall the skill with which they transformed the dullest sows ears into silken stories.

These attitudes toward the self and conversation were not dislodged by university, where most people I encountered had been brought up in the same tradition. I arrived in North America to discover what struck me as a dazzling openness. People talked about themselves. They told me about their childhoods and love affairs. They speculated about their inner lives. And they did not seem to notice that for years I provided an excellent illustration of the classic joke about British psychiatrists: that they have a hard time getting their patients to stop using "one," as in "one's mother was always telling one not to be a nuisance." From my American friends I learned that the self could be a subject of intellectual inquiry.

This difference between the two cultures is lessening, I think, as the years pass, but I still find that my British friends are more hesitant to talk about themselves. I can lay down a whole hand of secrets and have them respond with a nicely turned tale of office politics. For my part, after initial repudiation, I have come to a renewed appreciation of repression. There are things that cannot or should not be told. There are other ways of being friends besides simply pouring out one's heart.

When I do succumb to this North American habit, however, they listen patiently and make suggestions. Why not go to the RSPCA and get a dog? Why not learn something useful, like how to repair accordions or dig wells? They are much less likely than their American counterparts to advocate therapy. Of course therapy is not yet a major tributary in the stream of British middle-class culture. But more, I think, is involved than local customs. My British friends tend to regard problems as something to be endured rather than fixed.

Part of what we are all still enduring in Britain is the class system. Looking back over my childhood, I can see that whole populations of possible friends were annihilated by this system. It permeated the air I breathed, the books I read, the adults around me. When my father died of a heart attack, one of my stepmother's first remarks was how glad she was that she had waited for him, because he was a gentleman.

Like many British people who come to the States, I felt liberated from that inexorable yardstick by which I was judged and found wanting. Here my accent and good manners deceived people. They failed to recognize that I came from the shabby fringes of the middle class. People in Britain knew instantly; it was not only my enormous needs that made Mrs. Miller show me the door.

I found this freedom tremendously exhilarating and I still do, although over the years I have begun to apprehend that matters are not quite so simple as I first thought. Americans may not talk about class, mobility may be easier, but society remains highly codified. Thinking about the people I know, I discover that almost all of them are middle-class. There is an upper class here every bit as aloof as in Britain, and a lower class just as abandoned. But in the final analysis the judgments remain a little less severe, the barriers a little lower.

These two aspects of liberation — into new areas of conversation, out of class — were what made it possible for me to make friends here in a way that I had not previously been able to, and to carry that knowledge back to Britain. But over and above all the lessons of society, I had a teacher. At the age of twenty-five a woman came into my life who taught me how to live in the world, and how to be friends. Our conversation, which I trust will be lifelong, embraces both the self and the other. We talk about the secrets of our hearts and also the topics that Sally's parents regarded as important.

I could tell many stories of exchanging work and sharing pleasure, but what comes to mind is not really a story. Some years ago I went to visit Susan in New England. It was winter, January or February, and she was living in a beautiful, isolated house. We stayed up late that night, talking by the fire. Both our lives were in disarray and no solutions were in sight. Around us on all sides the dark, snowy countryside seemed to echo our sadness. In the morning we went out to my car. The sun was shining and as we stood there, saying goodbye, two deer appeared in the meadow at the back of the house. We watched them lope awkwardly through the deep snow and disappear into the woods. Then we laughed and embraced.

From that first friendship others have followed. Each enriches my life in ways I could not have imagined. I do not have those dark, thorny, inescapable relationships called family and I miss them all the time, but I feel hugely fortunate in what I do have.

Sometimes nowadays people ask me why I write, and although I have practiced articulate answers, my replies are incoherent. No reason seems sufficient; all seem spurious. But part of the answer is that I yearn to escape the narrow confines of my own singular existence. When I try to create a character on the page, that attempt gives me a sense of what it is like to be someone else. Friends, too, offer me that greatest of luxuries in a more profound way — the possibility of a life beyond my own. Ariosto went alone to the Valley of Lost Things on behalf of his friend. My friends go with me, take me with them, and together we bring back what we can.

X X X X X X X X X X X X X

Nones

I DREAM I AM A GIRAFFE. Across a chasm on a deep, safe ledge are my mother and father and sister. They are domesticated animals. I am not. I am on the edge. By myself.

I pay the price for my wildness, my undomesticated nature, my neck which sticks out, my mottled skin. In the dream my mouth splits apart, the jawbones break. I wake weeping.

I pay the price in life as well. I remain undomesticated.

My father used to imprint his hand across my mouth. "You're just like your grandmother."

My grandmother, my father's mother, was another undomesticated being. In some ways, my soulmate.

She was undomesticated in the simplest sense: she had husbands (three, in fact), but she never seemed married.

Her house was well-appointed but never lived-in. She spent little time there.

She vastly preferred restaurants to any meal at home, even if it meant convincing the waiter to take a postdated check. Perhaps that added an extra thrill. She almost invariably announced to me (her frequent dinner companion when I was a child), before we even ordered, that washing dishes might be our fate. It never was. And frankly the possibility never concerned me. I had absolute faith in her ability to make ends meet, or to make the

. . . .

waiter, or the maitre d', or the proprietor, if it came to that, see things her way.

Nor was the warning meant to inhibit our choices. We ordered exactly what we wanted. She was especially pleased that I ate oysters unabashedly at the age of seven.

She loved movement, the faster the better. Her car — and she always had a car of her own, up until her death at eighty-five — was her favorite possession. We called her "Paul Revere" because of her late-night arrivals and departures, often unannounced, always expected; and "Juan Fangio" because of her death-defying driving style.

The first car I remember was a silvery 1950 or so Cadillac with gray wool upholstery; that was succeeded by a jazzy Buick Special, turquoise with chrome portholes; in 1960, as if to commemorate JFK's election and its "youth must be served" message, she got herself a pure white Impala convertible with crimson leather upholstery. She bought the Cadillac in deference to her third husband's political aspirations, I suspect. It was not her style. When he was unsuccessful she reverted to type.

"I watched *The Sun Also Rises*," she wrote me in the eighties. "Read the book years ago. Your grandmother did all those crazy things — dancing on the table, men drinking champagne out of my slippers — I skipped the whoring tho' — Love you — write when you can. Nones."

We met when I was three years old. I'd spent the first years of my life in a large house in Jamaica, whose wide front yard edged Kingston Harbor, where yachts and fishing boats bobbed side by side, where my grandmother's sister took the place of my mother, and became the first love of my life. Her name was Irene and she died of breast cancer in 1950. She was fifty-two; I was three.

Irene and I came to America together. By boat to Florida, then by train to New York City. My first conscious memory is of running my fingers over the wicker of the train seat. My second conscious memory is of meeting my grandmother in Pennsylvania Station. She was wearing high heels with open toes and ankle straps. One strap had broken and the noise, the clack-clack of the loose shoe, overwhelmed any other sound or sight.

In the nuclear cluster of my mother and father and sister, my great-aunt was also the great secret of my life. Her sudden and irrevocable absence, the wreck her death was for me — all was silence. For years.

Dear Michelle —
In all consciousness I could not throw enclosed down the Incinerator — I got rid of all of Irene's things over the holidays — made me feel too miserable — The last day she was in this Country, she took you for a long walk — these hanky's were in her polocoat pocket — you wouldn't go any place without your "han-cur-shif" — I had to *iron* it yet — She made me promise not to ever let anyone hurt you — and I never will. . . . What you do with the hanky's I don't care.

I was sitting at the dining room table when I slit the envelope apart. Three handkerchiefs fell out. One a woman's, two a child's. Without reading the letter I knew what they were. The scent overwhelmed me. Thirty years later, her perfume lingered. I rubbed her scent against my face. Sniffed at the lipstick smudging one corner of her handkerchief.

I am taken back to a January afternoon in New York City. A Sunday, I think. No, I am certain. After church, the time when they take snapshots. I see us as if in a snapshot. Black-and-white and edged in beveled white. Irene tilts her head toward me. I am holding fast to her hand. She is speaking softly, taking her leave. Saying something like, "Be a good girl."

Then, she is gone.

My grandmother guided me through the wreck as best she could. I have a photo album and scrapbook we assembled together in the months after. Forty years have gone by and I, who have spent a lifetime divesting, still keep it, ponder it, study the snapshots: before we came to America, after we came to America; before she went away, after she went away.

This album marks the beginning of our friendship, my grandmother and me, the beginning of her becoming my champion, which she remained her entire life, in accordance with her promise.

My grandmother was an upper-class British West Indian — with a definite accent on the British — a daughter of the Empire and the nineteentn century, though born in 1905. She would be furious that I give the correct date. She believed Oscar Wilde's adage that a woman who would tell her age would tell anything.

A grandmother-granddaughter relationship was foreign in the world she knew, was raised in. One of servants, large houses, racehorses, sugar works, cricket, high tea, planter's punch, and day-long garden parties where ladies slept side-by-side in rooms where the louvers were drawn, avoiding the heat of the day. When the sun set suddenly, as it does in the Caribbean, the games would begin.

She originated in a world where lineage was only partly revealed. Where color was a stain.

She and I, inheritors of all that and more, were now in "this Country," as we referred to America, and grandmothers and granddaughters were best left to the pages of American women's magazines — the fiction of the American landscape — as vibrant, and as absurd, as Aunt Jemima.

We emerged from another fiction, another set of fabulous details. And this was our common ground.

We were joined there, and we were joined in our love for my grandmother's sister.

My grandmother had been an actress in musical comedy. In Jerome Kern's *Showboat* she was a bit player and Helen Morgan's

understudy for the role of Julie, quadroon or octoroon, I forget.
She had been a dancer in the Follies. A *Vogue* model.

In one show she performed a monologue dressed as a pirate,
"I am Adventure," it began, and she recited it to me again and
again, and I never tired of it.

My grandmother was a great beauty, as the expression went.
Pitch-black hair and green-green eyes and skin the color of, at
least, apricot. Her bloodlines as a daughter of the Caribbean
came together in her face, body. Arawak and African and European: the first was apotheosized in one female figure named
Pinto, a sort of renegade, possibly a Maroon; the third was
equally mythified, the trek to Jamaica traceable to 1066.

But she never spoke of the second, and later admitted her regret to me.

She told stories on herself, about the difficulties her beauty
caused.

She actually stopped traffic, her taxicab mobbed by screaming
women (women, mind you) on the day of Rudolph Valentino's
funeral, when she was mistaken for a lover of the Sheik.

She laughed telling the story.

The *bolero* "Ojos Verdes" ("Green Eyes") had been written
for her by a songwriter who was crazy about her. They'd met in
Panama, as I recall; perhaps Cuba. "Poor devil" was her comment. She wore her conquests lightly.

She was pleased with my looks, that I had inherited her
eyes, but I knew from an early age that she believed herself
the apex and was not interested in grooming a successor. That
was fine with me. My face, particularly the tone of my skin,,
was too much the focus of family interest; it made me uncomfortable.

The last time I saw her, her eyes were unavailable to me, as
they had been for some time. She hid them behind dark glasses,
which she wore morning, noon, and night, indoors and out.

I first remember the dark glasses under the big top at the old

Madison Square Garden, during the Ringling Brothers and Barnum & Bailey Circus. I was about eight or nine. The arena was dark except for the flashlights-on-a-string being spun by children in the audience. It was exhilarating, the flashing of light in the huge dark space under a curved roof. The beam of my light glanced across my grandmother's cheek just beneath her glasses, where a bruise was darkening.

I knew enough not to ask.

After the three-ring circus she took me downstairs, past the menagerie, to the sideshow of the Greatest Show on Earth, where I remember a girl of about sixteen or so, born with no arms or legs, writing with a pen fixed in her mouth. They advertised her as a poet, and I believed them.

Later, in one of my favorite restaurants, a place on the West Side called the Spaghetti Kitchen which featured white-hatted men in the window cooking for all to see, I thought more about the bruise under my grandmother's eye. From this distance I can't remember what I thought, although a process had begun. She was becoming more real to me. I glimpsed the woman behind the stories of dancing the Charleston until dawn.

These two memories, my grandmother's bruise and the limbless girl poet, are linked in my mind.

Our family could be the loneliest of places. Outsiders were not suffered gladly; freaks were treated as willful.

Within our kinship system my grandmother and I were two outsiders. This shared identity, or label, drew us together. At family gatherings we sat apart.

"I had thirteen abortions," she tells me one sunny afternoon, sitting in my sister's back yard at a niece's birthday party, amid a detritus of paper plates, half-eaten hot dogs, potato salad sweating in the August heat.

I don't know what to say. "How?"

There are squeals as wrapping paper is torn away and my grandmother's present is revealed, a life-size dollhouse, complete with kitchen. "Enjoy it, honey." She waves in the direction of the birthday girl.

"Oh, they were all arranged by producers, fixers. There were doctors all up and down Broadway, Park Avenue, too. Paid very well."

I notice the tone in her voice, lightening this awful fact, and note in that instant how similar we are.

We are friends, yes, huddling together at one end of this endless family gathering, but there is a formality to our friendship, perhaps born of our origins, the difference in our ages, even as we are able to exchange intimate facts of our lives. I cannot put my hand over hers; nor can she reach for mine.

She smiles instead, sips her highball.

I cannot imagine it no matter her bravado, her assurance to me that sunlit afternoon fifty or sixty years later that "It wasn't so bad." I cannot imagine thirteen abortions at all.

"Some girls killed themselves. Believe me, it wasn't so bad."

I didn't have the heart, or nerve, to ask how the pregnancies happened. She is my friend, I am afraid of hurting her. She is my elder; such a question would be impertinent. It is enough that she told me.

"Your sister tells me you had yourself sterilized."

"What?"

Again, we are at a family gathering, apart from the rest. Easter Sunday perhaps. Fourth of July? Her statement stops me dead.

"She said you had yourself sterilized."

"That's not what happened."

"What then?"

I explain to her that during a period when she and I were out of touch, when I was in college, I got sick. In the middle of the night my parents took me to the emergency room of a local hospital where a resident examined me. He found an extremely high white blood cell count. I asked him if he thought I had appendicitis, which is what I suspected.

Of course, doctors hate to be second-guessed.

"He said he knew what had happened. I'd had an illegal abortion and was paying the price."

He said this in front of my mother. I said he was mistaken. My mother said nothing.

He asked her to leave the examining room.

" 'Okay, she's gone. Now you can tell me.' I'll never forget those words. Those were his exact words."

"That son of a bitch."

"Indeed."

He sent me home with a sleeping pill. I developed peritonitis from a burst appendix, which nearly killed me, and left me sterile.

"Irene's only child died of peritonitis." She slides away for the moment.

"I remember." It was a terrible story. Irene's son was adopted, a little boy about two. She and her husband, a physician, were about to leave for the evening. They lived in Boston. The little boy, running to say goodnight, fell onto an upended three-legged stool. His father examined him and concluded he was okay, put him to bed, administered a sedative, kissed him goodnight. But he wasn't okay. He developed peritonitis and died in a few days. The doctor drank himself to death not long after.

"I was there that night."

This is new information; something has been added.

"I saw him fall; there wasn't even a bruise."

"Oh."

"Someone should speak to your sister."

"Don't bother. I imagine she has her reasons."

She introduced me to the adult female body.

Its terrain was foreign to me. My father was terrified of it, making constant comment often in the form of ridicule, while my mother seemed determined to make its secrecies and wonders invisible, or shameful.

My grandmother walked around naked in front of me, and I remember the joy at a very young age of watching her, and of realizing that this was all right, although I never spoke of it.

Her pitch-black thatch of hair, the fullness of her breasts, but above all the ease with which she waltzed out of the shower, into the master bedroom, and the rituals of adornment, gradually clothing herself — making herself up, as the expression went.

"Do you think I am too old for a lesbian relationship?"

We are at another family gathering, the mother of them all, Christmas, at my grandmother's daughter's house. There is something called a perpetual candle on the table that each year someone insists on lighting.

My grandmother has brought along a friend who has asked her to be her lover.

"Of course not," I respond; it's sometime in the seventies, she's in her sixties.

I don't know what happened. I only know that when I fell in love with a woman and my parents fell away from my contact, my grandmother was staunch. Either my new situation didn't faze her or she had the grace not to show it.

We came closer as I began to write.

I didn't set out to become a writer; I thought it was impossible for someone like me. My response to the armless, legless, girl poet tells me something: after all these years I still think about her, have a photograph of her snapped into my mind.

I began because I wanted to explain myself to myself. What did it mean to come from the place I come from? What did it mean to be able to "pass"? How was the female constructed in the Jamaican landscape, Great House, Quarters? Who were my ancestors and what did I remember of them? All of them.

As it turned out I was exploring crevices in our common ground that had intrigued, concerned, puzzled my grandmother also. But until I said in print what I felt, how the landscape, past, losses pressed into me, she was unable to tell me.

I was terrified to mail the package; then came her response.

Dear Michelle —
    Forgive my rudeness for not writing earlier — I've been
busy, reading your novel — 4 times, not finished yet. It's stu-
pendous . . . you've got to write a sequel — I cried at the end —
Now that I know where your heart "lieth" I have heaps to tell
you — e.g., my half-sister [her father's "outside" child] that I
snubbed — and spending my life wishing I'd gotten to know
her — secretly I admired her — she was gorgeous too —
    . . . . I got up and sang all the Ja. songs — Start the Sequel!
                                                    Love, Nones.

The novel was my first, and I blessed first her excess. Then, I
began to take in her truth.

I had written about the shattering of a female friendship
caught in the colonial cortex of fifties Jamaica. Two girls meet
across differences of background, class, and color. In private,
the privacy of deep country, they become friends, but their
privacy cannot be maintained; the tender thing that is their
friendship is overcome. At the end of the novel, the protagonist — the character most like myself — is sent to stay with
a family friend, a female representative of the colonial mind-
set who will instill proper behavior in a girl in danger of breach-
ing decorum. The protagonist ends friendless, remembering her
friend.

There is a terrible loneliness behind my grandmother's letter,
as there is behind my novel *Abeng*.

Now she knew where my heart lieth — as she put it, in
the Victorian tongue of our common ground — she dropped
the mask.

She'd lived a lifetime holding back. Behind the Auntie Mame
antics, the prodigious drinking, pub-crawling, nightclubbing,
fast driving, horseracing, was a witness who had until now swallowed her testimony, held her tongue.

Our Jamaica was not an idyllic, water-wheeled paradise. It was a place she was driven to leave in the 1920s, to which she returned only once.

We had been each other's company, had been company for each other. But with that letter, and with her subsequent responses to my writing, and my responses to her longings and revelations, our companionship deepened.

Dear Michelle —
    You take after me with the hotels — I used to make up trips just to stay in hotels — drove to Atlanta once to see my show business girlfriend Kay. Stayed three days in a beautiful hotel in Washington. Was the "cat's meow" in the elegant dining room — Spent Easter Sunday in a black neighborhood in a diner — and enjoyed watching the people come in after Church in their Easter finery . . . I'm enclosing a day in my life (I keep a diary) . . . got this new way of Writing from "Election Day" — I loved that story — I love you. Thanks. Nones.

A writer once told me to write every day. I visit her now. Sad.

In the elegant dining room she is the one being watched; she seeks out the attention, dressed to the nines, no doubt. In the diner in the black D.C. neighborhood she is the one doing the watching.
    She exchanges words only with those who wait on her.
    I can see her in each place; I have been in each myself. In the diner she is unobtrusive, she is not of these people and would not intrude. Neither is she of the crowd in the elegant dining room. Where does she belong? Where does her heart lieth?
    In a lonely place she keeps for herself and tells me about now and then. She realizes that the past is irretrievable and she longs for access to it.
    She is in a deep sense homesick. For place, for the half-sister shunned.
    From her diary:

When the past rushes back I jot it down. . . . Scraps of papers written on them — "For Michelle" — I remember myself as weeks old when I was lying naked on banana leaves — I'd lost all my skin.

I am crossing the Great Salt Lake, eyes trained on Nevada, racing. Rain is falling, the suddenly black sky crashing into the white body of water. She is falling. It is early summer.

I had seen her last in a restaurant in New York City, the same week Garbo died. I was taking her to lunch for her birthday. She'd just turned eighty-five, but the score went unacknowledged.

She looked wonderful; raven-haired, dressed in a chic light tweed suit, a silk scarf knotted at her throat. But she is smaller, and dark-glassed (When did I last look into her eyes?) — that never changed.

I put my arms around her and can feel her ribcage.

"Hello, darling girl."

She is my guest, but she corrals the maitre d' and gets a decent table. "Two women alone, you know . . ." she says.

She orders a cocktail, another, to be followed by wine and an after-lunch liqueur. I have a glass of wine to keep her company, say something about not being able to drink the way I once could.

"You never learned to pace yourself."

I smile at her and urge her to order. But food no longer seems to interest her.

"I wish I believed in God," she says.

I don't know what to say. I want to comfort her. I have a book in my bag, slide it out into my lap.

"This is for you." I pass the book across the table to her. My face flushes and I am amazed at my tentativeness.

She looks at my name on the front and I tell her to turn to the dedication, where her name and Irene's name appear.

Age, I guess, life, and what goes with it, have made her weep more easily.

"Don't. You'll make me start," I say without thinking. I sip my wine. She sips her drink.

"Nobody loves you as much as we do."

She is thrilled by my silver Mustang. Thrilled I am crossing "this Country" alone.

I am crossing the Great Salt Lake, and she is falling down a flight of stairs.

Cathy, Now and Then

SOMETIMES I THINK MY punishment for being a social organization dropout is an unerring memory for their oaths and
pledges, secret handshakes and songs. I remember every stanza
of "We've a Story to Tell to the Nation" from GAs (Girls' Auxiliary) at the Baptist Church (where I never made it past the
bottom rung of a rather lengthy climb leading to Queen Regent
in Service), and the Phi Mu Sorority's secret knock and *na nu na
nu*, Mork from Ork–style handshake. But the oath that reverberates most often is that little ditty in the front of the Brownie
and Girl Scout handbooks: "Make new friends, but keep the
old. One is silver and the other's gold." I'm not sure that's the
exact wording but it's certainly close enough and I regret that
I'm unable to get the little singsongy tune that accompanies it
onto the page for full effect.

I hate the song and yet I see people shining in such a way:
aluminum and bronze, silver today and gold tomorrow. Certainly making new friends these days is an entirely different process. No one has time for all-night phone calls and pajama parties; no one has time to ruminate over those stories from the past
that have made me who I am. New friendships rely on quick
meetings for lunch where I practically burst with excitement at
seeing another adult and then spend much of the time talking

about my husband, the children, my work. I don't have time to tell about the summer after third grade when I accidentally bleached my hair orange and then had to get a severe pixie, or about when a boy in the fourth grade told me that my legs looked like a chimpanzee's legs and I went home, snuck a razor, and shaved my kneecaps. I don't have time to tell that I barely graduated from college or that I once, while trying to make up for basic laziness in a literature class, rambled on and on about the bird imagery in a particular poem only to have the professor say: "Swan? What swan? I said *swine*." Somehow these things just never seem to come up. It's hard enough to give the good parts of ourselves to new friends; who has time for those moments of humiliation, heartbreak, and poor mental health? And though I really like meeting people as the person I am *now*, and though I look forward to years of slowly filling in details and stories and hearing theirs in exchange — seeing the elemental values of a relationship grow with each visit — there's nothing that can ever take the place of someone who knew you when and likes you, loves you, in spite or because of it. When that someone is a part of the present, then you have the rarest of all friendships; you speak your own language, a kind of shorthand only available to childhood friends, where a word or phrase conjures up major portions of your life. With such a friendship you know and accept all of the changes that have occurred over time; you know the past history that shapes the present, and you know the surface appearance and all that lies underneath. When a writer talks about having a strong sense of place he or she is talking about such encompassing knowledge — knowledge directly tied to one's roots. In the same way, the friendship that offers a strong sense of person does not happen suddenly but is one you grow with and into.

I have known Cathy Lewis for as long as I can remember. Our hometown, Lumberton, North Carolina, was small enough when we were growing up that it seemed everyone knew everyone.

Though we were never in the same class at Tanglewood Elementary School, we shared the same history and had witnessed the same events. We remember when Cindy Barnes broke her arm (white face, protruding bone, a circle of screaming fourth-graders) while doing the slide-to-slide on the playground; we recall with great detail the time Jim Connelly threw up in the cafeteria and set off a chain reaction down the yellow Formica table; we knew who got paddled in the hall and who had to stay after school beating erasers. We realize now that we were even in the same Brownie troop; we wore brown uniforms and beanies while eating stale Lorna Doones and drinking Hawaiian Punch; we wrapped cracked marbles in remnant pieces of net to make corsages for our mothers and sewed little squares of oil-cloth into "sit-upons." I quit when the troop leader said that we could not take our sit-upons home, that they belonged to the troop. Cathy endured a bit longer.

In the seventh grade we finally landed in the same homeroom. This year is marked in my mind with songs like "Na Na Hey Hey Kiss Him Goodbye," lovebeads, Indian moccasins which we all purchased at The Hodge Podge (a used shoe store), and by a boy in our class, Raymond Weston, who, knowing Cathy's dad was a veterinarian, provoked her to fury by saying, "Your daddy's a dog killer." Good old Raymond, a little piece of rawhide tied around his plump neck, talked nonstop about his minibike and his future plans of owning a Harley, and said things like "That girl's so ugly they could throw her in the Lumber River and skim ugly for weeks," or "Your mama had to tie pork chops around your neck to get the dogs to play with you." Raymond pressed my button by flashing big fake smiles my way and saying in an annoyingly sweet voice "Aren't you so nice? All the time smiling. Ain't you just the teacher's pet?" On those excruciatingly hot afternoons when the sun baked through the big wavy windows of our dilapidated school (the ceiling of our math class crashed in one day while everybody was at recess),

Raymond killed flies with rubber bands and lined them up in his pencil tray.

I think Cathy and I were first united by the mutual aggravation supplied by the likes of Raymond, but it was really in high school when our friendship as we know it began. Since our last names began with the letters *L* and *M*, we always shared homeroom and we quickly chose seats next to each other. It was natural that first thing every morning we had a lot to discuss (who was talking to whom out in the smoking area, who was wearing so-and-so's blue jeans jacket even though he hadn't officially broken up with what's-her-name, who was "grubbing" — the term that year for making out — up against the lockers before first bell, and so on). We had everything in the world in common: we both loved plants, and we both loved Elton John's "Madman Across the Water" album. We both knew a lot about everything even though we hadn't *done* anything. We were both tall brunettes, always in the back row in every group shot, we both hated cafeteria food and algebra and loved English. We were the types who would decorate for school dances and build the floats for the homecoming parade. If there are proms in the afterlife she'll be hanging old parachutes, Spanish moss, and crepe paper flowers in the celestial gym and I'll be tying balloons and maroon and gold pom-poms to the pearly gates. We both loved to talk about and analyze books and stories, songs and movies. As the editor of the high school paper she published my lousy poetry and I was grateful.

During senior year we even shared a job. We were sales clerks at the Smart Shop in downtown Lumberton, a clothing store owned by some of the kindest, most generous women I have ever known. They were interested in selling, yes, but they were more interested in honesty: "Lord now, child, I believe you need more bosom than you've got for a dress cut like that," or "No, honey, I can't let you buy that dress with it looking that way."

We learned to tell someone tactfully that she was too old, fat, young, or skinny for this or that. On Christmas Eve when husbands came in desperate to buy something, we were told not to think of a quick sale, but "to think of that poor sweet wife sitting there by the tree with the baby, stars in her eyes as she wonders what her husband will give her. She probably ordered him some nice things from the L. L. Bean catalog. Keep her in mind when he's trying to buy something that doesn't match." We heard our mentors say, "Now, I know your wife and I know she's no size six. Uh-uh, no, not a fourteen either. What about some costume jewelry or a nice pair of gloves?" and we also heard customers discuss their husbands and boyfriends and body parts. We never forgot the woman who patted her lower abdomen and referred to it as her "cooter." There was a lengthy discussion as to what constituted a plump, pretty cooter (an abdomen that rounded into the material) and a poor one (concave).

Cathy and I alternated afternoon hours but then on Saturdays we were both there, changing the clothes of the mannequins in the window and helping people decide what to buy. Mainly we spent our time adorning ourselves, putting things on layaway until we had used up everything we'd earned. Truth be told we probably both lost money while working there, but I can remember every piece of 1970s polyester that we purchased, especially my safari pantsuit complete with a shirt that had a lion's face on the front and his tail on the back. Cathy's taste was more conservative, her jumpsuit was yellow instead of orange, for example; her leisure-style pantsuit forest green instead of orange.

I admired the certainty with which she gave her opinions and the way she seemed to know instantly whether or not she liked something or someone. There was a self-assurance about her that I did not possess. She never buckled under the peer pressure to start smoking or to do anything else unless she *wanted* to do it. She decided who she wanted to date and it didn't matter what anybody else might think about him. I envied these traits. I tried to figure out why she had them and I didn't. For a long while I believed that she had escaped severe self-consciousness and guilt by growing up Methodist instead of Baptist. If only I'd never gone to Girls' Auxiliary at the church. The Methodist Youth Center on Sunday nights was much livelier than Baptist Training Union; they shot pool in a room they had been allowed to paint black and played loud music while pondering the larger questions of life; they smoked cigarettes and made out behind the building. Surely this exposure was what had given her such confidence. Surely if I hung around with her long enough I, too, could say "I *don't* want to go" (instead of "well, let's see, let me think about it") or "I *love* this" without all of the lengthy pauses and second guesses and musings.

We graduated from Lumberton High School in 1976 and that fall we were roommates at the University of North Carolina at Chapel Hill. We arrived on a hot August afternoon, our dads sweating as they carried box after box up to our lime green room on the third floor of an un-air-conditioned dorm, our mothers making sure we had toothpaste and soap and plenty of stamps. It was almost like going off to camp (a compressed social organization) except that I was happy to be there. Neither of us could stand for things not to match so we had a color scheme; everything we bought that year was bright yellow and green, except for my wardrobe which, despite Cathy's encouragement to branch out with color, was (aside from my orange items) in shades of basic brown and tan.

We still hated the thought of institutional food and the rules and order that accompanied a meal plan, so our domestic habits started early. We cooked canned goods on a little two-burner stove. It was going down to the hall bathroom to wash the dishes that posed problems, so freshman year we threw out enough Tupperware to have a king-size party. My contributions to roommate living were a love for television and junk food, things that both Cathy and now my husband claim they didn't indulge in before living with me. Cathy brought the stereo and the ability to shag. She gave dancing lessons to people on our hall, the beach music blasting as we took turns learning to twirl and dip. I was the local cosmetologist; I spent a lot of time trimming, perming, and coloring hair, and plucking eyebrows. I sat out in the hall smoking cigarettes while she sat under a space-age hair dryer and asked me if I liked the idea of having cigarette breath. We looked forward to football Saturdays, and neither of us ever went to the library, but we read our English papers aloud to each other. We took a math course that was filled to capacity by much of the football team; the course was the mathematical equivalent of the geology course I was also taking known as "rocks for jocks." But the worst course that I talked Cathy into was Geography 38. "How hard can it be?" I asked. "A few plateaus and mountains, maybe a bit of weather," but it was the hardest class we had ever encountered. The questions on the first little quiz went something like: "In Jakarta, Indonesia, on May twenty-second, 1900, at what angle was the sun to the horizon at 2:35 P.M." We couldn't even skip class to sit in the student union and do the crossword puzzle in the campus paper because this professor had a troop of graduate students who took the roll.

The night before our final, sympathetic friends wished us luck. We tried to study but we got so hungry we had to walk over to Roy Rogers for burgers and fries. Then we decided that maybe our minds would be loosened by just a little television. Then we opted to go down to the dorm basement and bake cookies for somebody we knew who was in prison. Finally, Cathy said she was going to hang it up and go to bed. When my parents called at ten to wish us luck, we were both asleep.

When we went to take the exam the next day, Cathy's Toyota was already packed to go home for the holidays. I looked at the exam and knew that my best option was just to eenie-meenie it. I got past the professor and the graduate assistants and then I ran. I was leaning against the car, smoking cigarettes as fast as I could, when I discovered that Cathy was right behind me. "Why did I let you talk me into this course?" she said. "'Little plateaus, an island or two.'" She was so upset she didn't even complain that I was chain-smoking in her car. Thirty minutes out of

town and we were laughing — nervous, but laughing. We returned to scan the grades, standing side-by-side in the darkened
hallway of the geography department, our fingers frantically
seeking out our social security numbers. "D"s. We had "D"s.
I was exhilarated; Cathy was relieved. This was not my first or
last "D," but it was her only one.

I was not soaring academically, so I decided to take some time
off from school. Come July, while lifeguarding at the Lumber
River, I knew this had been a dumb idea, but by then Cathy had
been assigned a new roommate who would live on my side of
that lime green room and I had to find a new place to live. The
good thing to come of that separated year was that because I
had not preregistered for classes, I had to pick up a whole sched-
ule at drop-add. At the time I had no idea for a major. I thought
it likely that I'd major in physical education and try to coach a
women's swim or tennis team or something. I signed up for English 23W (beginning fiction writing) because I liked to write
and assumed it would be an easy course.

When Cathy and I were reunited for apartment life junior
year, our color scheme of green and yellow still with us, I had
both a major and goals for what I wanted to do with my life, as
well as a brand-new Smith-Corona typewriter humming on the
kitchen table. Cathy was equally involved in her journalism
courses and the various romantic interests (photographers, news
writers, copyeditors) that had evolved therein. That fall I joined
her sorority and was formally taught all the secret handshakes
and songs and codes that she had already divulged. We went to
mixers and toga parties; I took care of the cooking and she did
the cleaning. We called ourselves Alice and Theresa after two
maiden sisters from our hometown who lived together and split
the chores in a similar way. Really, though, we were more like
Laverne and Shirley — Cathy with her zest for going out and
wearing monograms on her clothes, and me with a neurosis
about everything except school.

Although red polyester was not even our idea of a bad joke,

come summer that's what we found ourselves wearing. If we had been at the Smart Shop, we would have said, "Lord, girl, you do not have a butt for red polyester." And yet there we were, pushing slices at the Pizza Hut. Unfortunately, the owners knew that we tended to talk a lot, so they always put us on separate shifts on different nights. Our only time to see each other was while we lay out in the sun or in the wee hours when one of us came home, smelling of pepperoni, with a free large Super Supreme. These were given to us by Brent, the cook, a former reform school student who confessed to us that he had burned down his room there. In fact, he insisted that we take home large Super Supreme pizzas, and he also insisted — once the doors to the Hut were locked at midnight — that we play the jukebox with quarters from our tips and dance with him. He had long, greasy, black hair that fell forward when he bent to unzip his shiny boots so he could *disco* in his ratty socked feet.

Cathy and I often sat in our apartment at one A.M. eating pizza, one of us in a nightgown the other in the red suit, talking about Brent. We could complain that he made us dance with him but then he'd tell that we took home Super Supremes every night. Besides, we were scared of meeting up with Brent outside of work. One night, when my brother-in-law's Chevrolet Biscayne wouldn't go into reverse, I pressed harder on the accelerator and jiggled the gears; all of a sudden Brent jumped up from behind where he had been holding the bumper. Incidents like this reminded us that two of our friends from high school had been locked in the walk-in freezer at a Pizza Hut in Winston-Salem by a gun-toting man in a ski mask just two weeks before. It reminded us that people like Ray Weston were now *out there,* all grown up, with tattoos and Harleys and saying things far worse than "Your daddy kills dogs."

We were desperate to quit our jobs. Cathy was on the waiting list for a position at a clothing store at the mall and I had applied at a kennel and cattery. She liked clothes and I liked animals; by then we both hated pizza. It was while all of this was going on that we befriended our neighbor, the young woman who lived above us. Within the first afternoon of chatting she revealed that she was pregnant and that her boyfriend frequently beat her up. Now, during our carefree summer, beer in the fridge, Jimmy Buffett blasting from our apartment windows, we became therapists. Cathy has always had the great ability to ask just the right questions; people will tell her everything. I oftentimes get the same results by saying nothing. Together we were hearing more than we wanted. We were supportive and comforting, we encouraged her to seek help, to leave. We sat up in the wee hours waiting to hear if anything was happening.

A week or so passed and we were still at the Hut. We had begun coming in from the sun earlier to enjoy the luxury of an afternoon nap. One afternoon we both sat up at the same time, having just dreamed that we heard our door slam. We then heard the monotonous bass beat booming from the upstairs stereo and realized that the boyfriend was home. It seemed our neighbor, now noticeably pregnant, stopped by more and more frequently. We came home one day in the pouring-down rain to find her standing outside our door with a big trash bag that she had used to shield her head. Her boyfriend had locked her out and we invited her in to wait for him to get home. The conversation turned to one we liked discussing: clothes and how they fit people, outrageous examples of poor taste, and the kinds of things we'd heard and said at the Smart Shop ("Mmmm-MmmmmMmmmm, that's pitiful isn't it? Somebody ought to tell her that a bigger size would do wonders"). We talked sizes and shapes and then the neighbor shyly disappeared. We whispered about how sorry we felt for her. What could we do?

I was midway through my shift a few nights later, having been stiffed on tips at least twice already, when Brent loped his greasy way over with an occasional disco turn — shades of what I had to look forward to — to tell me I had a phone call; "The other one of you," he said. I barely answered before Cathy was asking if I'd borrowed the tip money on her dresser.

"I wouldn't do that," I told her. "Not without telling you."

"Well, I know that," she said with that little laugh that emerges when she gets nervous. "But it would be okay if you did." She was clearly stalling. "My watch is gone, too," she whispered and I could hear her beginning to open and close drawers. All of her earrings were gone. "My clothes!" she was shouting. "My clothes are gone!"

The owners were furious that I was leaving. "You girls don't take work seriously," the man said. Brent watched me longingly; he was going to have to use his own quarter to hear "Disco Inferno" and dance by himself. "Well, you don't get robbed every day!" I said. "It's not like we knew." But then I did know who had done it and I ran back to the phone. Cathy had the same thought at the same time. It all made sense. We *had* heard our door slam that day; someone had stood in the doorway of our room and watched us there on our matching little patchwork bedspreads, both of us in gym shorts and tee shirts. I drove home as fast as I could. I was sure that my typewriter was gone and Cathy's stereo and the small black-and-white television that my mother had won as a bridge party door prize years earlier.

When I arrived, Cathy and her date were in the living room with the policeman. The policeman eyed me and my attire and then went back to his little pad. "So," he said. "You girls have some grass?"

"What?" We both looked at him like he might be the idiot he was. Did he really think we'd give it to him if we did? Cathy told him that we had beer in the refrigerator.

"Most of these break-ins are drug related," he said and stared hard at us. "So I'll ask again if you're housing anything."

"No," Cathy said. Her hands were on her hips and her eyebrows were raised as they were in the seventh grade when Ray Weston barked at her. She was just about ready to take this guy out, and even in her Maleia sundress, bright green espadrilles, and add-a-beads, she could have done it. We tried to tell him that we knew who had robbed us. We went to look her up in the phone book but our robber had taken that, too. Maybe she thought we wouldn't know how to call the police without it. The officer said there was really nothing that he could do since we had no proof. I went on Cathy's date with her (a very brief date) and then we spent the rest of the night rehashing our clues. I was so relieved to see my typewriter that I hadn't even done a full inventory, so we sat up late going through our things. That's when I discovered that that woman had not taken any of my clothes! She had taken all of my shoes, bathing suits, and underwear, but she had not taken one damn article of clothing! There hung my brown sundress and my safari pantsuit. "I've been trying to tell you," Cathy said. "Haven't I been trying to tell you?"

The next day, every time we came or went, the crooked neighbors were watching us from above, hands holding back the curtains. We thought about faking an exit, parking on the other side of the building and then waiting inside for them, but we chickened out. We asked to borrow their phone book, thinking that they'd accidentally give us ours, the one with the sorority house and various friends and family members' numbers scribbled inside, but of course they weren't that stupid.

When the weekend came, we decided to take action. We went to the super of our complex and requested a solid door with a dead bolt instead of the standard glass door. He refused. Fire regulations, he said. So we said we were moving and needed our deposit back. We hadn't told our parents about the robbery. We were afraid they'd make us come home to Lumberton for the rest of the summer. We decided we'd tell them after we were settled in a new place. Once we made up our minds, we were out of there in twenty-four hours. We rented a U-Haul, packed Cathy's car to the gills, and were gone before the neighbors got home. By suppertime that night we were settled into a cute little duplex-type apartment on a wooded road. We had a deck, our own rooms, and were paying less rent. I had one pair of sneakers and no bathing suits but things were definitely looking up.

The good luck continued. We told our parents what had happened and they were more relaxed than we had expected. We badgered our former manager until he returned our fifty-dollar deposit. We turned in our red polyester and Cathy spent her days selling clothes (and steadily replacing her losses) and I spent mine joyfully hosing down dog runs. It seemed we were finally back on track. We had our nights off to go downtown or leisurely eat our Swanson frozen Mexican dinners while watching reruns of "The Andy Griffith Show." We drank enough Tab to sail a ship. I still smoked like a fiend either in my room or out on the deck. While nothing was going on at the kennel, I began writing what I called "The Jillzette," a paper I designed purely for Cathy's amusement. I wrote social columns describing our most recent dates (hers in great detail) and a "Horrorscopes" column where I profiled and drew pictures of people we didn't like.

One Saturday afternoon we unplugged the phone and went to take naps. I was asleep in my room, dreaming I was at a party and wearing this shirt I had loved. It was a nondescript sort of buff-colored Qiana oversized shirt that I had purchased at the Smart Shop and had worn with a pair of matching Candies that made me about six feet tall. I opened my eyes, wondering how tall Miss Crook — who now must have been about nine months pregnant — stood in my Candies, when all of a sudden I realized that one thing of mine had been stolen — that very shirt. I felt a momentary surge of pride and then an avalanche of fury. I ran to Cathy's room and woke her. I even lit a cigarette in the main room and she didn't say anything about it. "This is it," I told her. "We are *mad*."

We called our former neighbors and asked to speak to the woman. He said she wasn't there, could he help me?

"We know you robbed us," I said. "My roommate's daddy hired a PI who's been tracking you and now we've got all the evidence we need. The PI has asked us to take out a warrant but we thought we'd give her one last chance seeing as how she's about to have a baby and all." I know now that we must have been scared to death because we sat there looking at each other while I delivered that mouthful of garbage without one laugh. Finally, all those years watching "Kojak" were paying off. The woman came to the phone and said, "What do you want?"

"Return everything to us and we'll drop it. Otherwise you and your baby are going to jail."

"Why don't you come upstairs?"

"We don't live there anymore." I paused while she acted surprised. "Meet us in front of University Mall," I said, thinking we'd have a policeman there with us. Although they had fallen for the ridiculous story, they didn't fall for that. We finally got her to say that she would take everything downstairs to another neighbor.

When it was all over and we were safely back in our apartment going through labelless clothes, Cathy called the police to tell them that we had solved our own case. They said we were stupid, foolish girls but, of course, we knew better.

After that experience, we felt older and wiser. We felt too old and wise for secret handshakes and knocks; we were about to become Phi Mu dropouts. For the rest of the summer, we sat out on our teeny tiny deck and played albums. We read cheap trashy fiction aloud and we read good fiction aloud. We drank cheap champagne and practiced various shag moves. We played word games and had contests to see who could come up with the most outrageous stories about people we knew and deliver them without laughing. We talked about what we wanted to do, where we wanted to go.

The only disturbing incident after our move was when I accidentally killed an orphaned cat. I dipped it for fleas as you would a dog and the result was immediate poisoning. For nights after I couldn't close my eyes without seeing that convulsing cat. Today, in the midst of a group of people, Cathy will turn to me and with a blank face say "Tell about when you killed that cat. Tell about how none of your clothes got stolen."

That fall my first short story was published in the university literary magazine. Cathy and I had already celebrated this event many times over. We celebrated when it was accepted, celebrated when the issue came out. But the biggest celebration of all came when there was a very good review of the issue in the school newspaper with a whole paragraph devoted to my story. I know I didn't go to class that day; I just sat in the student union staring at the review. I remember getting to the apartment door and finding the review taped to it, that paragraph highlighted in yellow.

We shared everything that year. She read all of the manuscripts for my writing class and I brainstormed with her on ad campaigns for her journalism course. We could almost smell graduation, but it seemed the closer it came the less we talked about moving away; she had a job in Raleigh and I was going to graduate school for writing. We both knew that some things are just understood. There's no reason to say it or talk it to death, no need for little social hugs and kisses. If you've got it, you know it, it's that simple. I knew as our senior year was drawing to a close that we were about to experience a great loss. Oh sure, we'd always be there for each other; we'd live on the telephone. But what about the way we told each other everything that happened? What about the jokes other people didn't think were funny because they hadn't been in that seventh-grade classroom? What about our great album collection?

But there was no need to worry. We are still taping albums to fill in the gaps. Now we talk and tell everything that has happened during the week. We call to complain ("the baby has an ear infection," or "it's too damn hot to go outside"); to get reassurance ("who has time to just lie around in the sun and get skin cancer?"); to get that totally biased opinion that we all need from time to time (she always reads all of my work in manuscript); or simply to gossip (between the two of us we know all of the hometown news even though neither of us lives there). When I quit smoking we talked constantly, her cigarette cracks strengthening my resolve; and when her son was born I was there to assure her that she would (in a year or so) sleep a full night and get to take a shower by herself. I have learned to say *no* much more often and have improved my wardrobe. She relies on me to remember and entertain, to dredge up and record the kinds of sordid details from adolescence that most people choose to forget. We have huge phone bills but we always rationalize that they aren't as much as an hour with a really good shrink.

I've been surprised to learn that everyone doesn't have a Cathy, and every month or two — phone cords twisting as we pause and turn into our separate homes to say things like "get that out of your mouth" — one of us will remind the other how very lucky we are. The silver friend knows your present and the gold friend knows all of your past dirt and glories. Once in a blue moon there's someone who knows it all, someone who knows and accepts you unconditionally, someone who's there for life. I shudder to think how different my life would have been if I'd wound up in another homeroom.

JANE SMILEY

Ｘ Ｘ Ｘ Ｘ Ｘ Ｘ Ｘ Ｘ Ｘ Ｘ Ｘ Ｘ Ｘ Ｘ

Can Writers Have Friends?

NOT TOO LONG AGO, a man I do not know was approached by his pastor and asked whether he knew me, because he seemed to be a lot like a character in one of my stories. No, the man remarked, he did not know me, but his sister was one of my best friends. And I was in the soup again.

He called her. She called me. Their family was abuzz. Our family discussed the matter. Her husband thought a note of, not exactly apology but, well, something. When I agreed to do this, my husband asked me if I had any principles. I did, actually, so I didn't write the note, which was a relief because what would I have said? Unfortunately, Miss Manners doesn't cover the etiquette of inspiration. And there is a good reason why: writers don't exist, as writers, within the realm of social niceties.

I have to say that I have never met anyone who was depicted in a story or an essay who wasn't at least somewhat disturbed by the experience. While this doesn't always lead to a breach between friends or associates, the person depicted almost always has to assume an attitude about it — suppressed resentment is one possibility, resignation is another. I have never met anyone depicted who felt about it as writers feel they should — flattered to be so interesting, so inspiring, pleased to be given the compliment of such detailed and minute observation.

. . . .

44

Of course, there are plenty of people who can't wait for their lives to be made into a book or a movie, who approach any and every writer with the assertion that she could do nothing better than set aside her present project and immediately commence immortalizing this new acquaintance.

So maybe the world is made up of two kinds of people, those who can't wait to be written about and those who can't bear it. If so, then why do writers always end up writing about the second group?

Maybe the real question is, why do writers always end up writing about their friends, and since they do, is it actually possible for them to have friends?

It seems to be generally accepted that writers may write about their families and, in fact, must write about their families, preferably in the most caustic terms. This may or may not affect family life. Virginia Woolf is well known to have thinly disguised almost all of her relatives — her mother and father appear in *To the Lighthouse*, her adored brother became Percy in *The Waves*, and her sister Vanessa appeared, for starters, in *The Voyage Out*. Woolf's husband, Leonard, returned the favor with a novel he wrote called *The Wise Virgins* which discussed, observed, contemplated (what is the right word?) Virginia and Vanessa. It may be argued that the Woolfs and Stephens and their group understood each other and, more importantly, understood their devotion to art in the same ways — they accepted that loyalty to artistic truth was a higher calling than care for the sensitivities of earthly companions. Other writers, Samuel Butler, say, the author of the scathing autobiographical novel of Victorian clerical hypocrisy, *The Way of All Flesh*, and Ernest Hemingway, author of countless stinging portraits of all the women he knew, have not written about relatives or lovers with the affection Woolf and Woolf did. But even so, the hazards of producing a writer seem to fall acceptably upon the families in question. Somehow, if they had lived more normally, such a punishment wouldn't have befallen them.

At the other end of the spectrum are strangers. Supposedly, speculating about strangers, along with observing their mannerisms and eavesdropping on their conversations, is what fiction writers do.

Maybe. Not in my experience.

What I do is gossip. Now, I admit that gossip has a bad name. The very word almost always evokes a knee-jerk negative response. Ann Landers used to say in her column that only the pettiest conversationalists talked about other people — normal people talked about things, and the great-minded talked about ideas. Pardon me. I prefer to think that dull consumerists talk about things, dull abstractionists (usually male) talk about ideas emptied of their human content, and the most scintillating conversationalists are fascinated by human motivation.

Gossip is about the understanding and assimilation of daily events. There are five stages of gossip. They are: wait-till-you-hear-this (information), are-you-kidding (amazement), I-can't-stop-thinking-about-it (fascination), you-know-why-she-did-it-don't-you (speculation), and actually-I'm-not-a-bit-surprised (understanding). Every pair or group of gossipers is constructing a piece of fiction by making a logical character out of a mysterious person, or a logical story out of an untoward event. The story that emerges after all the facts are known and fitted in is, in my opinion, often a work of collaborative oral art, which I would define as life reworked by thought.

I frankly can't imagine how people could have moral lives without gossip — by listening to handed-down religious or moral precepts? By reading great philosophers? By adhering to rules? The trouble with precepts, philosophies, and rules is that they don't often fit individual circumstances and, more importantly, they are abstract — they don't bridge the gap between knowledge and feeling. Let us say that I understand a prohibition against lying, and yet my mother gives me a pair of slacks for my birthday that are not only ugly but are also unflattering. She is eager to know whether I like them or not — she *loves* them.

In addition to a precept at this point, I need a way to integrate my concern for my mother's feelings, my sensation of abhorrence at the sight of myself in these toreador pants, and my desire to set a good example for my ever-alert daughters. The way to figure out what to do is to compare notes; in other words, to gossip — to use your own and others' previous experiences as a guide. Discussing incidents and motives refines moral decisions and makes one's moral life participatory rather than reactive.

The most inveterate reader of trash fiction believes that there is at least a mote of instruction to be found in all that entertainment. The rest of us expect a reasonably large component of food for thought and potential enlightenment. Do we read *Anna Karenina* to find out about life in nineteenth-century Russia? Maybe some of those great thinkers do, but most people read it to experience vicariously, and therefore to contemplate, Anna's moral and emotional dilemma. Serious fiction is a game of contemplation, with rules of form and presentation that the writer abides by, and the requirement of suspension of disbelief which the reader adheres to. The payoff is joint contemplation of a more or less complex situation. The key feature, for our purposes here, is that the situation is always, must always be, a human dilemma. After laying out the ramifications of the dilemma, the serious fiction writer, with the aid of the culturally given tools of plot and language, proposes a solution to the dilemma, which the reader may accept or reject, but the heart of the game is the process of joint contemplation (tell me how this is different from gossip?), and the reader's deepest pleasure is contemplating, not solving.

Fiction writers, male and female, are committed gossips. But not every type of gossip is exactly right. Once I was sitting in a large group of writers, about half poets and half fiction writers. Everyone was leaning forward, clearly at the fascination point, as one of the poets told of a bat she had found in her house. She had just embarked upon telling us what the bat meant to her after she got rid of it when one of the fiction writers asked her *how* she had gotten rid of it. Unbelievably, she could not remember. At this point, the poets leaned farther forward, anxious for her to finish her thought about the meaning of the bat, but the fiction writers all leaned back or stood up and left the conversation. *How* was all we cared about. If she could not reveal how she had gotten rid of the bat, then she could not reveal the thing we most wanted to know: the nature of her character, her idiosyncratic but human way of encountering the world.

It is this fascination with character that drives most if not all serious fiction writers. Dilemmas are universal, and the interesting ones do not add up to a very large number. The variations of character and circumstance are infinite, however, and the moral being of narrative literature rests upon the instinctive need of the culture as a whole to make a bridge between precepts, rules, and philosophies on one hand, and character and circumstance on the other. Just as our lives are woven out of interactions between our emotional experiences and our intellectual interpretations and decisions, so the human world is a fabric of generally agreed upon rules interlaced by mitigating circumstances of identity or history. Stories, whether oral or written, whether narrated at an A.A. meeting or purchased in a bookstore or watched on television, make the necessary connections. Our culture is awash in stories — we have dozens of TV channels, for example, that turn everything from hard news to crimes to sports contests into investigations of character. I happen to think, in fact, that we live in a time when the precepts, rules, and philosophies seem largely to have failed, and so we turn to the accumulation of individual stories to find a substitute rationale for acting in a moral or at least socially acceptable way. Or, at the very least, in a way that has precedents on some cable channel talk show.

If we are all great consumers of stories, then where are the writers of these stories to find their material? The answer is more complex than it first appears. The simple answer is that they look around, they listen, they participate in the human world, which means that they have friends and associates who enter their work, sometimes in accordance with the writer's intentions, sometimes unintentionally. Many writers, especially beginning ones, do learn to create character by attempting to depict friends and relatives. The next step, which I often suggest to my students, is to juxtapose a well-known associate, such as an aunt, with an alien concept, such as serial killing. What if my aunt were a serial killer? How would she go about it? What elements of her character or personality would revel in such a career? How would she justify it to herself? What would she do if she were found out? I am not original in this suggestion; the early work of many writers — Dickens, Jane Austen, Virginia Woolf — abounds in such "what-if" constructions.

As a writer matures through a number of books, though, her methods of composing change as her skills and her understanding of her form become more sophisticated. She no longer needs to seek out models or think through the fit between plot and character. She no longer needs to find the theme — increasingly, themes find her, bringing with them their most compelling expressions of plot and character. The inspiration for a novel comes as a whole rather than as a laborious aggregation of this character and that incident. Novels and stories are no longer based so much on personal experience, more on ideas that are fed by experience gathered from many sources. In other words, the writer is less dependent on reality. Life is still the subject, but the energy comes from a plentifully exercised and well-developed artistic vision. In his memoir, *Speak, Memory*, Vladimir Nabokov noted that he was driven to write a memoir because he found that material taken directly from his experience no longer fitted very well into his artistic constructions and, in some sense, he could no longer stash it there. His novels' own integrity asserted a distorting influence over the real life that wandered into them. Thus it is with character drawing: earlier recognizable portraits of a writer's friends and family are replaced by wholly made-up figures who may share a recognizable quirk or set of ideas with someone, but about whom the writer feels entirely differently — figures who are not at all, in the writer's mind, the same as those friends or associates. As evidence of this, I would cite the experience almost every fiction writer has had of consciously putting a friend, or more deliciously an enemy, into a story or novel. The human side revels in the exposure and revenge to be wrought upon the bastard, but willy-nilly the artistic side goes about touching the fellow up here and there, finding charm or redeeming value, making of that hated and misunderstood (or loved and partially misunderstood) person an item of literary logic, a character.

A character, like all human productions, is far less complex than a naturally occurring person. Perhaps this is why no writer's characters seem, to her, to resemble the people she knows. But what about the perceptions of friends who, in spite of the writer's opinion, feel that they have been depicted, and therefore held up to the ridicule, or at least the observation, of others?

The writer could argue that the reader brings as much to the discovery of himself in a character as the writer has to the character's creation. Perhaps Hemingway's mother, who never recognized herself in any of his depictions of her, simply could not imagine herself from his point of view because she never knew his real point of view. Perhaps those who do recognize themselves are reacting not to how the writer has perceived them, but to how they perceive themselves. For example, in my experience the most resented details are physical ones. People mind less having been portrayed as a potential serial killer than having been portrayed with fat thighs or a disagreeable odor. They know, of course, that they are not serial killers, but they fear that their thighs do seem too fat or that their body odor is evident. It really doesn't matter that no one else in the world will ever link a person with the character he feels is him. He has made that connection, and that is enough. In fact, though, the offending physical detail may be the one thing about the character that the writer thought she made up.

The crux of the matter is inspiration. Inspiration is not confined to writers or artists — the word's Latin roots, which mean
"to breathe into," indicate a much more universal experience —
anyone can get the spirit (and everyone must lose it, since the
linguistic opposite of "inspire" is "expire"). I much prefer this
idea of inspiration being as ubiquitous as the air we breathe to
the old idea of inspiration as a visiting female, but the visiting
(and capricious) female icon evokes one of the truths of inspiration as I have experienced it — it is very closely related to love.

I am reminded of songwriter and ex-Beatle George Harrison, who was sued for plagiarizing the tune of his song "My
Sweet Lord" from an earlier song by the Chiffons called "He's
So Fine." Lots of people — including, apparently, the judge —
thought his explanation that the Chiffons song must have just
been in his mind was a little thin. I thought it was perfectly
believable. In the rush of inspiration, artists don't dissect the
sources of the images, sounds, and feelings that they are experiencing, they just get them down as fast as they can. I buy both
the connection Harrison must have felt between the love song
he was writing and the earlier one in his memory bank, and I
also buy Harrison's belief in the transmutation of the old tune
into an entirely different musical product through the applica-
tion of his own thoughts and feelings.

Nevertheless, however altered the product, inspiration may
have very real and sometimes recognizable sources, but they may
not be consciously chosen by the writer. I used to date. Among
the unpleasant consequences of dating was an experience I had
of listening to a very drunk date tell me a story that I found
inspiring. He was upset by feelings he was having about a phone
call he had just received. That, I suppose, was why he was so
drunk. At any rate, I made a specific request (my first ever) for
permission to use this incident in a story. The request was
granted so I made it again, to make sure that he knew, through
the fog of inebriation, what I was getting at. He did, and the
bone of contention was never that he hadn't given permission.

After I wrote the story (pure fiction, in my opinion), I showed it to him. He broke all further dates and wouldn't speak to me. A year or so later I showed the story to a woman who had known him well for a long time. She couldn't get over how deeply similar the main character, whom I thought was fictional, was to this man whom I barely knew. My explanation for this is twofold. The first fold is that I apprehended much about my date unconsciously — that he entered the story without my knowledge because I had just been with him, and as I was getting things down in the rush of inspiration, I was influenced by his recent presence. The second fold is that the incident he had told me of was specific to someone of his type, or even, specific to him. The very details that made it interesting also made it idiosyncratic, and his character clustered around the actions I narrated in some unavoidable way. Of course, as a fiction writer who asserts that character is destiny, I was gratified, if also surprised, to be proven right. Nevertheless, I didn't consciously put in the details that convinced my date that I was apprehending him, I just did apprehend him.

I am convinced that the real heart of my conflict with those who have inspired me is irony. Irony is a notoriously complex and difficult concept to define, but the word comes, through the Latin, from the Greek word meaning "to dissemble, to say less than one thinks." In that sense, an ironist is a liar, or, indeed, a fiction writer. I prefer to define irony as distance — the distance between the ideal, which is commonly understood between reader and writer, and the real, which is being depicted on the page. Serious realistic fiction is by nature ironic because that distance is its *essential* subject. What those who find themselves depicted in works of art object to is being observed ironically — being found wanting in terms of the subtextual ideal. Though ironic distance is necessary to how we see those around us, most people do not employ ironic distance in viewing themselves. Those who do, in fact, are believed to be cynical, depressed, unwell, etc. It is, therefore, a shock to see oneself portrayed ironically, to be distanced from oneself by the perceptions of an author. I suppose that to be assured that at least you are interesting is pretty cold comfort if the author has also made you perceive yourself as shallow, feckless, unpleasant, and physically unattractive.

Nevertheless.

Nevertheless, my experience has always been that strong feelings about someone or some incident are the first signals of oncoming inspiration. In the old days, when romance was the only thing I thought about, I couldn't not write about my boyfriends, or my crushes. Writing to them, as in letters or poems, was almost never successful — too much sweetness and light, not enough salty irony for my taste. My solution was to write about them. It may be that I loved them second, only after finding them inspiring first, and that I fell out of love with them after they ceased to have any inspiring tales to tell (my husband is partial to this thesis). It's also true I have always found my children inspiring. What the inspiration feels like is a curiosity about the subject that is too intense for simple knowledge — the curiosity can only be satisfied by deeply imagining the loved or desired one. This turning inward in order to discover what is outside the self is, I think, the paradox of imagination.

Strong feelings do not always cluster around a person, either. Sometimes they may cluster around an idea. In the late seventies, possibly as a reaction to having a baby, I went through a kind of nuclear panic similar to the nuclear panic I had felt as a child in the fifties. I worried constantly — how long would it take me to get to the daycare facility if the attack came? What if she survived me and her father? I even wondered whether the windows in my daughter's bedroom were dangerously large and too near the bed. These fears absolutely compelled me to write a story, later published in *The Atlantic,* called "The Blinding Light of the Mind." What with tinkering and fiddling and solving as well as I could the narrative problems presented by the material, I worked on the story for almost a year, which meant that I regularly contemplated my fears, which I had visited upon the main character. I noticed some time after finishing the story that I hadn't endured a bout of nuclear panic in months. When the story was published, I was even able to laugh at the artwork, which eerily picked up the state of mind I had once been in.

So it is with strong feelings — positive or negative — toward friends, people I meet, or even people I hear about. The disbelief and the fascination that obsess me are resolved through the piecemeal but systematic process of incorporating them into my psyche by imagining a story that distorts and changes the *person* into a *character*. Once I have finished the story or the novella or the novel, the character has become so different from the inspiration, and my relationship with the character so much longer and deeper than my relationship with the person, that I have almost forgotten to associate the two and, always, my original feelings about the person have been resolved into a kind of vague fondness. Or, if I actually know and am friends with the person who has inspired a character, I find that I am even more fond of that person than I was before, just through the experience of having thought about him or her so much, having filled in what I didn't know about him or her with my own thoughts or feelings, so that the resulting character is the both of us.

Finally, that's the secret. That's what I would like to tell my friend's brother — not that his less attractive qualities were communicated to me by his sister and then set down for all to see, but that in imagining a character based on an incident that she related to me, I ended up writing about myself as another sort of person. The inspiration for that character's failings came from my own experience of my own failings. The apparent likeness to him is the necessary costume and makeup covering the deeper and much more detailed likeness to me.

A piece of fiction or an essay is a piece of logic. Like any other piece of logic, it has a specious order to it that is not life, but an attempt to make sense of life. The component parts of the piece — characters and plots — are also pieces of logic. Every piece of logic makes a case for some method of ordering the world. A writer's logic reveals mostly the structure of the writer's mind and how that structure makes sense of the random world. Since emotion is a feature of a fiction writer's or essayist's logic, those people and events that arouse her emotion are driving forces in her logical constructions. Stories are pieces of logic that humans can't seem to live without, and that are uniquely human — I noticed that when they sent that time capsule into space some years ago, containing a brass plaque intended to define humanity but be understandable to intelligent nonhumans, it contained pictures, equations, and music, but no stories. As much as we need to tell ourselves stories, we can tell them only to ourselves, about ourselves.

Telling these stories, it seems to me, is a way of befriending each other across time and space, across the differences of culture. When a writer brings the friends of her everyday side into her work, she is introducing them to others, introducing what she deduces to be their "meaning" into the ongoing cultural investigation of what it means to be human. If any of my friends or family members ever writes about me with irony, detachment, and those mixed feelings that seem to be an intrinsic part of our human baggage, I hope I can take my own advice and remember that.

Best Friend, My Wellspring in the Wilderness!

WE ALWAYS WALKED HOME together, sometimes the back way, down Hyperion Boulevard, in the backwoods of east Hollywood, where we'd stop at a mom-and-pop store and get Cokes for a nickel out of those boxy machines swirling with ice water. Our hands played with bottles of orange and grape until our knuckles ached with cold, and the rest of our sweaty bodies cooled down a little. Then, since we lived on steep, steep hills, we'd begin the long climb, on streets that turned to staircases when they had to.

We took our time, without saying much about it. There wasn't much percentage in getting home.

Other days we took the regular way, leaving Thomas Starr King Junior High by its front lawn and walking up to Sunset Boulevard, and from there to the "junction" where Santa Monica Boulevard and Sunset join up and there was a flurry of red streetcars and noise. Another grocery store. This one, besides those chilled-out Cokes, sold huge dill pickles that we bought for a nickel each. Gnawing on them, we wandered on down along the bottom lands of the Micheltorena Hill, knowing one way or the other we'd have to climb it.

We went past the S.O.S. Bar, where my divorced mother took her boyfriends. Past a poverty-stricken Catholic school. Took a look at a little store that sold horsemeat — with a great big cut-out dog standing at the ready, saying, in effect, that this was only *dog food*, no big deal! But World War I had barely ended. The people all around us lived deep down in the lower-middle class. I'd had some fairly suspicious hamburgers up at my house, and Jackie had told me her mother shopped here.

It would take an hour, at least, every day, to get on home. We'd turn up Maltman Avenue, climbing slowly if we were going to my place, or turn on steep Micheltorena to get to Jackie's. I lived farther up than she did so we usually went to her place. I don't remember what we talked about. It seems to me our conversations were dreamy and morose. We were in the seventh grade, or eighth, or ninth; this went on for years.

At my house it would be clean and neat and empty, and God help us if we made a mess of any kind, left a saucer on the scrubbed-down sink. At Jackie's, the last of a set of ramshackle bungalows built up into the hill, in a California structure called a bungalow court, our conversation would get quieter and quieter as we got to Jackie's door. We whispered. All around us, on splintering, inviting balconies shimmering in the glinting sun, bright red geraniums dried out, jade trees dried out, those fluffy purple flowers that mean *California* grew in pavement chinks along with parched, dry rye grass. Jackie pulled out a house key and opened the door. She always looked to her immediate left.

The door to her mother's bedroom was on the immediate left. Stairs went directly *up* to the living room. The trick was to cross about six square feet of red-painted cement (meant to look "Spanish"), get to those stairs, tiptoe up, get to the living room, cross to the kitchen, see if there was anything in the refrigerator. Half the time, Jackie's mom would be in the room at four in the afternoon, still taking a snooze, sleeping off some magic night or other. Sometimes, she wouldn't be snoozing alone. Some guy would be in there, the soles of his feet pointed our way. Wow!

It was something you'd never see at my house; never, never, never, never.

My mother had a steady boyfriend — large, sad, dependable, broken-nosed Charlie — but she never let him get to first base, as the saying goes, except for *once*, to my knowledge, when she kept the three of us up all night, screaming about the outrage of it all. My mother felt about men the way most people felt about Gila monsters: they were all right in their place, *perhaps* — out in the desert, or sulking in a glass zoo cage — but take one of them to bed with you and you'd definitely be up, screaming all night, not in passion, but horror and rage.

So Jackie's mother, Belle, was a mystery to me. To be in bed by choice. Far out. I loved the living room — so far from the parched, lace-curtained, Irish "good taste" of my own mother (which I, in spite of fifty years of trying not to, have inexorably inherited) — flowered couches, "good" prints, white lamps, full bookcases, all that. Jackie's mom had set up a wonderful femme fatale parlor: green carpet, green couches, green lamps with green-flocked negro heads as bases. The only pictures were of Belle, eight-by-ten glossies, looking glamorous and beautiful, letting cigarette smoke come out of her nose.

Here was what Jackie and I had in common: we were alone in the world, living with mothers who, on a *good* day, didn't like us very much. On bad days, they hated us with all their strength. My mother beat me until her arms got tired. Jackie bore scars on one arm where her mother had stabbed her with the jagged end of a broken hair brush. Other times, Belle could be a lot of fun. She'd come home with a sack of hamburgers and we'd sit down and eat them all up. Or she'd take us out to an all-you-can-eat chicken place and the three of us would fill our purses — which we'd already lined carefully with wax paper.

What Jackie and I had in common was that we were poor, so *poor!* My mother worked as a typist. My dad, when he sent the child support, usually had his girlfriends pay it, out of their waitressing wages. Money, in our house, was basically unheard-of.

Jackie's mother, for a while, actually owned a liquor store on Skid Row. She'd drive us — fourteen years old — downtown to work for her. The police never arrested her, because she was going out with the police. She'd swoop in around two A.M., grab us from the store, take us out to an all-night restaurant for huge steak dinners. Can you see why I loved quiet, dreamy Jackie, and both feared and loved her beautiful, crazy mom?

Jackie and I were orphans in the storm. The other part of our life was an unspoken, inarticulate *lust* to get out of the place we were in life and get into another place entirely. As we left junior high school and went on to the tenth grade, the dynamics of high school friendships had made us into four: besides Jackie and me, there were Joan and Nancy, daughters of wealthy Jewish fabric merchants. Joan and Nancy had enough clothes, and they were more than generous about loaning them to us. So while I went through John Marshall High School with a total of two straight skirts, Joan and Nancy lent me at least two dozen more, and they did the same with Jackie. If you didn't know better, you'd think the four of us were from the same economic class.

Nancy had a beach house. Her family was generosity itself in inviting us out to the beach for weekends, where Jackie and I would puzzle (but always silently) about how the maid knew to come in and remove plates after each course, never figuring out until much, much later that Mrs. Stone was stepping on that little button on the floor.

In high school, Jackie grew some gorgeous breasts. It became more depressing that I had a birthmark on my cheek. My mother told me that boys would think I was "an easy lay," that I'd be so desperate to go out on dates I'd sleep with anybody. The strapping youths from John Marshall High got it into their thick heads that Jackie's voluptuous breasts meant that *she* was voluptuous, when, it seemed to me, no two girls in greater Los Angeles could have been less interested in sex than we were. We were so busy *scrambling*, so busy borrowing a blouse to go with a borrowed skirt, so busy being in drama and journalism and getting dates for the prom that lying down in the back seat of a car with our legs waving in the air would have had to come in one hundredth on a list of one hundred. What we did want was love but wouldn't have known it if it had slapped us upside the head, since we'd never seen it. Didn't know what it looked like. Had only read about it in books. Had only seen it on film.

This story is about a friendship that has lasted forty-six years. A story of female friendship in a patriarchy, except that when Jackie and I were little, we couldn't even afford a patriarch! Jackie and I should have ended the way my little sister did, out on the streets doing drugs, going to jail from time to time. We had no prospects. Our saving grace was that we were too ignorant of the world's ways to know it.

The September after we graduated from high school — with high grades and many honors — Jackie took the streetcar over to Occidental College where she'd been accepted as a freshman. They asked her for six or seven thousand dollars, tuition for the year. She took the streetcar home, thought hard about her options, and decided to enroll with me at Los Angeles City College, where the tuition was two dollars and fifty cents a semester. Our two rich friends split off a little from us, with regret. Joan went to UCLA to study art. Nancy invited us over one last time to her beautiful house, to inspect her going-away wardrobe for Stanford. Nancy wrote me a last letter, imploring me to go to UCLA. She saw me sinking, in a forest of furnished rooms, to a bottom of society she couldn't even dream of. (I had run away from home and was living alone now, at seventeen.)

Jackie and I took to L.A. City College two different ways. I studied, became an "intellectual," was never seen outside without my Modern Library edition of *The Brothers Karamazov* or *The Idiot*. Jackie took her gorgeous body and sweet singing voice to the drama department. She learned to sing and dance. She tried out for commercials. Dostoyevsky brought us together one last time. In a pitifully bad student dramatization of *Crime*

and Punishment, the inspector general tapped his arm with a
letter opener and rapped out ominously, "Listen here, Perfori
Pepplevitch . . ." instead of Porfiry Petrovitch. Jackie, sitting next
to me in the auditorium, began to laugh. So did I. We laughed
so hard that our souls left our bodies and floated together in the
dark air above the other, earnest students. We laughed at long
afternoons in homes where they didn't want us, at the humiliation of wearing clothes we'd never pick out for ourselves, of carrying our possessions to a rich beach house in worn paper bags.

    We laughed because we'd got free. The student inspector gen-
eral, an actor who I believe grew up to be Hurd Hatfield, went
solemnly on, waving his letter opener. Pepplevitch! We'd lived
through a lot to get to this sweet, free evening.

In that same set of drama courses, drama productions, somebody decided to put on a medieval Spanish play in which, during
the second act, the romantic leads stopped everything and recited what they'd do for each other once they got married. They
were so specific about all of it! "You bring in the lambs if they
get lost in the hills!" "Yeah, OK, but you have the lamb stew
ready in the stew pot when I get home — and no lying about
why the vegetables aren't done when you just put them in five
minutes ago, because I'm not buying it!" "Yeah, well, OK, but
as many kids as I have, you're going to stand by, and never let
them go hungry!" "Absolutely right, but you're going to have to
teach them good manners, and how to be dutiful children, and
solid members of the church!" "Of *course* I will! What do you
take me for? I'm a good woman. I know what I'm supposed to
do!" "Well, cool. Because I'm a good man, and I know what I'm
supposed to do, too."

    Just great, wasn't it, that back in twelfth-century Spain they
knew what they were supposed to do, and then, in theory at
least, they went ahead and *did* it?

    But it was — to say the least — a little different for untrained
women let loose in a crumbling patriarchy in greater Los An-

geles in the late middle of this century. Of the four young ladies of whom I've been speaking, only Nancy, the Stanford one, appeared to have gotten her instructions clearly. She finished school, worked — as I remember hearing, because I didn't see her during this time — in New York publishing for two years, came into some inherited wealth of her own, married a business-man, lived in a beautiful home in Greenwich, Connecticut, raised three fine children, began taking graduate classes in ar-chaeology, was first a docent, then a professor, always kept her cute figure, and minded her tennis game.

Our other comparatively wealthy girlfriend took the adven-ture-and-alienation route. She skipped off to Paris for a year. (My first husband and I went with her.) Joan came back, went to some more art school, and, trained for absolutely nothing, married a nice guy who also appeared to be trained for abso-lutely nothing. Faced with their parents' irritated scorn, Joan and Harry artfully slid down the American economic ladder, so afraid were they of ending up like their merchant parents.

I was stuck by then in graduate school, with that sweet, Eu-rasian first husband who wanted to be an anthropologist. We managed an apartment house in the slums, "working our way through college." My idea of homemaking was this: take one stick of butter, one pound of cheese, one container of sour cream. Mix with the contents of four baked potatoes. Brown. Serve. We were so poor I washed diapers in the bathtub. We were so poor that when a young lady-novelist, Alison Lurie, came visiting, she looked into my closet and made me — with-out asking — a purple cotton dress. My in-laws came over every day with king-size cans of peaches.

Jackie, it seemed, had broken out. She had been appearing in a wonderful little show in L.A. called *The Billy Barnes Revue* — eight or ten kids dressed in black, with eight or ten chairs and an upright piano, singing Billy's songs. For years they were a hit. Jackie, with a great deal of emotional effort, had moved out of her mother's house. She worked as everything. She wore polar bear outfits. She gave out Vanda orchids in supermarkets. She sang in the Sacramento Light Opera. She worked as a Vegas showgirl. And around seven years after we'd graduated high school she married a dancer from *The Billy Barnes Revue* in a charming show business wedding at the Hollywood Roosevelt Hotel. Buster Keaton was in attendance. Our friend Joan, looking stunning in yellow chiffon, wandered around with her hands on her chest, saying, "My marriage is on the rocks." Jackie — in a wedding dress borrowed from Nancy — looked radiant. And I felt ashamed and poor, twin emotions that took up the first twenty-five years of my life.

Four of us had married. Three of us were still in town. And this is how *out of it* we were, in terms of the world we were living in. Joan decided to give a dinner party. She invited me and my husband (actually my second husband by then, a dour Slovak with high cheekbones and a terrible temper), and Jackie and her tap-dancing husband. Of course, Joan's own sweet-natured, untrained-for-anything husband was in attendance.

The small house was spotless and perfectly decorated. The meal, copied from Joan's mother's Albanian-Jewish recipes, was perfection itself. Medallions of veal. Red cabbage simmered in wine. Homemade potato pancakes. Watercress salad. *Crème brûlée* — nostalgic homage to the year Joan and I had spent in Europe. All this in the early sixties, when haute cuisine hadn't yet properly come to L.A. All this in a three-bedroom tract house on the crumbling lip of the concrete-lined L.A. River. It should have been swell, right? But even after thirty years, I remember it as one of the most trying social events of my life.

Because, though Joan's husband scurried around quoting García Lorca and speaking of the merits of Mortimer Adler — his "Great Books" program called, I think, the Syntoptikon? — we had reckoned without the other two human beings who sat, slumped and sullen, in the living room. The Slovak — who was studying romantic poetry at school — squinted at a copy of *Popular Mechanics*. The graceful tap dancer with the beautiful singing voice pored over another edition of *Popular Mechanics*. They didn't speak *one word* all night. They didn't eat their cabbage and they never smiled. Because Jackie and I were so scared of our husbands, we twittered for a while, and then fell silent.

What was lacking, I see now, was a clear code of conduct: one of those peasant pageant plays like the one we'd seen at City College, where the man says, "Whenever we go out to dinner parties it always has to be with *my* friends and never with *your* friends, because the Patriarchy is slipping, and there can never be a time where men aren't the center of attention!" And then the woman could answer back: "That's OK by me as long as you do your share with the children, and I'm talking particularly about child support in case you run off, because the traditional family is going down the drain along with the Patriarchy!"

If there had been that kind of dramatic blueprint, maybe it would have been possible to strike an offstage devil's bargain: "Listen, I'll eat the red cabbage, I'll make ten remarks an evening to your loathsome girlfriends, if I don't have to pay child support ten years from now," and the lady could have chimed back in, "It's a done deal, buddy, if I can go out and work without catching hell for neglecting the kids. *And* if I can have a lover on the side to talk to, you can read all the *Popular Mechanics* in the world!"

But we didn't have that. That didn't happen. We lived for years in our husbands' worlds, fixing meals for men who talked bullfighting and Hemingway in my case, or pretending to be decorative and dumb and marginal in Jackie's case, even when — considering the vagaries of show business — the wife of the tap dancer at times made more than the tap dancer did. And the kind husband who wasn't trained to do anything never did anything.

There was a good ten-year period when I saw more of rebellious Joan than showgirl Jackie. This probably happened because Joan split with her husband and took up with a writer friend of my husband. And even now, after twenty years, after that poor writer friend is dead, it *gripes* me to remember how much *attention* my husband and his various friends demanded for themselves around these manuscripts they were going to write — Jim, who loved bullfighting, and suffered, and wrote a bad book; Cody, who subsisted on lentils and wrote a bad book; Gerry, Joan's friend, who caused serious trouble and wrote a bad book; and even my husband, who wrote eleven pages of what could have been a swell book, but retreated from that project and turned his talents instead to writing love poems to his editorial assistant (and leaving them where I would be sure to find them). But women all around me, with no attention at all, were beginning to write, beginning to publish, with no attention at all.

During this period, when my husband was off at a demonstration in Berkeley, saving the world in the company of his editorial assistant, I drove over to Jackie's lavish Hollywood house, where she was living with her husband. She had taken in her mother, Belle, who had stomach cancer, and installed her in the maid's room.

But what a maid's room! Balloons covered the ceiling, the walls bristled with photos and movie posters; Belle's bed was piled high with toys. A Nixon dart board hung at the foot of the bed, within easy playing distance. Belle greeted me cheerfully, demanded Chinese food from Jackie, ate a few bites, labeled it tasteless, chatted a while, laughed a lot. She was dying. Afterward, Jackie took me for a tour of the house. They had adopted two children, and perhaps because of this the living room was filled not with furniture of the couch variety, but with enormous toys: slides, cars that you could ride around in, plastic mazes and tunnels you could climb through. When Jackie's husband came home, he came in the back door and went straight to the refrigerator for a beer. He didn't look too happy to see me, and I vamoosed. To drive home, out of Hollywood, the length of the San Fernando Valley and up into Topanga Canyon, where we lived in a minuscule, book-lined cabin that you could only get to by going up in a tram or trudging up a switchback path, was to cross two or three worlds. It seemed, at that time, that Jackie and I weren't really friends anymore — not from any ill feeling, but because time, place, space, different husbands, different lives had separated us, would keep us separated forever. Earlier, when Jackie had had a baby and he had tragically died after only six days, I hadn't even written. It seemed I didn't know her well enough. Also, Jackie and her husband had gotten rich and comparatively famous, and with the obdurate pride of the snotty poor, I thought it would be best to keep my self to myself. Stupid!

Joan and I lived for some years in the harrowing land of divorce. (What women don't remember to say very often is that, as you get used to it, it's a fair amount of fun.) Many evenings she and her three kids and I and my two kids and whatever semi-boyfriends we could round up would drive on out to a great restaurant called the China Palace. The kids would go hog wild and we'd giggle and laugh and fall about, and nobody would get on our case. We could play! Nobody could order us around! Although we were dead broke and had our troubles — some of them would develop into tragedies — at the time, we had some fun.

The lanyard goes on weaving itself. After eight years as a single person (my older daughter recalls me perhaps more accurately as a "tramp"), I found a wonderful man who looked to me to be the real thing, the authentic article. After nineteen years we're still together. Joan found this unbearable. "I can't stand your happiness," she told me frankly. "I can't stand that you've found a man that you really like."

Writing this down, let me interject, it seems so strange to even *look* at this material. You live in a dream world — *I* live in a dream world — where friends get along easily, as in a beer commercial. In reality, you may meet three or four real friends in a lifetime, and your friends may not get along with your social circle or with your family. (I had a strong friendship once, a ten-year one, that was destroyed because we both loved the same very undeserving man. When she flew off with him to the island of Yap, I was devastated — not because of him, I wanted to *kill* him, but my heart broke for the loss of her.)

Meanwhile, over in an even fancier house that almost qualified as a mansion, Jackie's husband was getting migraine headaches. They were so bad that finally, just to cure them, he had to move out of the house. He didn't move in with an editorial assistant, but dance's equivalent: a sweet and pretty female who was ready to throw in her lot with the tap dancer and needlepoint a million throw pillows, one of which averred most touchingly, "God is Love."

Jackie wouldn't let herself notice this (ah, does this sound familiar?) but the day came when she finally did. Once again, a woman alone, locked within that configuration in which we had both grown up: it's you, just you, in a house, with children who die before your eyes, of loneliness. There's a rope, hanging down through life. A divorced woman hangs at the end of it. You thrash and thrash, and go into free fall, and if you get lucky, you land on something.

Joan had taken to the divorce life. Something in her liked hanging out with the raffish sort and never having to go to a "couples" dinner party again. During my own eight years I'd met some "pretty miscellaneous people," as my father liked to call them, and gotten something out of my system. I'd also begun to write, which my husband had frowned upon almost as much as he did my friends. Coming home early from work one day, he found me in tears trying to piece a short story together with scissors and tape: "I suppose it won't hurt for you to do this," he said. "I suppose it's good therapy." (And all the while that little snake was dipping his wick in his *editorial* assistant!) But I had my writing now, so I found ground, shifting ground, under my feet.

Jackie, in free fall, noticed a different kind of material than Joan and I had seen. When Jackie got a movie paycheck after the separation, she had the temerity to open her own account. The bank *tattled* on her, basely throwing its loyalty to her husband since they considered him to be the better investment. In the show business circle, divorce was different. One wife of a man-in-the-movies widely considered to be a saint had been left their mansion, except that her husband hadn't paid the taxes on it for years. A year later, the government took it away. Another dumped wife of a famous person lived in a mansion but couldn't pay the utilities. My own therapist told me of another actress who had been forced to perform a lot of blow jobs (with a gun to her head) on her husband and then had been dumped, turned in for a younger, cuter model. (Jackie never told me any of this, but as a journalist, doing interviews, I came to see this material, too.)

Like Jackie, some of these divorced women had been showgirls, singers, dancers, actresses. Their working days were done. Many of them had been waited on and catered to for so long that — like Chinese women teetering on bound feet — they were in great part physically and emotionally helpless. They suffered terrible rejection and *then* they got to see their husbands clutching new babes in sleazy tabloids. Talk about your cruel and unusual punishment!

Jackie, Joan, and I ended up like many divorced women — without an income, with children who yearn for their fathers with a terrible yearning and are ashamed to be seen in (just) your company, and with loneliness that stares and stares at you like an endless Escher engraving. I only wanted to annihilate one Slovak long-distance runner and his (actually rather likable) editorial assistant. Jackie had *always* thought big, or else she wouldn't have made it from poverty into respectable show business: her own talk show for a while; places in ongoing TV series as the beautiful, ditsy, and dumb girlfriend; even a part in the very first *Little Shop of Horrors* where, with greats like Jack

Nicholson, she played Audrey Plant, the demented female lead. Jackie got *mad*, not at the tap dancer, but at the whole American system that trained women to be pretty and dumb, used them for a while, and then spit them out with no apologies, no alimony, a pack of lies, and a lifetime ration of self-hatred.

Jackie decided to change things. Nobody thought to tell her that she couldn't, that she had no credentials — not even a college degree. (She'd been too busy kicking up her heels in Vegas, or taking care of her dying mom, or trying to take care of her husband and kids, or singing her head off in various light operas across the country.) Jackie decided that she was going to change the system, change the way people thought about women alone with children. She started right where she was, with band-singers and starlets, secretaries and dancing gypsies who, in their thirties, forties, fifties, had been unceremoniously dumped, and found themselves in despair and in free fall. She became a founding member of LADIES (Life After Divorce Is Eventually Sane). There would be no badmouthing The Boys, she insisted. They weren't women scorned; they were women inventing new ways to live. They would take this chickenshit hand they'd been dealt, turn it into fertilizer, and grow a beautiful garden. No more loneliness! They would band together in defiantly joyful crowds.

By the time this is published, Jackie Joseph and I will both be sixty. We will have been — with that ten-year hiatus — close friends, best friends, for forty-seven years. I've gotten fat; Jackie's deaf in one ear. But I don't see that we've changed much. Jackie went to the Democratic Convention, unofficially, and managed to shake hands with Bill Clinton so many times that, as she said, "If I'd been him, I'd have had the Secret Service check me out!" When I went to New York (still the scared Californian) and spoke on a dais with Jimmy Breslin, E. L. Doctorow, and Joyce Carol Oates, Jackie went with me. Afterward, as the writers signed books, she drifted up to the dais, filched the place cards, and stuck them up on the toilet tank in our hotel suite for luck or for fun. Jackie ballroom dances, I drive fast cars. The days of my silver 911S Porsche with the Targa top are gone; I drive a Nissan NX now and a car salesman, upon finding that out, eloquently expressed his feelings at the unseemliness of it all: "Ugh!"

Jackie has rounded up the LADIES and put them on television talk shows, but, more to the point, she's hauled them out to small desert towns where dumped women, too scared to leave their houses, will conquer their fear to come out and see the lately discarded Mrs. Michael Landon, Mrs. Pat Morita, Mrs. Jerry Lewis. To these frightened, lonely women, the lovely LADIES say: "Listen! It's bad for all of us. But we can get over the personal hurt, and we can change the system." Jackie works with state government, persuading our leaders that they can do more for women. She works for an outfit called Displaced Homemakers, again for those housewives whose husbands have strolled out and never come back, never honored their responsibilities. Jackie gets residuals, most recently from "Gremlin" movies, but she takes in boarders, too, so that she can tell the saddest of the sad, "Well, you can always take in boarders. That's what *I* do!"

And I have my writing and my family, including the authentic man who made Joan so unhappy. One of my daughters writes and one works with the homeless. They light my life with their loyalty and competence. And, like any other writer, I like to think I change the world with every word. It's true, too, I know. Every word a woman writes changes the story of the world, revises the official version. Every book a woman buys changes the economic balance of the country by ten or twenty bucks. They say women only get paid sixty-nine cents on every dollar paid to men. They forget to say that women work at least one and a half times as hard as men, and all those extra thirty-one cents are bound to add up. What Jackie and I want — although we go about it differently — is to jigger around with the world so that there will be fewer penniless, unloved children dawdling on their way home after school because their sad, unloved, rejected mothers don't want to see them and have no idea how to care for them. We don't want an America where bright young women work their butts off making great dinners for unmannered churls, or suffer blows, or watch some husband on a toot put his fist through the wall or pitch the family barbecue into the swimming pool to make a point.

Above all, we want women in their forties, fifties, sixties, *seventies* to get together after they've been left and make a lot of money and have a great big party. Not for revenge, but for the fun of it, and for our children so that they don't have to be scared when they look at us — or at the future.

Why haven't Jackie and I quarreled through the years? I believe, more than anything, it's because our taste in men has been radically different and our interest in "passion" comparatively muted. It would have never occurred to us to scramble for the same man because, without saying anything bad about the men we like, we don't like the same kind. Speaking more generally about my friends (with the single exception of the dear one who ran off with a mutual lover to the dreaded island of Yap), there's always been a *noblesse oblige* kind of sharing of ex-husbands and ex-gents — *You* take him! Oh, no, you like him better, *you* take him! Oh, I wouldn't dream of it. *Well*, if you *insist* — And these transactions continue, down through decades.

Last summer, when my younger daughter was getting married, she registered at a good department store but the woman in charge began to behave strangely. She changed coffeepots on the computer list, she wouldn't sell certain tablecloths — it turned out that she was devising a trousseau for Clara's *divorce;* what she would need after the marriage was over. "Let's face it," the saleswoman raved to me on the phone one day. "Men come and go. All you ever really have are your kids. And your friends." I don't know if she's right or wrong.

Finally, I want to say something about physical appearance, since it's competitiveness over men and over physical appearance that allegedly drives wedges into relationships between women. Jackie was always very beautiful, showgirl beautiful, and still is. "God damn it!" my stepmother (my age) once remarked crabbily, "Jackie still looks about fifteen. How does she do it?"

I, on the other hand, was born with that birthmark on my face, a neat map of North and South America. My mother inadvertently channeled thousands of dollars into the profession of psychology when she told me men would only sleep with me because they felt sorry for me. My answer to my mother about that and every other matter has always been an enormous *NO!* My birthmark is there and part of my life's "work" has been to take the scariness out of it by having a good time and making a life I like.

Only very recently have I begun to realize that Jackie has had to struggle with her looks, too. When confronted with big creamy breasts and a beautiful face and a laugh that sounds like crystal bells it's hard for men — and women — to get past that material manifestation. It's hard to argue cogently in the state Assembly when you know those drowsy old guys are just checking out your chest.

Hard for a woman — even now — to be important. Hard to imagine that what we have to say means anything at all. Even now! But when the car salesman says "ugh!" when he sees I drive a bright red NX, I can call up Jackie. When a crass producer calls up Jackie, asking if she knows where he can find "a young Jackie Joseph–type," she can call me.

I know I've rambled here, but I'm not sorry. I could talk about us parasailing together in Mazatlán, or spending various weeks at various spas, or the wedding showers we've given for each other's children, or how when we collaborated for a while writing episodic television we ended up doing one of the very last segments of "Barnaby Jones," and the meetings went terribly because we couldn't come up with a suitable murderer: "Why would they do that?" Jackie kept asking plaintively. "Why don't they just sit down and talk things out?"

Finally, we settled on a guy who deserved to be killed. An adulterous husband, naturally. I believe we wrote the worst-ever episode of "Barnaby Jones," in which an autistic child solves a murder (but can't talk, of course). It contains the immortal line: "Not now, Frank! Can't you see I've got a problem?" which ranks as our personal fave, right up there with: "Listen here, Perfori Pepplevitch!"

The world is full of distressing things. But I count it a miracle that two desperately poor, desperately lonely semi-orphans could, day after dopey day, put together a friendship that can last up to (and further than) half a century. I know the world is better because Jackie Joseph lives in it. I'm lucky, so lucky, to know her.

ANGELA DAVIS-GARDNER

✗ ✗ ✗ ✗ ✗ ✗ ✗ ✗ ✗ ✗ ✗ ✗ ✗

The Ginger Dreams

I STILL HAVE THE journal I kept the year I turned thirteen. It was my first work of fiction. Aside from lists of my best swimming times, swoonings over various boys, and jeremiads against my parents for such crimes as curfews and telephone limits, the life I recorded was largely an invented one. The central strand of lies had to do with friendship.

My actual friends — and I did have a few, in spite of being a shy, bookish creature — hardly figured in my journal. Not mentioned at all was Trudy, my soul sister from elementary school who had deserted me, once we arrived at junior high, to try to make it in the "in" crowd. It was this inner circle (which Trudy did not, to my satisfaction, ever really penetrate) who were the intimates of my journal. They were the dazzling galaxy of Southern belles at the center of the universe that was Jackson Junior High. All these girls were pretty, of course (or, even better, "cute"), sumptuously dressed (cashmere sweater sets in shades of Necco wafers), and supremely self-confident, sashaying down the halls in a susurrus of crinolines, bestowing their dimpled smiles and honeyed "Hey, y'alls" upon the favored. One of these girls, Ginger, who in real life barely acknowledged my existence, was the best friend of my journal. Her phone number is at the top of the list in the directory inside the front cover; in the text are notes on Ginger's "Raves" and "Pet Peeves," and numerous conversations with her, recorded as though they had actually taken place.

Ginger, along with her handmaidens Lundie and Boots, was the collective sun around which the inner circle revolved. Lundie was blond and willowy, with smoky blue eyes; Boots was a slightly less pretty version, but she made up for it in "personality," chattering nonstop as she bounced from class to class, her ponytail in constant motion. Ginger had such lustrous, red, wavy hair that people called her The Breck Girl. But there was nothing soft about her brown eyes, ever on the lookout for objects of scorn. With my burdens of gawkiness, inferior clothes, and wrong neighborhood, I was occasionally a target of her derision. More than once, in the hall and in the locker room getting ready for gym, I sensed those brown eyes upon me, then heard the verdict in whispers behind my back. But no stranger reading my diary could have guessed I felt an outcast. "Lundie and Boots said I looked darling today," I gushed in one entry. "They all just loved my new skirt, and Ginger asked us all over for a slumber party Friday."

Writing, Jean Rhys said, is consolation therapy, and I consoled myself with a vengeance, fabricating in entry after entry evidence of my acceptability. There are accounts of imagined mutual conspiracies (including several variations on the humiliation of Trudy), double dates with Ginger and her boyfriend Ned, and an initiation into a secret, exclusive club. "Dear Diary," I wrote,

> Last night I was inducted into the Royal Omegas. It was the most thrilling moment of my life, so far. The ceremony was held at Ginger's house. All of us wore white dresses and carried candles. There were some beautiful prayers and poems, and a vow which is so secret, dear diary, that I pledged never ever to breathe it, so I guess I'd better not write it here, but what it means is, friends to the death.

Even those actual triumphs of my life recorded in my journal were embellished with notes of Ginger and Company's envy or

approval. On the day I was chosen editor of the school newspaper, I added this gloss: "Ginger, Lundie, and Boots were
thrilled for me, I could tell." The first time my name appeared
on the special honor roll, I recorded that fact, then added a reaction from Ginger, a wistful "Gosh, I wish I was smart." (This
was surely the height of my self-deception: smart was the last
thing most girls in the South of the 1950s longed to be.)

Only on one occasion did I attempt to make reality and fantasy merge. Encouraged — in spite of the surprise in her voice —
by Ginger's comment that my new dress was cute, and buoyed
by her question about where I'd gotten this enviable item, I was
emboldened to ask the three of them if they'd like to go to a
movie with me the next Saturday. They consulted one another
with quick, ironic glances, then Ginger said, her voice sugary,
her smile mean (that oxymoron of affect for which Southern
belles are famous), "I'm sorry, we're busy." I did not, needless
to say, record this remembrance of "friendship" in my journal.

Ninth and tenth grade were happier years for me. My ugly
duckling phase was over; I began going out with boys; I was
active in school politics. I made a number of new girlfriends —
including, eventually, a few members of the Jackson Junior High
inner circle (which remained prominent and intact even in the
larger high school). Though Ginger never became my friend, I
did not (with the exception of a post-prom party to which she
did not invite me) think I cared.

But the curious part of the Ginger phenomenon — which
otherwise might have seemed a more pathological version of the
imaginary companions of my kindergarten days — was her endurance in my psyche. For well into my adulthood, years beyond
the time I'd known her, Ginger appeared in my dreams, a powerful specter of a not-friend, hanging on as if she had something
to teach me.

Children are infamously cruel, as every parent knows. But even
so, I have to take several deep breaths when my child gets in the

car after school and wails that so-and-so "doesn't like me anymore" or "won't let me in their club." I have to remind myself
that he does have friends, and that he, unlike his mother at his
age, has learned to voice his feelings. While that doesn't erase
pain, it does help him endure the rejections that are an inevitable
part of growing up.

Just how fierce the exclusionary instinct is in young children
was documented in Vivian Gussin Paley's recent book, *You
Can't Say You Can't Play*. A teacher at the University of Chicago
laboratory schools, Ms. Paley tried to teach her kindergartners
to stop rejecting others on the playground. There was considerable resistance, bluntly summed up by the child who said that if
kids can't exclude those they don't like, "then what's the whole
point of playing?" Older children Ms. Paley consulted were
equally discouraging. "You're not going to go through your
whole life not being excluded," one fifth-grade boy told her,
"so you may as well learn it now."

Most solutions offered the outcast child tacitly celebrate the
supremacy of the group. The kid who is "different" is encouraged to lose weight, to acquire the one-hundred-dollar sneakers
"everyone else" is wearing, or to stop using "big" words. Even
Ms. Paley's admirable efforts to ingrain a sense of fairness in her
young pupils suggest that the real power lies in the group. But
as these kids grow up they all need to learn, insiders and outsiders alike, that the center is not in the circle but in the self.

In his essay "The Inner Ring," originally a speech delivered to
students on the verge of adulthood, C. S. Lewis describes the
dangerous seductiveness of exclusive circles. While a group of
friends may be drawn together by shared interests or mutual
sympathy, the charm of the exclusive circle (or inner ring, as
Lewis calls it) lies in a perceived sense of its superiority. Inner
rings are pervasive in every sphere of human activity, he points
out, not just in society, but in schools, the professions, business, the arts. At some point in everyone's life — and for many
people, throughout all their years — one of the dominant pas-

sions "is the desire to be inside the local Ring and the [attendant] terror of being left outside." But this is a quest doomed to failure, for within each ring are more rings, like the skins of an onion, with nothing at the center.

Old age and death hold their worst terrors for those who have wasted their lives. Tolstoy's "The Death of Ivan Ilyich" is the story of such a man, an inner ringer facing the consequences of a life dominated by the desire to be inside.

The story opens with the announcement of Ivan Ilyich's death and his "friends'" chilling reactions to it. All wonder who will get his place. One is irked to have to leave his card game to commiserate with the widow (whose main distress, it turns out, is financial). Each friend is mainly relieved that it is Ivan Ilyich and not himself who has died.

The narrative then doubles back in time to tell the story of Ivan Ilyich's life, and death, from his point of view. His life had been "most simple and most ordinary, and therefore most terrible." There is a connection between his superficial friendships, his loveless marriage, his ultimately meaningless work. He has lived to please, and to get ahead; consequently his was a shallow, skimmed-over life. Only as he faces death does it occur to him that his own quickly suppressed impulses might have been the real thing, "and all the rest was false." But it is this realization that allows him, at last, to reclaim his own life; in the end, honesty is Ivan Ilyich's salvation.

For many writers, there is a connection between lonely childhoods and writing. The novelist Jose Luis Doñoso, when asked why he became a writer, said, "I wasn't invited to the party."

Being a solitary child shaped me as a writer, too, since being an outsider has the great advantage of making one a keen observer, and I was that. But perceptiveness and the pleasures of consolation — even combined with a talent for language — are not enough. I was a failure as a writer — and not much of a friend, either — until I learned Ivan Ilyich's lesson, the crucial value of honesty. And it was, oddly enough, from my not-friend Ginger that I learned it.

When I began writing seriously in my early twenties, I took as my models Eudora Welty and other Southerners, writers I had read for years. I suppose I gained something from this — there is value in imitation — but what I wrote was an echo, not a voice. I grew up in the South as a somewhat aloof outsider, in an intellectual-artistic milieu; my parents were both writers and there were always painters and poets at the house. We didn't live in a neighborhood but in an isolated part of the countryside (I could not be, like Eudora Welty has said of herself in Jackson, Mississippi, "locally underfoot"), nor did we go to church or eat Southern food. My brother and I were corrected if we dropped our g's; Southern accents were discouraged.

Mine was not the South of books, so I thought it wouldn't do as a source of fiction. I perceived my own family, my own South, as not "colorful" enough to write about — no Snopeses, no Milledgeville peacocks — so I borrowed my settings. The more serious problem was that I avoided writing about the very pain that was the source of my material. Instead, my characters were charming eccentrics, mindless as clams. "Why don't you write about people who *think*?" my teacher Peter Taylor said to me once: it was the closest anyone came, in my waking life, to trying to make me confront the truth.

The truth lay in the past at Jackson Junior High; it began to emerge when I was in my early thirties, in dreams about Ginger. The Ginger of my dreams had aged with me but she was the same scornful nemesis she'd been twenty years before; she seemed to be reminding me, again and again, how unacceptable I still was, unlovable, hopeless, failed. Some of the dreams were about exposure; many — for reasons I did not understand — were about writing.

In one dream, Ginger was inspecting my unkempt back yard while I watched from my bedroom window. Dressed in pink suit, hat, and high heels, she disdainfully picked her way across the

weedy grass, shaking her head over ragged beds of flowers and neglected shrubs. Occasionally she paused to make notes in a book.
She interviewed my neighbor, the two of them gossiping over the
back fence while Ginger continued to scribble in her book. Then
Ginger came to my door and held up the book she'd been writing in; on the front her name and the title — *Biography of a
Garden* — were printed in gold. "The critics just raved," she
said in that nasty-sweet voice, "I know you're happy for me."

In another dream I met Ginger and a man who looked to be
her twin at the University of Illinois Chicago Circle Campus. She
was chewing on a strand of licorice. "Have you met my husband?" Ginger said with a malicious smile. "Marc Davis? The
writer?" She stuck out her tongue — black, from the licorice —
then began to chant, in grade school singsong, "Nyah nyah ni
boo boo, go stick your head in doo doo." Only when I woke did
I realize that this husband of hers had my own last name — my
maiden name. Clearly, in both dreams, Ginger had appropriated
something of mine, but it was years before I discovered the significance of this and other similar dreams.

My epiphany came when I was on a flight from New York to
Chicago, where I was living then. It was a bleak period in my
life: I was recently divorced, and lonely; the few friendships I
had were superficial. What little fiction I had produced during
that time was derivative and pale.

On the plane I happened to sit next to a woman named
Sandra. She was an English professor at an Ivy League university, on her way to deliver a paper at a conference. In the course
of our conversation about academia (I was debating about going
for a Ph.D. in English) she noticed my Southern accent (which
my parents had not been able to eradicate after all) and asked
where I was from. It turned out that she'd lived for a while in the
town where I grew up and that we had been, though briefly, in
the seventh grade at Jackson Junior High the same year. At the
mention of the school, Sandra cackled with delight. That laugh
of hers, and her dominant feature, close-set eyes behind thick

glasses, brought back my memory of her. Though she hadn't been in my homeroom, I recalled the slightly anxious stir she'd caused throughout the school when she'd arrived mid-year, a transfer from the North and said to be "smart as a whip."

I asked her if she remembered Ginger. Indeed she did. "Honey, do you like my hay-ar?" she mimicked, patting her own hair and batting her eyes. When I confessed that Ginger had made my life miserable, she hooted. "That little twit?" Abruptly she fell silent and looked out the window. "A bitch actually," she said, "they all were."

Then she told me her story. Her father had been transferred from Connecticut to manage a textile mill in our town, and they had moved to a large house in the neighborhood where Ginger and other members of the inner circle lived. Sandra became chummy with these girls, partly because of her parents' connection, but also because of her gift for parody. She entertained Ginger, Lundie, Boots, and the others with imitations of our teachers and various "losers" among the students. When I asked — a bit hesitantly — if she'd ever done me, she looked vague, then a little embarrassed. "I really don't remember you," she confessed. "I wish I had known you," she added, "having an intelligent friend might have saved me."

She had kept a diary, Sandra told me with a deep sigh. In it she set down her true evaluations of the inner circle: Ginger, Lundie, Boots, and the others were superficial, vain, pea-brained. Thought they were so pretty, but weren't, with their washed-out, waspy faces and dumb blue eyes. But at country club gatherings, birthday parties, spend-the-nights, Sandra went on amusing them, trying to charm her way into friendship with them. Until the day they found, and read, her diary.

They were all at her house for lunch on the patio. "Mother had outdone herself — vol-au-vent, duck in aspic, things they didn't see at the country club." As the chocolate soufflé was served to oohs and aahs, two or three girls went upstairs, "to powder their noses." They were a long time coming back. Sandra heard giggling through the open window of her bedroom just above and went inside to investigate. She met the girls coming down the stairs. We have to go now, they murmured; they would not meet her eyes. Back on the patio there were whispers, then a sudden mass exodus.

In her room, Sandra discovered her open desk drawer; the journal was gone. She managed not to go to school the next day — convincing her mother she was sick — and when she did return, Ginger, Boots, all of them, looked through her as though the space she occupied were empty air. But bits of her journal, sentences and paragraphs in her handwriting, showed up throughout the day, one scrap taped inside her desk, others on her locker, in her cubbyhole in the cloakroom.

"What did you do?" I asked, horrified. I could imagine a sentence in my florid hand, "Ginger and Lundie and Boots are my best friends now," pasted to my Latin book.

"Went home sick," Sandra said with a laugh, "very sick." And she managed to stay sick all that year, with aching joints, weakness, recurrent low-grade fevers ("the old thermometer-in-hot-water trick," she said, grinning), polio-like symptoms that terrified her mother and mystified the doctors. She didn't go back to school that spring, and the next year, at her insistence — with a passion her parents never questioned — was sent back North, to boarding school.

"What an awful story," I managed to say. Shivering, I thought about, but did not mention, my own journal. We ordered drinks and sat silent for a while. Then we plunged into an orgy of analysis, laying bare the petty foibles of Ginger and Company in adolescence (their prime, we were sure) and speculating on the particulars of their present lives: face-lifts, tummy tucks, liposuctions, repairing everything but their souls.

We ordered a second round; Sandra launched into parody mode and we grew hilarious. The Japanese men across the aisle looked alarmed, then packed up their briefcases and moved forward. "We're regressing," we cried to each other, doubling over with laughter. As the plane began to descend, we wiped our eyes, exchanged addresses, and told each other how cathartic this had been. Walking away, I envied Sandra her honesty. How much stronger her scornful diary had been than mine, with its pathetic fantasies; how much worse to have had my journal exposed and read. But then it came to me as I got into my cab: she'd pandered to those girls; she hadn't been any more truthful than I was. She was just the flip side of myself, because I'd been scornful, too; the difference was I'd kept my judgment a secret, even from myself.

I had admired nothing about Ginger; that was evident in the pleasure I'd just taken in her dissection. And my disdain had been there in my dreams, all that time, waiting for me to claim it. Biography of a garden, indeed! And gathering material from gossip — ridiculous. I had been longing for someone I didn't respect or like.

It was a simple revelation in a way, but it ended the Ginger dreams. And it was the first inkling of what I began to learn about friendship and writing.

I have been lucky, these past few years, to belong to a circle of writers, a group of novelists that meets each week to discuss one another's work. Two major strands of my life, writing and friendship, come together in this circle; the common strand is honesty. Honesty about reactions to the material we read to each other; about difficulties we're having writing a particular piece, or with hearing criticism; occasionally, about feeling competitive with one another, though we're always pressing one another toward our best and richest (which often means darkest) material. From all this, other feelings naturally flow, too: warmth, kinship, a sense of connectedness that helps in every other part of life.

There are seven in our group, two men and five women. As writers we have quite different material and voices. As critics our points of view are so distinct that when one member is absent, we may fill in part of what he or she might have focused on in a particular piece. What makes our group work well together in spite of our differences is mutual respect, trust, and similar values about what matters most in writing: being true to one's material, getting at the characters' real feelings, and using language which, however fine, does not throw a veil between the reader and the page. As a critical body, we are greater than the sum of our parts: by the time a piece has survived several sessions, it's received a synergistic commentary that wouldn't have been possible if each person had read the story alone. Partly this is because one comment inspires another; it's also the locus of the circle, the warm security it offers critic and writer. It is the kind of friendship I'd been looking for all along.

Last year the daughter of one of my friends from Jackson Junior High — she had also been what I thought of as an outsider there, like myself — appeared at a signing for a book I'd just published. It was like seeing a ghost, she was so like her mother, tall and graceful with a sweet, shy smile. "Mama told me you were talented even then," she said. I felt, at that, twinges of regret and guilt. There had been someone who valued who I was, yet I'd wished for another set of friends who did not, and whom I did not even care for. In that I had betrayed my friend, and myself. If I'd been candid with myself, back there at Jackson Junior High, I might have found myself in a warm circle even then.

And I might have gotten to my real writing sooner. Only as I've composed this essay has it occurred to me that the dream of Ginger in my scruffy back yard was a dream of possibilities as well as of misplaced scorn. For everything I've ever written in what I think of as my own voice has had its origin in an image of a garden, or a tree. Once I told Ginger to get the hell out of my yard, then the book that she claimed as hers, that biography of my garden, became mine to write.

Now that I've demasked her, I feel a certain fondness for the Ginger of my dreams. Had she not persisted in my unconscious, tenacious as a weed, I might still be living, and writing, a lie.

X X X X X X X X X X X X X

Road Trip: The Real Thing

THE THING ABOUT Thelma and Louise *was, if they'd had any children, they couldn't have driven off the top of that precipice. The thing about us is, we have six children between us, and we have to come back in shape to make it through next week.* How to describe my friend Pam? We met in childbirth class; she was having her fourth daughter, I was having my first son. On Christmas Eve she called from the hospital to say her baby was born; I immediately went into labor. Pam went to Brandeis and NYU film school before she married a divorced pediatrician at twenty-three and had a set of twins. The year her youngest was born she was thirty, trying to finish a master's thesis in fiction at Boston University. She still hasn't finished that thesis. When a magazine offers to rent me the car of my dreams and pay expenses if I'll reprise a currently topical cinematic road trip with a female friend, I invite Pam. She has to call nine mothers before she finds someone to fill in as soccer coach and drive the girls' team all the way to Sudbury. *This isn't* Thelma and Louise, *this is* Escape of the Suburban Mothers. *We're like two animals let out of a cage: we don't know what to do first.*

What I do first is examine the Dream Car, a red Jag convertible delivered this morning by a beefy blond male who drove it up in the rain from New Jersey and departed immediately via a waiting taxi. He did show me how to put the top down, which had to do with engaging the emergency brake, but he failed to advise me of the nature of the car, which is long, low, and essentially female: if she thinks anyone is fooling with her, she shuts down completely and pulses, reflecting the sky in her red flanks. Her doors have to be locked and unlocked with a certain decisive turn to the left; if the key is perceived to hesitate or tremble, the locks freeze and simply won't work for two minutes. Then one tries again for that essential flick of the wrist, a subtle movement which inspires confidence throughout the car's delicate circuitry. I discover all this by locking my little boys into the car before I even start the engine. They'd jumped delightedly inside to play: the three-year-old is perfectly happy pretending to turn the wheel, but the six-year-old is getting a little perturbed as I walk from one door to the other, nervously turning the key, imagining telling the troubleshooter at the end of the toll-free number how I've locked my kids in the Jaguar and can't get them out. But the key eventually works, the kids go off with the babysitter. I position myself in the driver's seat and try to start the engine. Nothing. Bear in mind that I didn't really start driving until I was twenty-three (a magic age: Pam had children, I started driving). In a decade plus of mobile freedom I invariably owned secondhand American tanks whose primary function was to get me from Point A to Point B, cars that absorbed abuse and rough handling on numerous coast-to-coast treks to this job or that writer's fellowship, cars that spun off the road in snowstorms, hit the ditch, rocked and rumbled their way back onto the two-lane, and kept going. I've never driven a car that preferred to start with the driver's foot nowhere near the gas pedal. But that's how Pam starts the Jag, after I phone her to rescue me in the Dodge van she uses for carpooling, grocery shopping, and (still) working on her thesis. She writes in the van, alone, for an hour at a time, parked in front of her own house.

Now we stand in my driveway, listening to the Jag purr. Pam ruminates. *You know, I saw the movie again after you and I*

*went. Remember that part when Darrell is offscreen getting
ready to go to work and Louise is on the phone to Thelma,
saying* Are you ready? Are you packed? *And Thelma is saying*
Uh, no, I haven't told Darrell yet, *and all the time she's talking
and cooking breakfast she's biting off pieces of this frozen candy
bar. She takes a bite, puts it back in the freezer, takes a bite. . . .
Watching that scene the second time, I realized I was crying.
That part was terrible, it was much worse than the ending.*
When Pam gives me presents, she often gives me food, a pretty
bag filled with jars and tins of exotic edibles. And I often give
her food, more basic food, like a huge jar of organic strawberry
granola, then wonder later if she ate it or foisted it off on her
kids. Pam is seriously thin, fast, vibrant, like something's burning inside, and she takes evasive action by steering into the center of the physical or emotional energy. Many times, she's said
astounding things to me in less than the fifty-minute-hour, and
I'm not even expected to pay her. Talk between women friends
is always therapy, but Pam has access to depths of feeling and
insight I seem to approach the long way around, in the two to
five years it takes me to write a book. Pam calibrates way up
there in AWWP index (Ability to Work with Pain) and she's fun,
she laughs, she loves books and films. She's worked a few shoots
in Boston as a production assistant and was so good at it that
directors asked her back on jobs for two years, but by then she
was working full-time in public relations *I could make a film, I
know I could — all I need is an editing machine. I could dedicate it to all the people I knew in film school who've already
made films, and I could call it* Remedial Ambition.

Pam rushes home to pack. When the car and I pull into her
driveway, she's coming out of the house with bags and hangers.
I tell her she doesn't need all that stuff, but she pulls it off the
hangers and starts stuffing it in the bags anyway. We're laughing
already. *I need coordinated playclothes like yours. See? You look
nice. And I don't even have my own sunglasses, I had to steal
these from my husband. What about my hair? Do you really like*

the haircut? She's in what I would call a frenzy of detachment, a state I recognize, right here beside her own privet hedge. She pulls out a navy bandana à la *Thelma and Louise* and tears it in half, except she tears it the wrong way, and the two pieces are so short we practically strangle ourselves tying these symbols of camaraderie around our necks. Road trip! She takes our picture, a lopsided view of two dissolutes on the lam, and we almost get going, except I insist on double cappuccinos to go, and we buy notebooks and pens and a blank tape (the better to record the marathon discussions we fully intend to have, uninterrupted, over the next two and a half days). Pam dashes into stores while I keep the engine running, afraid we'll have trouble getting the Jag started again if I turn it off. I realize we don't truly have a handle on the intricacies of the machine, but if we come to a dead halt I want it to happen hundreds of miles away, not here on Union Street in front of the Coffee Connection.

Next we look at maps but realize we need music — forgot the music! — and we go back by my place for the Toni Childs tape that was on the movie soundtrack, then to Pam's to get more tapes, then back by my house for my lucky hat, since I'm on the way to the Mass Pike anyway, and by now it's four in the afternoon and the rain has cleared and we're speeding along under a pure cerulean sky in New England in an infant October. So what if I was up with the kids at five thirty this morning? I don't ever want to get out of this car. We have the top down and the feathers in my hat are so disturbed I think they're going to blow off, so I turn it inside out, transforming a svelte black velvet number into a sort of quilted purple shower cap, and I drift across into the wrong lane, distracted by Pam, who is laughing so hard she appears to be choking.

At the toll booth we (seriously) check the map. Seven hours from our destination on the coast of Maine, a long hike up 95, bypassing the scenic route. Sunset is by now a scant hour off, and that blue sky is mauve at the horizon. *You know this is the very toll booth where that woman on heart medication rear-*

*ended a Jeep at sixty mph last winter. Remember? The Jeep slid
and turned over and exploded on the ice and those two men,
brothers-in-law married to sisters, were killed. They were on
their way back from a football game.* I tell her what's important
about the story is that minute and a half before the Jeep exploded, when no one thought fast enough to help them. Pam
covers her eyes and tells me that's the thing about me, I can
always be counted on to remember the worst detail. In fact, I
don't tell her the worst detail, which I read in a follow-up account and thought about for weeks when I woke up in the dark:
one of the booth attendants, questioned about that time lapse,
said she saw someone's arm moving behind the filmy window of
the Jeep, trying to open the door. I do tell Pam there was speculation in the press about requiring toll booth operators to take a
course in emergency preparedness. Can you imagine? Not only
do they stand there in all kinds of weather, breathing exhaust
and grabbing quarters, they're supposed to save lives and pull
people out of burning cars. Pam fixes her gaze on the horizon.
*Men remember tragedies if they happen to be part of them. For
women, personal tragedy is not enough; they have to incorpo-
rate whatever they scent on the wind, because they have a Jeep
or a sister or they know how toll booths are metaphors for some
rite of passage, some admittance or farewell.* Farewell? We speed
up 95 under the shadow of a pink sky, and I'm saying that's not
the whole story, women are obsessed with death: women are
obsessed with everything, it's associative thinking, the connec-
tive life, how we deal with tragedy by learning the pain in someone else's story, break down the anonymity and make it real.
Pam talks about the birth of myth, how myth is essentially feminine, like Jaguars, the details intuitively, perfectly selected,
how the willingness to feel is not hysteria, it's spiritually courageous and basic, then she lapses into a Manilow-like rendition
of "Feelings" in the cold Maine night. Time to put the top up,
so we pull over somewhere past Brunswick, decide not to talk
about women, we'll talk about men instead, but we begin by

discussing our mothers. We work together over the convertible top in a kind of perfect syncopation, unsnapping and hooking, unfolding the black vinyl cover like a flag between two Girl Scouts. Utterly absorbed in our mothers, one of them back in Boston, the other on the far side of death, we get back into the car and go another mile before we realize we forgot to actually put up the top, and that's why we're still freezing. We pull over again but now we're nearly crying, and laughing so hard we don't concentrate, and the emergency brake doesn't believe we're supposed to be driving this car. We press the button on the console and the top goes up and down, up and down, but the brake won't disengage. Finally, magically, the brake light goes off, we proceed onto Route 3. Road trip!

At last we pull into Bar Harbor, squinty-eyed with fatigue. Unlike Thelma and Louise, we actually have an expense account and a reservation. We pull up to the Bar Harbor Inn, which looks to be a kind of tastefully aged Down East dude ranch, lots of trees, several white buildings, the sound of the sea. We could head for a decent restaurant except that we can't lock the Jag due to the jammed rear windows, and we can hardly leave such an expensive machine to fend for itself. The very helpful concierge recommends consulting Karl the Security Man, who is on duty at the Inn nine to six. Karl is a long, lanky Scandinavian sort who can't figure out the windows either but says he'd trade his Honda for this car regardless. He says he'll watch the Jag so we just give him the keys and the manual and go off to dinner. When we come back the windows are up, the car is locked, and there's a little note folded under the wipers: "I figured it out. Karl."

We call home, and then sleep with our balcony doors open, hearing the sea, watching the lights of boats. Three islands visible in the inlet are solid ovals, crouched animals whose rounded backs are visible in the dark water. The memory of our children's voices approaches us like rain across the same black sweep.

There's weight in the air, moisture in the cool fragrance forced across the bay. Pam is talking about freedom. *That summer after graduation, the French teacher took some of the brightest girls to the Dordogne, near the medieval town of Sarlat. I was seventeen, free for the first time, the only time, like this but for so many weeks I didn't count the days or think it would end. Free of my family, free of school, and all I had to do was wash dishes for the older couple I lived with. Oh, that old woman cooked! Every night seven courses: soup, omelets, meat, garden beans and tomatoes, pasta, cherry clafoutie, yogurt and cheeses — I gained twenty pounds, and the boy I saw was a soldier. He lived with his family above a mill. We would stay alone in his room and there was always the sound of water rushing. . . . . I* fall asleep and she's still talking, a wash of waves backing up behind her words.

What else? By day we drive all around the island; hike to where the cliffs rise above the trees; sleep on the beach; go to bars; watch the sunset from Cadillac Mountain, where all of Desert Isle turns blue and green under the risen moon. We shop — Pam for presents for the girls. I for presents for the boys. We hit one antiques shop, where I fall in love with a set of children's blocks. They're from 1900 or so, in a fitted wooden box with a sliding lid, with a little booklet in pastel fever colors: various constructions to be made from endless combinations of the blocks. I touch some of the tooled surfaces and discover the blocks are stone, some of them vanilla, green, or rose granite, some of them black and cold. Has life really improved? This is what children played with then, so intricate, so beautiful. And permanent, more permanent than they were. *That's just it. Think about having children and no recourse to antibiotics. You had a retained placenta, remember? You would have died in your first childbirth, never known your children or experienced all the gut-wrenching conflicts you deal with now.* Pam gets out her credit card and pays for the blocks, since I'm broke, and there's no way we could count children's stone blocks as expenses. *You have to pay me back, immediately, when we get home, because I could never explain paying this much for a set of kid's blocks.*

Kids will be kids, I tell her, and in fact kids, male kids, congregate around the Jaguar every time we park it downtown. A couple of the older boys ask to look under the hood, a request duly granted. The one with long hair mentions fuel consumption and shrugs. "Mechanically," he says, "it's state-of-the-art, twelve cylinders, perfect, like a Swiss watch. It's so beautiful it has a right to exist for its own sake, but, I mean, if I had this much money, I wouldn't buy a car with it." I tell him some people have so much of this much money that they do buy cars with it, and other toys, too, but that we didn't. That actually the car was rented for us by a magazine, and we're just now on excellent terms with its delicate mechanisms.

We leave town in a rush; we want to drive the long way back, the scenic route, and we step on it as dark falls, wanting to see our children before they go to bed, thinking we'll turn the car over to our husbands and invite them to go out for a drink together on the last of the expense money, but we miscalculate driving time on the coast road. When we get in it's quite late, everyone is in bed, I take Pam home. Early the next morning, another driver arrives to speed the car on to its next recipient.

A week or so later, Pam comes over to borrow a Henry James essay on the writing of "The Real Thing," which she'd read in one of my books on the trip. She and my husband have coffee and begin to discuss what exactly a real thing is. Was our getaway real? I find myself trying to explain the trip, what we did and laughed at, and what I've written about it. My husband says, "You know, you could write that I stayed here and took care of the kids so you could go."

Pam sighs.

We study the man I live with. Once, pre-kids, he and I made

our own getaways to Italy and Greece and Finland and Russia. Upstairs, his share of the bills, the lion's share, is lying on his bureau, neatly stamped and addressed, unmailed because his entirely spent paycheck hasn't cleared yet. I smile a little sadly and say, "I know you did. And that's what the story is all about, really. I hardly mention Pam and me at all."

Where People Know Me

LATE AT NIGHT, long after the other residents in the senior care facility have gone to sleep, Big Grandma is wakeful. She cruises the hallways of the fourth floor wing in her electric wheelchair, making occasional forays — when the night staff at the nurses' station is not watchful — into the forbidden region of the elevators. On one occasion, she made it down to the ground floor, where security finally caught up to her, headed out the lobby doors, toward the parking lot. When they asked where she was going, she answered, in Japanese, "Where people know me."

This is what the Japanese-speaking night nurse reported to Aunt Tee, my mother's oldest sister, who tells my mother, who calls long-distance from Honolulu to tell me. Meanwhile, Aunt Tee has gotten in touch with Aunt Emma, now the second oldest since Aunt Dorothy's passing, and Emma is offended at not being notified — as "age etiquette" dictates — before my mother who is youngest, even though she, that is, Emma, hasn't spoken to Grandmother in years. Emma then complains to Dorothy's daughter who gets back to Tee's daughter who tells her mother, who phones my mother again and claims the whole thing is making it so she can't sleep nights. "You're the trained social worker," Aunt Tee says. "Why is Mama doing this to me?" It takes days more of burning up the city phone lines before family peace is restored. For a long time, this is what it meant to me to live in a place where people know you.

Here in Grand Rapids we've been having a week of record cold when my mother's call comes. The day's high was ten degrees, and the mercury's dropping as darkness falls. "You probably don't get many attempted escapes from the senior home there," my mother observes.

This is one of our private afternoon conversations, when Dad has gone to a meeting of his retirees' union and she has the house to herself. I can hear "Days of Our Lives" playing on the television in the background. The first time she called like this it was a few months after I left the Islands, nearly ten years ago. But even now I am obliged to remind her, out of the thriftiness she has taught me, that she is phoning long-distance in the middle of the day. I still relish the thrill of stolen pleasure when she replies, "Oh never mind," as if we are old girlfriends settling in for a good chat.

After the family news, she gives me the rundown on her Birthday Girls Lunch Club, her arthritis exercise group, and her General Electric cooking class. The cooking class, which has adopted the motto, "Encounter the good tastes of American cuisine," has moved on from ethnic desserts to ethnic salads. I am relieved to hear this since my waistline cannot tolerate many more encounters with the good tastes of Turkish baklava or Hungarian chocolate rum torte, which have been arriving with regularity by two-day priority mail.

It is hard to believe, laughing with her, that she's recently had cancer surgery. My father and I, who are much less resilient, are still recovering from the scare of almost losing her. But the doctors found the tumor early, and after a few months of recuperation, Mother has resumed her full social calendar. "It's like calling the sickness back to keep talking about it," she finally tells me, exasperated with being cross-examined about her latest medical checkup.

Now, before going off to prepare one of her ethnic desserts for a housewarming party, she fills me in on the neighborhood news. The Blums' divorced son has moved back in with them. The Shigetas are traveling in India. The ugly Labrador retriever puppy next door has turned out to be a rottweiler. "I know you're very busy," she segues, and before she says another word I know that someone will be requiring birthday greetings, congratulations, or get-well wishes.

After we hang up, I sit in my darkening kitchen and watch the lights come on in the surrounding houses. It occurs to me that it's been days since I've seen any of the people who live in them. I think of the old man who stopped by one afternoon the previous summer, while my husband, Bill, and I were unloading groceries from the car. As we exchanged pleasantries, it was clear that the man had something on his mind. "By the way, you didn't happen to be around this time a couple days ago, did you?" he finally inquired. All around us, our neighbors' air conditioners were humming and their houses were tightly shuttered against the heat. Bill said he did not recall, then asked why. The man explained that his wife had been out walking alone when she'd fallen on the sidewalk across the road from our house. "Broke her wrist clean through," he continued. "And no one saw or heard a thing." After he'd gone, we realized that neither of us had caught his name.

This incident is still on my mind the next time I speak with my mother. "We'd have helped that woman if we'd seen her," I begin.

"Of course you would've," Mother answers.

"It's just that everyone around here keeps to themselves," I say. "Not like it is back home with everybody in each other's business. I can never work when I'm at home."

"I bet you get a lot of work done there." Her reply is without irony. "What are you writing now?"

I can't help laughing then. "Oh, about what it's like back home."

My next visit to the Islands is in late May, a few months after Big Grandma's near-escape. As soon as we arrive at my parents' house and unload the car, my mother starts reminding me to call people. "Don't forget to get in touch with Aunt Tee," she says. "And Aunt Emma — you know how she is. And your dad's sister Winnie has been phoning every day for a week . . ."

The following morning we drop by Emma's on our way to pick up Aunt Tee, who is going with us to visit Big Grandma. My mother worries about Emma, who has turned more and more reclusive in the last several years, since her husband died and her daughter has moved off the island. My aunt has developed a fear of prowlers, so she keeps all her windows fastened and her curtains drawn, even during the day. From the outside, it is impossible to tell that anyone is home, but my mother assures me that Emma hardly ventures out, unless accompanied either by herself or Tee. Aunt Emma has also had a locksmith install a deadbolt and a couple of additional locks on the living room door, and we can hear her undoing these as we stand on the front stoop, in the drizzle, with our cardboard boxes of homemade food.

After she lets us in, she disappears into the kitchen with the boxes, while we make our way through the stacks of newspapers and magazines lining the dim foyer to the cluttered living room. A reading lamp glows on the end table next to the couch and a game show is playing on TV.

"Oh, 'Hollywood Squares,'" my mother says. "I watch that sometimes."

"I never do. I just keep the sound on for the company." Aunt Emma has materialized in the doorway. Her gaunt face is framed by stiff gray curls, and she is wearing a pants outfit of bluish gray.

When we leave, we invite her to come with us, but she declines, as she always does. "You were always the favorite," she tells my mother. "Mama would never know that I was there."

The senior care facility, where Big Grandma is staying, occupies an entire wing in what was formerly called the Japanese Hospital and has now become one of the largest medical centers in the Islands. It was in the Japanese Hospital that my grandmother watched her twelve-year-old son, Masahiro, die of septicemia more than seventy years before. It is in another wing of the same hospital that my mother was operated on for pancreatic cancer.

As she, Aunt Tee, and I step out of the elevators, my aunt explains that the night staff has tried using medication, even physical restraint, to curtail Big Grandma's nocturnal activities. They have yet to overcome her determined resistance, which includes occasional episodes of biting. "They have confiscated her dentures," Aunt Tee says, barely able to contain her mortification. Now, if you bring any edibles for Big Grandma, you must go to the nurses' station and ask for her teeth. My aunt stops there to do so now, and also to drop off the loaves of mango bread she has baked. "Penance food," my mother whispers, as Aunt Tee distributes mango bread and expresses our thanks and apologies all around.

Big Grandma is sitting up in bed, dozing or pretending to doze, when we arrive at her room. Someone has dressed her in a baby-blue duster trimmed with lace, and braided her white hair with pink and yellow ribbons. It is a new look for my one-hundred-eight-year-old grandmother.

"Isn't that nice?" Aunt Tee says too brightly.

"Easter egg colors," my mother adds. They both have the same fixed smile on their faces — the same smile, I suddenly realize, that is on mine. As we stand grimacing at my grandmother, I resist the impulse to reach over and pull the ribbons from her hair.

Big Grandma opens her eyes and lies back on the pillows, looking us over. Seeing that she has wakened, Mother gestures at me to approach, then says, "Look, look who's come to see you all the way from Michigan."

Big Grandma regards me blankly.

"It's Sylvia," my mother persists. "From Michigan."

"Where?" Big Grandma asks, turning her good ear toward us.

"Mee-shee-gen," Mother repeats, louder.

"Ah," Big Grandma replies. She glances around the room, then back at me, comprehension dawning on her face. "I was wondering where this was."

In my memory, she is always dressed in midnight blue. She wears black *tabis* and straw slippers on her feet. Her hair is neatly oiled and pulled away from her face into a knot that is held in place with brown plastic combs.

Her sense of fashion, if one could call it that, was not guided by vanity but by what she thought appropriate to who she was. Even in very early photographs, she wore dark colors, muted pinstripes and inconspicuous floral prints, though the kimonos were eventually replaced by mama-san shifts with high collars and elbow-length sleeves. She seems always to have thought of herself as old. This is not to say that she was resigned to aging; for her it was not a process of defeat. She told me once, "You can't be free until you're old. After I came to Hawaii, there were so many young men looking for a wife, I married your grandfather to get away from them. We had a good life. Then he died. Someone else wanted to marry me, but I'd already had one husband. I didn't need another."

It seemed curious to me that she should speak of freedom with such spirit, when she had more rules than anyone I ever knew. She had rules for what colors and styles to wear, and rules for when you took a bath or were served dinner (the oldest and youngest, which meant she and I, were always first), and rules for eating at table (take less than your fill, never leave a single grain of rice in your bowl, refuse the last piece of chicken). I recall, when I was six or seven, being seated at the dining table and instructed in the proper use of chopsticks. After she'd showed me how to hold them (thumb on the bottom, middle finger between, index finger on top), I was handed the pair and a bowl of Rice Krispies, then told to pick out the grains of cereal, one by one.

Big Grandma also had rules she never expected anyone else to follow, like her strict diet and exercise regimen, invented by a doctor in Japan. The diet, which allowed fish but no meat and touted the curative properties of icicle radishes, was taken in five small meals a day. The exercise regimen consisted of twenty repetitions each of thirty-seven different routines — including ones for every major organ in your body. Each morning, Big Grandma woke at five, performed her exercises, ate her first small meal of the day, and was out puttering around the yard by six. She took a half-hour nap after her midday meal, spent the afternoon on her quilting, and had her bath at four. In the evening, she performed her waking routine in reverse and was in bed before nine. On Saturdays she attended matinees at the Japanese movie theater in Chinatown, and on Sundays spent the morning at the Buddhist temple. From day to day there were small variations in her routine, but in general this was how she lived from as far back as I could remember, until she lost the use of her legs when she was past one hundred.

As a young child, until I was old enough to begin school, I spent a great deal of time in Big Grandma's company. Every weekday before work, my mother dropped me off at Aunt Tee's house, where my grandmother lived. By the time I arrived she was usually out in the yard. I'd sit under a big mango tree and eat my breakfast while she worked nearby. Often, she'd pick fresh fruit from the yard to accompany my milk and toast. Sometimes there were fresh lychees or pomegranates. "This is what silkworms eat," she'd say, giving me a handful of purple mulberries. In mango season she'd harvest the bright red and golden fruit from my aunt's tree. I'd help with the spotting, gazing up into the shady branches, and we'd pick mangoes until she'd gathered a whole fragrant apronful. Then we'd sit on the grass and eat them together, with Big Grandma saving all the peelings to put on the compost later.

Despite the strictness of her dietary regimen, I was quick to notice that it did not exclude experimentation. For years she listened to a talk radio program, broadcast over a local Japanese-language station, in which people would call in with their favorite (and usually bad-tasting) cures for everything from rheumatism to temporary amnesia. She took note of all the call-in remedies and if one particularly interested her, she had no reservations about trying it out on me. I was a sickly child, subject to allergies and "bronchial conditions." For a while, after I was diagnosed as anemic, she took to feeding me duck eggs. When I objected to their taste, she tried to disguise them in egg salad, a ploy which did not fool me one bit. To this day, I immediately get suspicious whenever I hear ads for turkey bacon, soy bean ice cream, or any other kind of undercover food which claims to be something it is not. But the worst things my grandmother gave me were the brownish-green drinks she concocted out of unconventional vegetables. Tonics of chives or aloe. Pureed mountain yams. The bitterest bitter melon tea. She'd pour some of whatever concoction she'd come up with into a large tumbler, so there'd be just about an inch of the stuff down there at the bottom, and she'd say, "See? You can polish that off with no trouble at all."

Big Grandma's quest to restore me to health also included visits to sundry healers and prayer ladies. I don't know how she heard of these people — perhaps from the radio or at church — but there was a tacit understanding between us not to mention our visits to anyone else. We'd wait until my aunt had gone to work, then we'd change into our going-out dresses and, hand in hand, set out for the bus stop on the corner. We visited a shiatsu specialist who treated your ailments with finger massage; an herbalist who made you inhale scented steam; and an acupuncturist nun who stuck you with needles or applied heated glass suction cups to strategic places on your back and chest. Big Grandma herself claimed that she had the power to perform *reiki,* that is, to heal with the energy flowing from her hands. I still recall her sitting up nights beside my childhood sickbed, the touch of her cool palms upon my forehead, while her lips moved silently, chanting prayers.

"Your grandmother and I were never friends," my mother remarks, after I tell her these memories.

When I ask why, Mother answers, "For one thing, she was never around." After Grandfather's death, Big Grandma had gone to work as a cook and live-in housekeeper for a wealthy businessman's family and was away for days at a time. Then my mother adds, "Besides, it would never have occurred to us to be friends. That wasn't how it was."

"So, how was it?" I persist.

She explains that children were bound to their parents by duty and gratitude. Then she smiles. "Isn't it a pity that all that's changed?"

Another time we are sitting out on the porch, sipping iced coffees, and she tells me, "When I was a girl, we always heard stories about fathers who signed their financial obligations over to their grown children, then headed back to Japan. In those days, children were so brainwashed to be dutiful, they'd work their whole lives to pay off those debts. Usually, the heaviest burden fell to the eldest."

I think of Aunt Tee and how she left school when she was fourteen to help support the family.

Mother continues, "Your grandmother taught us that nothing is stronger than the bond of obligation between a parent and a child. All of us felt it. But I couldn't help thinking, she'd cut those ties, hadn't she? And what about those fathers who dropped everything to go back to Japan?

These are stories she'd told me many times, but now in the cool reflective light they cast, it chills me a little to remember what my grandmother described as the "freedom" that comes with growing old. It seems that widowhood had not simply freed her from the expectations of men. It had also freed her to create — out of that closed, tightly knit world she inhabited with her daughters — a female version of the old way she knew so well. I can't pretend to know how this came about, so I try to imagine how it was for her — a mother, alone, with four young daughters, and work always keeping her away from home.

Yet, even as we slip the ties that bind us to that old way, I can't help asking, when we are free of all this, what holds us then?

To which my mother answers, sighing, "Who knows?" Then adds, "Friendship maybe. A kind of love."

Whenever I am home, my mother cooks. On most mornings, when I come out into the kitchen she greets me with the question, "What would you like for dinner tonight?" By the time I sit down to my first cup of coffee she has already hung the laundry, swept and mopped the floors, and is taking a break, clipping recipes or coupons from the previous night's paper.

On other days I wake to the smell of baking. A few mornings before Easter, a wonderful yeasty fragrance fills the whole house, and when I emerge from my bedroom there are pans of sweet rolls cooling on every available surface in the living and dining rooms. Mother reminds me that they are having a bake sale for her General Electric cooking class. While she was at it, she decided to make extras to give away. None of it penance food.

She believes that everything to do with eating should be a pleasure, and she takes as much care in selecting the food she will cook as in its actual preparation. When I am visiting, she rousts me out of bed on Wednesday mornings way before six, so we can get down to the open market when the produce vendors are setting up. Afterward, I drive her to Chinatown, where she is acquainted with the specialties of every shop. She sniffs and pokes, quizzes the vendors about prices, and periodically offers me bits of cryptic advice, like, "buy fish whole," or "the sound of a pineapple tells you if it's sweet."

After my return to Grand Rapids, Mother and I continue to keep in frequent touch. On one occasion, she reports that Big Grandma has decided that she is visiting at her uncle's estate back in Japan. "The last time I saw her," Mother says, "she complained of what a long stay it's been. Then she looked around at her roommate and the other residents out in the hall, and whispered, 'I can't figure out what all these strangers are doing here.'"

During another call, my mother announces that she and my father are accepting our invitation to come out and see us the following spring. This will be their first visit in the five years since my husband and I moved to Michigan. She also says that she's been losing weight and may have to buy a whole new wardrobe for the trip. This cheerful declaration implies darker possibilities, but I refrain from delving into them. Instead, she volunteers that her doctor is keeping track of her progress and isn't concerned a single bit.

Every week she reports losing another pound or two, but her monthly checkups turn up nothing unusual. She's developed a bit of a backache, but both she and her doctor agree that it is an old muscle strain flaring up. I begin calling her several times a week to keep track of how she's doing, and she, surprisingly, seems to welcome my concern.

In March, when my father and mother arrive for their scheduled visit, I am nevertheless surprised by the change in her. She has gone from 110 pounds to less than ninety, and her clothes hang loosely on her small frame. Her hands tremble when she unbuttons her jacket or lifts her fork to eat, and she hardly eats — just tiny bites.

But she loves everything. Our little house. The crocuses blooming in the yard. The unpredictable March weather. She loves that it can be 70 degrees and sunny one day, and snowing the next. When it starts to snow, she grabs her coat and boots so she can be outside in it. She crunches wet snow into little balls and throws them at us when my father and I step out the door. I take pictures of the two of them — in the snow on the front walk, in the snow on the side of the house, and in the snow in the back yard. Mother takes naps in the afternoon but she is always up by dinner. She sits on a stool in the kitchen and watches while I cook. I teach her my recipes for *tabouli*, refried beans, and meatless marinara sauce. When we go to the market, she is enthusiastic over the strawberries and asparagus that have just come in season.

One day, my husband drives us all out to Lake Michigan. It is a forty-minute ride, and on the way over my mother begins to sing. I remember summer evenings back in the Islands, when it was too hot to stay inside, and she and I went for rides beside the sea. Then in the middle of telling me about some dance she'd been to when she was young, she'd start to sing, and I'd join in. We'd both sing, riding the night roads, all the way home.

A few weeks after my parents return to Honolulu, Mother takes to her bed. Her back is worse and she complains of "hunger pains." When I ask my father if she gets out at all, he replies that she doesn't, then adds that he is doing all the housework now. I ask if she ever cooks anymore, and when he hesitates, I realize that something is very wrong.

However, Mother refuses to give in to panic and insists that there is no reason for my return. Meanwhile, she goes from doctor to doctor and they turn up nothing. One performs an endoscopy and diagnoses gastritis. Another prescribes swimming therapy for her back condition. She regards all this as good news, but meanwhile the weight keeps slipping off her. "You have to feed her," I tell my father. "We have to fatten her up." To which he responds, sadly, "She's lost her joy in food."

I begin making plans to fly back when he calls and says she's taken another turn for the worse. She has a fever and can't keep anything down. Before I hang up, she gets on the phone. The last words she ever says to me are, "I don't know what's wrong." That afternoon my father takes her to the emergency room and she is rushed into surgery, where the surgeon finds an abscess covering two thirds of her liver. He inserts a drainage tube then closes her up. "I've never seen anything like it," he tells my father.

I return to the Islands the next day. One of my cousins meets me at the airport. My mother is at the same hospital where she had surgery two years before, and when we arrive at the waiting room of the intensive care unit, my father and Aunt Tee are there. I put my arms around my father, who keeps saying, "We've been through this before, I just know she is going to get better."

The rules of the unit allow us to visit my mother in pairs for ten minutes, three times an hour, at twenty-minute intervals. My mother lies unconscious, with tubes running in and out of her body and a respirator to help her breathe. During one of the breaks between visits, I phone Bill in Michigan, and he says that he'll be with me soon.

Over the next few days there is no change. Aunt Tee drops by again. The Birthday Girls come. The ladies from the General Electric cooking class bring food for our vigil. The long hours are beginning to tell on my father, who decides to go home in the afternoons to take short naps.

One afternoon I am alone with Mother when Aunt Emma enters the room. I look around for Aunt Tee, but Emma has come alone.

"I rode the bus," she says, positioning herself on the other side of the bed.

After we exchange a bit more small talk, I turn back to my mother and pick up where I'c left off. "Remember the time . . ." I say to her, listing things we've seen and done.

A few minutes go by this way, when Aunt Emma suddenly speaks up; she has been remembering, too. She leans close to Mother's pillow, and murmurs, "Remember when we were kids, and you got a new pair of shoes, and I didn't get any? Remember the lady at the corner store who gave you free ice cream that you never shared? Remember how you wanted to tag along wherever I went and how Mama beat me for not taking you?"

More days pass. Bill arrives. The doctors move Mother out of intensive care. It's not looking good, they say. The antibiotics aren't working, and the infection is in her blood.

In the new room we can be with Mother all the time. We stand by the bed, massaging her icy hands and feet. Her circulation is poor and her toes have turned black. Dad quits talking about miracle recoveries. One afternoon, while Bill is getting a cup of coffee and I am half-dozing in a chair across the room, I can hear my father talking to her. "It's okay, Betty," he is saying. "You can let go now. You can let go."

She doesn't let go, just yet. The blackness spreads upward from her toes to her legs. She is so full of fluids they are leaking from all the places where she has been stuck with syringes and IV needles. The fluids are causing her body to swell, and it has become impossible to find a pulse to take her blood pressure. Nevertheless, the lab technicians come by like clockwork to check her blood pressure and shoot her up with insulin, which immediately leaks back out. I finally ask for permission to have them stop this futile routine, and her doctors give it.

None of our friends or relatives comes by anymore. There is a sign on the door that says *Visitors Limited to Immediate*

Family. I sense that it is difficult for my father to be there; the air conditioning, the hours of sitting on a hard chair are bad for his arthritis, so I tell him that it's all right if he leaves early because we'll call if anything happens.

When the nurses come in to change the bedding, they instruct Bill and me to wear rubber gloves whenever we touch my mother. This is to safeguard against infection from the fluids leaking out of her. Periodically, someone comes in to vacuum out her mouth and throat with a suction device on the side of the bed. The necessity for doing this becomes more and more frequent, and finally, one of the nurses shows me how to do it. There is the smell of blood, perhaps of earth, around my mother's bed.

With just my husband there in the room with us, I sing to her. She lies in the same position she's been in, with her head turned to one side, and one leg slightly bent, as if she's dancing. I sing, "Sunset glow the day is over, let us all go home . . ." I close my eyes and imagine myself large, large enough to hold all of her, her dying, within me.

Bill and I have rented a room in the hospital where we can catch quick naps during the day or grab a few hours of sleep at night. The room is in the same wing as the senior care facility, a floor below my grandmother's. At one or two in the morning, after a day of sitting with my mother, he and I squeeze into the narrow, twin-size bed and, still in our street clothes, almost immediately fall asleep. We have slept less than an hour when we are wakened by banging at the door. We stumble to our feet, and I feel as if I've plunged into a pool of icy water. I am so cold my teeth are chattering and it is difficult to catch my breath. Bill steadies me, then opens the door. There are two nurses on the other side. They tell us, in a businesslike way, to go to my mother's room. As we follow them down the corridor, I think of Big Grandma somewhere upstairs, wakeful, among strangers.

WENDY WASSERSTEIN

🌾 🌾 🌾 🌾 🌾 🌾 🌾 🌾 🌾 🌾 🌾 🌾 🌾

The Ties that Wound

MY BEST FRIEND isn't speaking to me. The falling-out was both of our faults. Maybe we had become too close, too dependent on one another. But I ran into her the other night, and I realized how very much I miss her.

All my life I have counted on the compassionate nature of my own sex. Men can be romantic, bright, and interesting, but when times get tough or genuinely funny — cutting Hebrew school, experiencing young-career-gal anxiety, reassessing middle age — my most significant others have always been a circle of intimate women friends.

What I have constantly been afraid to acknowledge, however, is the difficulty of sustaining these friendships. Perhaps I never speak about soured female relationships because men are always so ready to portray women as competitive, jealous felines. Furthermore, men claim to have the joys of male bonding on canoe trips and hunting sprees, while women are relegated to gossiping in car pools. I have always felt I was betraying my sex by uttering even a passing thought of criticism. In my mind, if I can't maintain a female friendship, which should be warm and supportive, then I must be not only a competitive and jealous wench, but also politically incorrect.

Recently, girlfriends of mine have confessed that it's hard to make new friends because women's lives have become so segmented. Those with family obligations juggle the demands of personal and professional lives, and those without seek the comfort of others in similar positions. Ask any single woman who's been to a we're-having-a-second-child baby shower how it was, and she'll tell you she immediately ran home to have a Scotch with an unmarried friend.

Something more complicated and insidious than scheduling seems to be in the air. Unlike the days of support groups, when women felt the sudden surge of excitement in realizing that they could bond, there now seems to be a female Olympics of getting one's life in order. Maybe this was all fostered by those fabulous surveys that found a single woman's chance of being blown up by a terrorist greater than her possibility of meeting an available man. But it seems as if there is only room for so many of us at the table of satisfaction and, therefore, we are all forced into competition.

This competitiveness, however, is hardly only about men. I notice women in aerobics class (the two times I've been there) checking out one another's body tone. There is no reason to believe that just because the adjacent number in a purple body thong loves to do doggy lifts she is taking away any potential opportunities. Or that it is only another woman who could stand in the way of a promotion. Rather than support one another, we've ghettoized ourselves into a constant and tenacious race.

The relationships we have always been told to "work on" or to speak about in therapy tend to be those with a primary partner, that is, the person with whom we are tied romantically. I've seldom sat through a dinner where a companion weeps over buffalo mozzarella because a friendship is falling apart, and yet ending a friendship can be a deeply wounding experience. When my best friend stopped speaking to me, I felt as if I had failed. I had never thought female friendships required the same attention or could have the same bumps and turns as other loving relationships.

I have always measured my life by the lives of my best women friends. In seventh grade, when it became time for Susan to begin thinking about men, it was time also for me to begin considering a personal life. My sense of order has come from sharing a well-considered point of view. If in high school Kathy decided so-and-so was crazy for befriending so-and-so, it was in fact a truth. There is nothing as comforting as knowing two opinions are right, to hell with what everyone else thinks.

Maybe, then, what I am missing these days are those complete and trusting alliances. An older and wiser woman friend suggested that my best friend wasn't speaking to me because I was obviously ambitious and my friend wanted to move on to a more domestic life. I became sad because I felt not only completely misunderstood by both of them, but startled at the idea that when friends move on to change their lives and images, friendships have to end.

Nowadays I think about if I were to have a party of women friends, exactly who I would invite. I worry that when I meet women I am always wondering if they approve of me, or I of them. Are they like me? Are they funny? I wonder if we will be secretly checking out one another's lives, measuring ourselves by the other's accomplishments.

I can count at least four deep female friendships that have been ruptured over the years. I think of all these women with great fondness. In many ways I wish we could have sat down and talked our differences through. But for some reason, even though the splits were irrevocable, we never gave the relationships the time that was probably spent on far less important male alliances.

This problem is difficult to talk about perhaps because I want my feelings of competitiveness and inadequacy to go away; or because somewhere I have learned to become suspicious of women and I hate that about myself. When I meet a potential friend, I find myself sizing her up, being harshly judgmental. When I befriend younger women, I fear that they won't approve of how I've lived my life, or that they'll find my choices obsolete.

I keep reminding myself that this isn't a race. There's plenty of room for many of us at the table. And I've made a resolution to pay attention and treasure my long-standing friendships, and honestly try to form new ones. Recently a new friend, who is a married actress and has a child, and I went to a dinner for Texas gubernatorial candidate Ann Richards and out for drinks afterward. We chatted at a swanky hotel bar about our diets, her career, my career, her child, my desire for a child, her husband, my boyfriends. For the first time since my old friend stopped speaking to me I felt back on track. It was the same comfortable feeling I'd had with childhood friends and it was good to have it at an older age. I felt that my life was coming back to order.

I am afraid of being guarded around other women, and I am afraid of moving on from friends when they no longer suit my life plans. I know women's friendships have their ups and downs. It isn't always Bette Midler and Barbara Hershey sunlit and loving in *Beaches*. But it isn't the jungle red frenzy of *The Women* either.

Over the past year I've made contact again with the friend who had stopped speaking to me. At first, like any splintered relationship, our contact was very delicate. A passing hello at a party, a dinner where at least three other mutual friends were present. And every time I thought to myself this is too difficult, women's friendships should be easy, I realized I didn't want to stop trying because the truth was her friendship was irreplaceable.

Now we chat around once a month about her love life or my mordant insecurities. We even had a lunch alone together in California across the room from John Travolta and his new baby. As we sat there checking out the baby, the wife, and the man-

ager, there was a moment when all the murky feelings went
away and we were "girlfriends" in the best sense of the word,
giggling slightly and defiantly secure in our mutual affection.
Great friendships with women are some of life's most difficult
and caring intimacies. If I work harder at them, I hope to have
them forever.

CONNIE PORTER

𝕏 𝕏 𝕏 𝕏 𝕏 𝕏 𝕏 𝕏 𝕏 𝕏 𝕏 𝕏 𝕏 𝕏

GirlGirlGirl

BEING INSIDE. When I was growing up in a small city just outside of Buffalo, the long days of winter made me appreciate the comfort of what was on the inside. Winter was like a dark and endless tunnel I entered when I left the house for school. The clouds pulled themselves down around me, reducing clear sky to a place just above my head. I could almost touch those gray clouds that blotted out the sun for weeks and weeks on end. The cold was sometimes so intense that my nostrils would freeze, sticking together, and the coldness could transform the snow. There were days when it did not melt, or adhere to anything, but lasted as a fine powder that squeaked under my boots. The prowling winds skulked through the maze of buildings of the housing project where I lived, waiting behind corners to attack, to shoot icy blasts up my nose, down my throat. And then there was the inside.

At home, my family was burrowed in, comforted by forced-air heat, buttery cinnamon toast crusted with sugar, cocoa rich with Pet milk, the lemon glow of electric light, and storm windows that tried their best to keep the outside out. In the coldest of weeks, the glass inside would frost over, with ice as thick as a half-inch growing in the bottom corners, but the outside could not touch me. I could touch the ice that had no hold over the world inside. Finally the feathery, ethereal patterns melted away, leaving the windows covered with a film of water. I would draw on that film, movies of my life, sun and stars and girls jumping rope. The pictures would run and blur as the water dripped down the window. The thick ice at the bottom would lose its grip, and I would break off and eat pieces, vanquishing its power.

Once, when I was twelve, my mother ventured out into the tunnel of winter on a Saturday morning long before my sisters and I had risen. She'd gone the few blocks to the beauty shop to get her hair done. Our father had gone out, too. He had a habit of rising at five or six in the morning — even on weekends. But my older sisters, already teens, and my younger sister and I, heading for that nebulous teenage world, looked forward to Saturday, the one morning we could lounge in bed. That morning, from the safety and warmth of my bed, I gazed out at the driving snowstorm that had been blowing all night, its baleful winds moaning through the tiny cracks around the windows. Then there was a knock at the living room door, and I bolted downstairs to answer it. I pulled back the curtain at the door to see my mother's face, soft and brown on the other side of the steamy glass. I opened the door, and she stepped to the inside. Before I could close it, the wind forced its way in, pushing a swirl of snow into the house. My mother stood on the rug, a small bag in her hand. She was out of breath. Her hat and coat were covered with snow.

"It's so bad out there. I picked up this much snow from Eli's to here." Eli's was a small store just a block away. "That Eli is going crazy. He had the door locked and didn't want to let me in," Mama said, taking off her wet things. Her hair looked beautiful; each black curl was shiny and had been set in place with a curling iron. She continued angrily, "Talking 'bout he don't want no teenagers in his store. He so scared of black people, he think a fifty-year-old woman a teenager! Standing on the other side of the glass in his warm store, had me standing out on the step in this blizzard until he decided to let me in."

I could understand my mother's anger. She had been left on the outside because she was black, and it was brutal out in the storm, and some white man had to decide if she deserved a place on the inside. And I could understand Eli's fear. He was an old Slavic man who knew little English and teenagers did shoplift — chips, pop, beer, ice cream bars, anything they could tuck under their shirts or slip inside their pants. In the clouded window of the store, he had not seen my mother at all. He had seen a reflection of his own fear.

I had just begun junior high, and some process that I did not understand was actually causing me to think and to question my world. Though my family lived in a housing project, I never thought we were poor, but in junior high I received a free lunch. Once a month the names of all those who received free lunches were called out over the loudspeaker. In small, alphabetically ordered groups we went to the principal's office to get a book of lunch tickets. It was a humiliating process, an hour-long calling of names of the poorest students. I would leave my seat when I was called, looking around to see which kids were watching. It mattered when it was all over, who had never left her seat. Being poor was disgraceful and generated such a sense of shame in a few kids that they didn't eat lunch. They gave their tickets away and usually ate nothing, or occasionally showed up with a dime for an ice cream bar. I felt sorry for them, but I ate my lunch every day. Black, Puerto Rican, and white kids ate for free. There was some solace in that for me — that we were all in it together.

At school, black and white kids formed friendships. I was friends with a white girl, Sherry. We were in advanced studies classes together. I was in this phase when my brain had jump-started, and I began to think about how people came to be friends. Sherry and I had been assigned to the same seating group. Chance brought us together. But we were school friends, never seeing one another once the day ended. She lived in the white neighborhood, I lived in the housing projects. Her name was never called for lunch tickets, I received a free lunch and extra milk. We each went our own way, that I did not question or think much about. It was the way of our world. The fears of the older generation visited us, gathering speed like those winds in the tunnel of winter. Adults feared the ability of children to destroy. Children like Sherry and I had moved on from combing the hair out of our dolls' heads, breaking all our crayons, bending the frames of our steel skates, and had turned our attention to the world. A friendship as innocent as ours was a threat to social order. Our giggling over lunches made of surplus government food was threatening to destroy the world. The winds generated by the older generation blew unrelenting over the next three years of junior high, and what happened to Sherry, I saw even then as contemptible.

She mixed easily with black kids and had a number of black friends, and for that she was ostracized by many white girls. She was harassed by those who were bolder. They slipped hate mail into her locker, letters accusing her of being a nigger-lover, of wanting to be a nigger. They felt she had betrayed not only them, but the entire white race. A few black girls harassed me, but not as badly. I was an Oreo, a Tom — a Thomasina, really — I was told. I was angered and hurt by the slurs, but refused to be baited, refused to be drawn into a fight. Being small for my age, I did not care to have my face ripped off. But there was another reason I refused to let them draw me out into the howling winds of their ignorance — I felt deeply that they were pitiful girls. Sherry felt that way, too, but she would fight if provoked, pounding her detractors into silence. I understood her anger, though I never fully gave in to mine. Those girls who hounded us cared nothing about me or Sherry. Friendship for them, back then in our small steel town, was a matter of keeping all of the wrong girls outside, of repeating and imitating behaviors they did not even understand. Those girls wanted Sherry and me to think that they had somehow locked us out in the cold, kept us breathless and expectant at the door of their lives. But I was the one who refused to even walk up to their door, refused to stand before a pane of steamy glass in which they would only see my dark face, the reflection of their own fears.

My mother had sought out Eli's door for very different reasons, and she had stood before it until she was recognized and let in. Sherry and I, and the other girls, were all seeking the same thing — to find our way to the comfort of the inside, to a place we felt we belonged. The search for our place on the inside is one we make all our lives.

In Toni Morrison's *Sula,* the character Nel Wright also searches. In mourning Sula (who died many years earlier), she says, "We was girls together . . . girlgirlgirl." Her lamentation serves as a reminder of what was lost when Sula betrayed the trust of their friendship by having an affair with Nel's husband. Later Nel recalls what Sula once said about hell, that it was forever. But Nel thought, "Sula was wrong. Hell ain't things lasting forever. Hell is change." It was the change that hurt her. More than the loss of her husband, Nel had lost someone to be girls with when she locked Sula out of her life. And only after Sula is dead twenty-five years can Nel name the sorrow that has gripped her. *Girlgirlgirl.*

Sherry and I were girls together, stumbling through the vagueness of our teen years. Eventually we lost sight of one another in the tunnel. We moved on to our city's mammoth senior high school with its long stretches of hall and homerooms assigned by last name. I was a *P* and I was assigned to the homeroom from hell — the auto shop. It reeked of gasoline and oil. I was one of only two black students in the homeroom; the other was a boy who sat on the other side of the room and said little. The homeroom teacher was a stoic who showed no interest in anyone. Maybe he wasn't a stoic. It is possible that his brain cells had been slowly eaten away, picked off by the fumes that filled the room morning after morning. Every morning at 7:45, come rain or shine or snow or wind, the huge metal garage door was cranked open with a chain and the cars, parked just in back of our seats, were started, sending billows of carbon monoxide into the room. I don't know where the cars went. I think driver's ed used them.

The only other homeroom that could have been as bad as the auto shop was the cosmetology lab, filled with ammonia and peroxide fumes and lined with dryers and disembodied practice heads covered with human hair. I did not know which home-room Sherry had been assigned to since she was an *A*, but I liked to imagine her in a better place than that. I liked to think she was in a real homeroom, one filled with nice kids who left her alone. We did not have one class together, not even lunch. We did not ride on the same bus. For weeks I looked for her as I made my way through the hall between classes. I only caught glimpses of her, and neither of us had time to talk as we hurried down the long hallway to another class. We lost touch. Just one year later my mother, sisters, and I moved to Buffalo. It is ironic to me that it was not the girls with the big fists and big mouths who pulled us apart. It was simply change, that hell that Nel came to know.

She is a girl I think about still, because I feel it is as girls that we begin to figure out what friendship means to us. For me, it is still the place inside. What is outside and is not the wind, not the snow, nor the creep of ice, is change.

It is that threat of change that I felt as I stood sweating in my friend Lisa's apartment four years ago. She and her husband were moving from Milton, Massachusetts, to Durham, North Carolina. Though I felt a great deal of joy that she was going to attend Duke on a fellowship and pursue a doctorate in history, I felt a sense of profound sadness.

We had met two years before when we had both been hired to teach English at Milton Academy. I had just finished grad school, she undergrad, and our presence at Milton was a rarity. There were no other black women teaching in the upper school

at that time, and only one black man. I cannot say that Lisa was
so much drawn to me as I was drawn to her. From the first time
I saw her, I knew I would approach her and introduce myself.
Perhaps it is hard for white people to understand that feeling, of
looking around and not seeing yourself, not seeing yourself, not
seeing yourself, then seeing yourself reflected in the face of someone else. I was used to it because as my education progressed,
the fewer and fewer blacks I saw — especially women. As an
undergrad there were a few handfuls. In graduate school, I was
down to the fingers of one hand. It was not that I did not form
friendships with white women — I did — but when I looked
around me, I would rarely see myself.

There is a moment when we are searching for a place of be-
longing when we see ourselves in the glass of our lives — a liquid
presence staring back at us, a reminder of our presence in the
world. What confirms our existence is not just the reflection. If
we merely had to see ourselves to be affirmed we would be nar-
cissists, needing only a house of mirrors to comfort us. It is seeing our image merge with that of someone approaching from the
outside that affirms who we are.

When I interviewed for the job at Milton Academy, I had liked
the school very much — the small class sizes, the intelligence of
the students, the dedication of the faculty. But once the job began, I was not totally prepared for my sense of isolation. I had
never lived in New England, and before my interview at Milton
I had only been in the Boston area once, when I was a teenager,
attending my brother's graduation from Boston University. The
wealth of Milton Academy left me feeling breathless: the red
brick classroom buildings, the girls' dorms — really converted
mansions — the volume of food served in the cafeteria, the im-
peccable grounds and sweeping lawns manicured by a crew of
black men. I felt sick at times, drunk from this opulence. The
other faculty seemed at ease, as if they wanted their glasses re-
filled while I had fallen onto the floor in a stupor. But seeing
Lisa made me feel a bit calmer. I had no reason to believe we

had anything in common, other than the fact that we were both black and both women, but even from a distance, I felt there was a possibility of seeing myself reflected in her.

She had grown up in the inner city of Chicago. Like mine, her parents were part of the great migration of blacks who came up from the South. Like me, she felt the swirl and tilt of the school, and we were both looking for the comfort of the inside.

We would go to her quiet apartment and have tea, and there we would analyze the political-racial structure of Milton, of America, of the world. We would reorganize it while we ate pie, or Jamaican beef patties, or curried goat, as we turned from tea to ginger beer. Or we would engage in one of our favorite activities, grazing our way through a local shopping mall, nibbling in Filene's Basement, only looking at the clover on the other side of the fence at Ann Taylor, finding the greens good and tender in the Limited.

We did not spend our time there turned in on ourselves. Anyone who goes into teaching, especially at a boarding school, must be willing and able to talk to and be supportive of children. Lisa and I shared the feeling that we did not want the black students at Milton to be stuck somewhere on the outside looking in. There was a minority student group that many black students on campus took part in. It was part support group, part social organization, part political committee. Lisa and I worked with the group, though we were not its official sponsors. And it was Lisa who noticed that some black girls in the school who had come from inner cities were in "the Walkman stage."

By the time some of them reached junior year, they had retreated into a space that no one could enter, even themselves. They would walk around campus with headphones on, tuning out what was going on around them. They had few friends and rarely had boyfriends. Sometimes my white colleagues would comment on these girls, outside of the swirl, seemingly antisocial in their sweat pants, their high-top sneakers, surrounded by the thumping bass of the rap they listened to. But Lisa and I did not see them that way. We both knew that these black girls did not see themselves enough, or see themselves at all. So they turned to what was on the inside, the blasting music that screamed in their ears and confirmed who they were.

Lisa and I reached out to these girls, often finding them sullen, and sometimes angry. We befriended those who let us, braiding their hair, taking them shopping, inviting them into our homes for hours of long talks. Girls who walked around during the day saying little or nothing would come alive when they burst into my apartment on Thursday nights. They would sit with me, four of us jammed on a love seat, and watch "The Cosby Show" and "A Different World." And we would fall into call and response — a black American, a Jamaican, an African girl, and me, a black American woman. We would talk back to the television as if the characters on those shows could hear us. I would like to think they found themselves there in my house, in Lisa's house.

It was painful for me to see them sometimes, with the paucity of black girls around them, a condition I did not encounter until I was older. But even in their Walkman years, when they had almost completely shut down, they still reached out. The girls who came and sat on my couch were girls together. *Girlgirlgirl.* The tears on their faces at graduation were those of joy, but also of sorrow. They had drawn close together, now only to have to face the hell of change. I did not cry with them. Sometimes sorrow does not come all at once.

The day my friend Lisa moved, it did not. Her house was packed with boxes and friends. It was hot that day, and she and her husband lived three flights up. As we all pitched in to load the truck, I felt hot, but I kept climbing through the rising heat of the upper floors to help bring down carton after carton. We had a barbecue afterward that lasted until the sun set on that June night. When I went back to my apartment in the basement of the dorm, I wrote the following journal entry:

June 30, 1989 — Today is sad. I'm leaving for Buffalo tomorrow. I went to a final dinner at Lisa and Sid's, a barbecue. It
was so depressing. Lisa cried. I nearly cried. She has been like
a sister to me. She braided my hair earlier in the week. It came
out great. I'll write more later.

I did not have much to say later, really. I was in too much pain
to talk, even to myself. It was not until the school year began
and I had returned to Milton that I wrote:

September 18, 1989 — There is no one here to be "girls" with,
like in *Sula*. I feel that way with Lisa, like she's a sister, a girl.

It took that long for me to really name my sorrow, to fully
accept what had happened, and I was scared there would be
nothing left. I was not fifteen anymore, and not many more
Lisas or Sherrys would be coming into my life, not many more
women to be girls with. I wanted to make sure Lisa and I did
not lose contact, float away from one another. We haven't.
We do the traditional things like call and write. Actually, Lisa is
far better at writing. I am more inclined to pick up the phone. I
cannot honestly say we are best friends; we never really were.
But I find Lisa to be the most amazing woman. She has an eclec-
tic group of friends, black and white, girls from years back,
many from her college days at Oberlin. But I felt, and still feel,
a part of her life. She is generous, funny, kind, brilliant, non-
judgmental, and she has the greatest collection of shoes I have
ever seen.

What I feel keeps our friendship alive, even when months go
by when we don't talk or write to each other, is that we are
kindred spirits and we are girls together. Our friendship is not
subject to the flames of change that push their way in from the
outside.

I hope my friendship with Lisa will last over the years, but I
know the love I feel for her will. The love between Sula and Nel
endures, despite the breakup of their friendship; it is symbolized

by a rose-shaped birthmark just above Sula's eye. I see the love Lisa and I share as a flame, a fire contained, incapable of being destroyed by fire because it is fire itself, warming up the house I live in, steaming up the windows in a place she will always be welcome, where I will throw back the curtains to find her face. In it I will not see fear; I will see myself, and I will let her in.

🦎 🦎 🦎 🦎 🦎 🦎 🦎 🦎 🦎 🦎 🦎 🦎 🦎

An Unsolved Mystery

AN UNSOLVED MYSTERY is a thorn in the heart.

Many years after my friend Barbara's death I still think of her with a stir of hope and dread. As if she hasn't died, yet. As if there might be something I could do to prevent her dying.

We were eighteen years old, the final time we spoke on the telephone. It has been that long.

I can't claim that I was Barbara's best friend in high school — Barbara wasn't the type to have a "best" friend. But we saw each other often and, for each, the other was the measure of sincerity: the opinion that mattered. We did not flatter each other, nor did we withhold praise out of envy. Sometimes I wondered if Barbara, with her quick, frequently sharp tongue, was capable of lying.

Since Barbara lived in town, in an attractive residential neighborhood, and I lived twelves miles from town, I was sometimes invited to stay overnight at her house — which suggests, in retrospect, that we were close and might have shared secrets. In fact these overnight visits were rather formal. Mainly, Barbara and I did our schoolwork. Being earnestly, indefatigably "bright" students, we invariably did more than our teachers required of us. Amid classmates aggressively mature for their ages, the girls in particular (in those years girls *hoped* to become engaged directly out of high school, as a way of being shielded from seeking a "career"), we were anomalies: intellectually advanced for our ages, yet clearly young, immature, in other respects.

Barbara was large-boned, not fat, nor even plump, but thick-bodied; with a pale, smudged complexion; close-cropped, unstyled hair; a weak-muscled left eye of the kind called "wandering." It was the right eye that engaged you. She was shy, yet aggressive; seemingly withdrawn, yet capable of surprising, and wounding, with a sudden sarcastic or cynical remark, as if resentment built up powerfully in her, awaiting discharge. Because of my teenaged appearance — diminutive, dark, watchful — I was perceived as shy, though in fact I was not shy; yet I lacked Barbara's outspokenness. Even in self-defense I was incapable of a razor-swift, cutting remark.

We did not resemble each other physically at all. Yet in some mysterious way we were like sisters. Or twins.

I recall several occasions when, to my bewilderment, I was confused with Barbara, or Barbara with me. Once, swimming in the school pool, myopic and blinking, and hearing the teacher call out, "Barbara? — I mean, Joyce." Another time, overhearing a mutual friend say, "It *was* Joyce, wasn't it? — or, no, Barbara."

Barbara was scientific-minded, and competed successfully with the most favored boys in our class. I was literary-minded, a tireless reader. Yet we shared each other's interests and obsessions, to a degree. When I became caught up in reading American plays, especially the long, somber tragedies of Eugene O'Neill, Barbara read the plays, too, and my own awkward attempts at writing "tragedy." In turn, I read through *Scientific American* (to which Barbara had a subscription) and I accompanied Barbara to special exhibits at the natural history museum and the planetarium. In spring of our senior year, Barbara was awarded a scholarship to Cornell University, where she intended to study chemistry; I was awarded a scholarship to Syracuse

University, where I intended to study comparative literature. So close were the Cornell and Syracuse campuses, it seemed certain we *must* see each other often.

Yet, for some reason, our friendship began to dissolve almost immediately, as soon as we left for college.

Barbara was a poor correspondent. If I wrote her three or four letters, she might be prodded into writing me one. Her letters were brief and apathetic; she mentioned several times the size of the Cornell campus — it was "unreal" and it was "strange." After Christmas break, Barbara stopped writing altogether. I telephoned once, in February, and was hurt by her affected coolness. "*Who* —?" she asked. As if she hadn't recognized my voice. Half-accusingly she said, "You sound different, somehow."

Not just why Barbara took her own life, in May of that year, but how — this is part of the mystery, for me. Sleeping pills, slashed wrists, poison? — I never knew, and never wanted to know. (Of course there were rumors, the most convincing being that Barbara had swallowed a corrosive chemical taken from a university laboratory.) Barbara's stunned, grieving parents spoke to no one outside the family about their tragedy. In those days it seemed reasonable to keep private facts private.

Yet memories of Barbara missing from my life actually predate her death. Why this is, I don't know.

At Thanksgiving, a mutual girlfriend invited a number of us over for an impromptu party, and I was to pick up Barbara; but, when I arrived at her house, she'd changed her mind, greeting me wanly, unsmiling — "You go on without me, nobody's going to miss me." She had a migraine headache, she said. Her eyes did look swollen, reddened.

I tried to talk her into coming with me but she was stubborn, sullen. Standing in her old bathrobe regarding me with something like amusement. "Go on, go alone. Nobody is going to miss *me*."

So I went to our friend's house by myself and, it's true, no one exactly *missed* Barbara, as she'd predicted. This fact made a strong impression on me, in retrospect. *Don't die willfully, you won't be missed.* Yet, that evening, there was a sense of my being somehow incomplete, as if lacking someone — something? At one point a girl asked, unthinking, "Oh where's Joyce? — I mean Barbara," and everyone laughed; I joined in the laughter though feeling suddenly very strange, as if about to burst into tears.

SHIRLEY ABBOTT

Understanding Julien

> What kind of man am I? Do I pos-
> sess good sense? Good sense of a pro-
> found kind? Do I have a remarkable
> mind? To tell the truth, I've no idea.
> — Stendhal,
> *Memoirs of Egotism*

I STILL SEE BILL JAMES'S square midwestern face, his gray
eyes, the heavy glasses, the flat black hair — exactly as he was. I
see the anxious look that did not let up even when he laughed.

When I dream of him, as I sometimes do, I awake grieving.
Bill James, where are you? Phone home. I must have loved him,
or at least I love him now, thinking of the turns my life took
because of him. For example, in the unruly, untidy pile of books
on my bedside table are at least four books I live by, that never
fail me. All these Bill first put into my hands. Perhaps I'd never
have become a writer without him — for he assured me that I
could write. I'd heard that before, of course. All aspiring writers
have heard it. (The English theme in ninth grade comes back
with an "A" and an admiring scribble, and we're hooked.) But
when Bill James said I was a writer, it was different from when
my father or my English teacher said it. Bill really knew writing — I'd never known a person so married to the word.

As I sat with him at a tiny round table in the Café Anglais that
winter in Grenoble, I certainly did not love him. Squinting at

him through cigarette smoke, I tried to observe him clinically, half listening to his voice, trying to dissect the anxiety in his face. (I was making notes for a novel, of course, about a young woman who comes to France in search of her identity.) Was he in physical pain? Did he yearn for love? He'd told me, briefly, that his parents had abandoned him as a baby; his mother had left him with his farmer-grandmother in Nebraska. I could see the obedient boy who weeded the garden and lugged pails of water from the pump, but lived only through the word on the page. "I don't know who my father was," he said. "I never asked." Growing up like that, I supposed, would make you permanently anxious. I knew about weeds, pails of water, having myself spent part of my childhood on a farm.

It rained unendingly in Grenoble that winter, jailing us behind the dripping windows, hiding the distant ring of mountain peaks, sealing off the valley where the city lay grimy and cold. The Anglais was immune to time or place or singularity — the same smoky, unclean café with the same chairs and tables all over France — but preferable to our rented rooms and to the vast, chilly amphitheaters at the University of Grenoble. The year was 1958, and the American government or the French (I wasn't sure which) was paying the bill (more or less) for a large group of American students here. We spent our stipends on Gauloises, *café au lait,* and watery French beer. And books — cheap editions with pages you had to slit. Jean-Paul Sartre and Albert Camus lay as heavily on our minds as Alpine fog. So did Algeria — for the war was on, France's last colonial war. The French had pulled out of Indochina in 1954, leaving the trap Americans so eagerly fell into. But as yet I'd barely heard of Vietnam, did not even think of my country as a colonial power. "*Paix en Algérie*" was scrawled on every wall. I knew a young Frenchman who planned to beat the draft by eating two dozen raw eggs the night before he reported for his physical — albumin in the urine. Among ourselves, we Americans at the Anglais spoke of anomie, *la nausée, engagement,* the existential hero. I see from my notes that we tried ceaselessly to define "the great soul," or "the great man." "Man is condemned to be free," we said. But we were angry, depressed.

"You been to class?" Bill James would inquire when around two in the afternoon I arrived and ordered breakfast. Palms upward, eyes rolling, I would do my French shrug. "*Eh b'en, mon vieux, qu'en penses-tu.*" He would laugh. His copy of *Le Monde* would be neatly folded beneath a pile of books. I would inspect the top book: he went through one or two a day, so something new was always on the stack. I suspected that he sat there every day waiting for me, but at twenty-three I had no use for predictability or fidelity in a male, especially one with an internal injury detectable at fifty paces.

"How did we land here," I would moan, "the most boring spot in France?" Before enrolling at Grenoble, our group spent a few weeks in Paris, polishing our spoken French, and learning with every breath that Paris not only *is* France but is superior to it. Thus we came to the provinces as newly made exiles from the gorgeous heart of civilized life three hundred miles to the northwest. Bill didn't mind. He thought Grenoble was as good a place as any. I had come because of Stendhal, whose birthplace this was.

In fact, the one French novel I'd really read was *The Red and the Black,* the story of Julien Sorel, the handsome, amoral youth and would-be priest who somehow rises from his peasant background and finds work as a tutor in first one and then another wealthy household. He seduces the wife of his first employer and the daughter of his second, who becomes pregnant. Ladyfriend no. 1 denounces him, and after he tries to kill her he is executed, leaving ladyfriend no. 2 to solve her own problems. (They're both still crazy about Julien, of course.) Toiling through the novel with a dictionary, I myself had been seduced. I too came from the depths and was determined to rise. I too was fiercely proud, a secret radical who loathed all aspects of Eisenhower's America. Like Julien I hated the French, yet wanted them to love me. (Every generation of Americans must discover anew that the French don't like Americans, but I took the news badly.) I too intended to advance in love, to make conquests — without shooting anybody, of course. I was thrilled with Julien's ruthlessness. Yet I wanted both to be Julien and to be loved by him. To be a conquest and a conquistador. However, I could identify spiritually only with males. The women I knew, both in and out of novels, were passive and boring. Surely the term "mankind" or "civilized man" included me, not just people with Y-chromosomes. Man was condemned to be free. I could be both Julien and myself, be Sartre (*not* Mlle de Beauvoir) but still be a woman. Why not?

"If I want to study Stendhal, I should go to someplace that he loved — Paris, maybe, or Italy." I would complain to Bill, day after rainy day, since he always was willing to listen.

"Well, forget about Stendhal. He was just a fat, bald little man. Not much of a lover. All talk." Bill would answer happily, as if he knew Stendhal personally. "Also, he wore a corset. Did you know that? Anyhow, there are better novels than *The Red and the Black*. Actually, *La Chartreuse de Parme* is a better novel than that. If you want to stick to Stendhal, read the good stuff. You'd like Fabrice better than Julien. In the *Chartreuse,* there's a brilliant description of the battle of Waterloo, where Fabrice gets lost on the field — a worm's-eye view of war. The only morally defensible view of war, I think. The worm's-eye view. Or you could read Flaubert — a better writer. And Emma Bovary would interest you a lot more than Julien." He would talk on and on. But I was not ready to abandon my persona, my prefabricated discontent, let alone to plow through all those tough books.

Though I was always the only woman at the table, sometimes other young men joined us. Americans from the scholarship group, or French students worrying about the draft, or even Richard Van and his entourage, an older and very attractive bunch who hung out mostly in another café. Richard was a

high-status catch whom I coveted, for he had already published
a short story in the *Paris Review*. And looked like Gérard Phi-
lipe. Richard's idol was Hemingway, and he planned to be in
Pamplona for the running of the bulls next spring: material for
his novel-in-progress. I yearned to go with him. Often, he entertained us with opinions about existential aspects of fly-fishing
and the *corrida*, as well. Richard Van dominated any and all
tables he chose to sit at, and I noticed that in his presence Bill
James said nothing about Emma or Fabrice or Stendhal's stays.

Secretly, I liked my life, though the angst I recorded in my journal was genuine. The accommodations I'd dreamed about — a
spacious bedroom, plentiful food, a smiling mama and papa
eager to help me speak proper French, rosy children climbing
into my lap — did not exist in my price range, if at all. I lived in
an unheated fifth-floor room that opened off the same foyer as
my landlady's apartment, where she and her husband and their
four children (not rosy) lived. At night the water froze in my
drinking glass. The only member of the household I regularly
saw was the scullery maid, a bright-eyed child of twelve who
scrubbed the floors on her knees with brushes strapped to both
hands. "*Bonjour, mademoiselle*," she would say, smiling and
ducking her head, as I emerged in the early afternoon and tip-
toed around the wet spots. I could smell the *pot-au-feu* simmer-
ing in the kitchen, hear the dishes rattling, but the family never
invited me in. At the student cafeteria, the food was white:
pasta, cauliflower, potatoes, rice, yogurt, tiny carafes of white
wine. Even meat and eggs, if any, were colorless.

But the only meal I ate there was dinner. At five or so, I would
leave the Anglais to change my clothes and prepare for my evening's adventures. Which presented problems. Like all of metropolitan France, Grenoble, and especially the shabby quarter of
town I lived in, was filling up with Algerian immigrants. My
landlady had advised me they were dangerous, had hinted at
rape. Indeed I sometimes passed dark men on the street who

gave me odd, lustful looks or even turned and followed me, pairs of them, speaking Arabic. I was frightened at first, but soon realized that except for being swarthy, they were no different from other Gallic assessors of female flesh. More terrifying than the men on the street were the women.

I knew, in the abstract, that France had plenty of prostitutes — it was a national trait, like wine-drinking — but in Grenoble, prostitutes seemed to outnumber the men. By late afternoon, women in tight dresses and high heels stood in every doorway and alley. I skittered past them, trying not to spy on them but spying. I was shocked to see that they were mostly teenagers. A friend of mine, a Los Angeles man who was on good terms with some of them, told me the girls came by busloads every week — shipped in fresh from Marseilles like produce. No wonder the French called them *poules*. Some were failures and were moved on. Some got steady work in one of the scores of brothels. Now and then a very pretty girl might be set up as some local businessman's mistress.

I wondered obsessively what it meant to stand in doorways and make love in the shadows after the man had given you a few bills, or to take him to a room somewhere. What if he hurt you, was dirty, had sores, wanted (ugh, that word) fellatio? Did you have to do it? Why would a woman be a whore? To survive, of course, but would I do it? How many customers a night did you have to have? Why was it okay for the men to buy but immoral for the women to sell? What cut did the madam take, the pimp? What did you do when you got old? Sick? My close-cropped hair, flat shoes, and heavy sweaters clearly marked me as a student, but men always felt free to approach me, whispering words I half understood. They enraged me. Did they think whores came out in olive drab duffle coats lugging a book bag? With no makeup, their hair a mess, and an American accent? I'm an intellectual, I wanted to shout. Could they not see the difference between me and the girl in a fur jacket and satin dress?

Bill James, when I brought all this up, explained that they could never see it, "Not until you're thirty-five or so, and then they stop looking at you. You should read some Zola. This noble writer *engagé* who defended Captain Dreyfus despised prostitutes. He thought they killed French virility, sapped soldiers of their ability to fight. He blamed them for the loss of the Franco-Prussian War. He didn't blame the men."

"Well, he's an ass," I replied, "and I don't want to read him." I hadn't intended to read him, anyway. Naturalism, as an aesthetic, was old hat.

Nevertheless, I roamed the cafés and other student hangouts after dark, restlessly seeking the relationship I wanted. At least I had no trouble finding male companionship: an American painter who liked staying up all night, a French Communist who kept live grenades and loaded rifles under his bed, and a succession of other relentlessly casual acquaintances. One evening I came into the student cafeteria wearing a scarf — a breach of manners that called down instant punishment. Shouts of "*Chapeau! Chapeau!*" whistles, and stamping feet rocked the room as I put a few items on my tray and my scarf in my pocket and fled to a table at the back of the hall. Unable to swallow but too angry to leave, I noticed that a tall dark-skinned man in a shirt, tie, and elegant sweater had sat down next to me.

"These people are animals. You mustn't cry." His English was perfect but with a lilt. "Would you care to come around the corner for some coffee?" His hands were the most beautiful I had ever seen, very long and thin with well-articulated knuckles, velvety brown with white nails and palms. The little finger of his right hand was a stump. "You're an American. I've noticed you before. You're usually with your Amurrican pals" — he gave the phrase an ugly, parodic twist — "and I haven't dared speak to you." I put on my coat; he took my hand. "My name is Ali Mirza. *Je suis musulman.*" As it turned out, he went unpredictably from English to French and sometimes to Urdu. "I hail from Karachi, Pakistan. Where do you hail from?"

"I hail from somewhere near Hot Springs, Arkansas. *Je suis* Southern Baptist. *Pas tellement.* Not so you'd notice."

Laughing, he insisted we stop at the first plate glass window, to compare our reflections, both tall, one fair, the other dark.

"A beautiful couple. Good thing your parents can't see us."

"Or yours. I can't imagine they'd approve of you going down the street with a white Baptist lady in tow."

"I have no parents. But you're right. My guardians wouldn't like it either. But they'd like it better than yours. White women want nothing to do with us, except those ladies on the street."

Later, at the café, he said, "You noticed my little finger — I saw you wondering what happened to it. Well, look here. Did you notice this?"

And he pointed to his right ear, the outer shell of which was mutilated. "When I was fourteen, a gang of Hindus raided the district where we lived in Karachi — this was ten years ago, when Pakistan and India were partitioned. The Hindus came with swords and scythes, killing and burning. We heard the screams from next door and tried to leave by the back way, but they caught us. I watched while my mother and my father were hacked to pieces. They didn't have time to kill me properly — they just slashed at my head and cut off half my ear. I must have put my hand up because I lost my little finger as well. So much blood — they probably thought I was dying. At least they didn't set fire to the house."

Unable to think of a comment, I took his hands in mine. I kissed them. I began to cry again. "My love is black but comely, O ye daughters of Jerusalem," was what flitted through my head. From then on we spent at least one evening a week together, in cafés, of course, and walking the city parks and the countryside as the weather improved toward April. I was deeply in love with him — but only on the nights I saw him. His kisses, bestowed in doorways or under the dripping, budding trees of spring, were as chaste as a nursemaid's. He politely rebuffed my efforts to sexualize them. He was determined to be a virgin when he married, he said. Because of the turmoil in his family, and the trauma of partition, however, no bride had yet been selected.

Richard Van and his set, whose headquarters were the Café Victor Hugo and a pizza parlor nearby, became steady company, too. They had come to France on the G.I. Bill, unlike the students on scholarship, or in some cases on family money. Most of the men in the group had sleep-in girlfriends. Richard had a girl named Nancy who was always with him in the evenings, never the afternoons. The one readily available male in the group, Arthur, a boy of eighteen, spoke Russian. His mission was to find a language into which Dostoyevsky could be perfectly translated. He had thought that language would be French, and thus had come to Grenoble to begin work. But he had been in error, he now felt. French had proved incompatible with a Slavic tongue. Perhaps Italian was the answer. Soon, therefore, he would move on to Bologna. He watched me eagerly, insanely — and always tried to sit next to me. Richard called him Raskolnikov, because of his wild, wiry, black hair and eyebrows, and his enormous yellowish overcoat with its vast lapels, which he never took off. We assumed he slept in it. Once or twice, at odd hours of the morning, I let him walk me home.

I tried timidly to get Richard to show me his half-finished novel. Referring to the thick, disorderly batch of sketches typed single-spaced on onionskin and stored in the case of my portable Olivetti typewriter, I told him that I was working on a novel, too. But he showed no interest, particularly after I told him the novel was about me. Most evenings, Richard talked with other men and left me to Nancy, who was the only woman friend I had. Like me, she gravitated to smart men, but in a spirit of servitude. And there was another difference, too. Love — the concept that to me was a dark, essential mystery, the center of life — was the center of life to her as well, but not dark or mysterious. It meant somebody in the bed beside you. It was as ordinary as your shoelaces, as ordinary as morning coffee. Sex every day.

"You can't be a woman without it. Richard and I have sex all the time. Sometimes all day every day, when we feel like it."

My previous sexual experience was slight, but of high quality, I'd always thought. At nineteen I had been initiated by a much older man who'd not only scrupulously avoided risking pregnancy but had fallen in love with me as well. That was not quite the only item on my résumé, but was the one I thought about the most. Though I fancied myself searching systematically and ruthlessly for love, I had certain unspoken inhibitions. Even with a condom, sex could be scary. Without a condom, it was worse than scary. Though I loved the afterglow of sex — the aura of true womanliness it imparted — and with my first lover had loved the sex itself, the payout was slight when you woke up worried sick the next morning and had to pore over the calendar and do arithmetic and count days on your fingers for two or three weeks. And then maybe get your period a week late just from sheer terror.

I asked Nancy how she kept from getting pregnant.

She gave me a look. "I just don't think about it when I'm with a man I love. If I get pregnant, I'll get an abortion. Or I'll do whatever I do. Maybe I'll just have the baby. Richard would take care of me. I wouldn't make him marry me. I'd never do that to a man. But he'd take care of me."

"Did he tell you he would?"

"No, but I know. Anyhow, maybe I'm infertile. Maybe I'm just lucky. Do you really worry a lot about that?" Another look.

Maybe I wasn't a woman, really.

"Anyway," she went on, "you're the dolly who's swinging with the spades. Does he use something?"

"Spades! What are you talking about — Ali Mirza? You must be kidding. He's no spade, and I don't swing with him."

"Come on now, how can you miss out on that? Oh, he's so dark and tall and beautiful. Did you ever try black cock? I love Richard, but black is better."

"He's Pakistani. That's brown, not black. And he's not doing it with anybody. He wouldn't even do it if I offered. He won't do it till his wedding night."

"Well, are you after Richard? If you are, I can tell you it's okay by me. We can all go to bed together. We do stuff like that sometimes."

"My God. I'd die before I'd get in bed with two other people, and one of them you! How can you say you don't care if another woman sleeps with your boyfriend, especially when you're right there?"

Nancy laughed. "You're really from the sticks, aren't you, honey? My God, are you a virgin? It's okay to tell me."

Compared to Nancy, I was a virgin. In my soul, I wasn't Julien Sorel, I was just a contemptible virgin. Richard and Nancy probably did things every day that I'd never even heard of. Shocking things I probably hadn't even read in books. All I really wanted was to see the running of the bulls at Pamplona. To watch Richard gather material for his novel. To find out if his novel was any good. I wanted him to read mine. I wanted to be his peer, not his woman.

The closest I came to sexual intercourse in Grenoble that winter was with a stereotypically handsome German — my partner one evening at bridge. We played till well past midnight, and he courteously insisted on seeing me home — Algerians were around, he murmured, and they could get nasty. His arm was heavy on my shoulder, and got heavier as we walked along. He'd drunk six or seven beers, at least. I'd had one or two myself. Stopping here and there, we kissed beerily but without much interest. However, when he cornered me at the entrance to my building, pinned me against the wall and somehow thrust his hand inside my coat and under my sweater, he seemed brutally sober. "Give me your door key," he commanded, planting his mouth on mine, twisting my arm with one hand while he searched my coat pocket with the other. "You might as well take me to your room, or I'll screw you right here on the stone floor. If you scream, you'll wake the concierge. I'll tell her you're a whore, and your lady will throw you out." I struggled and whined, lapsing into English as he lapsed into German.

No man had ever laid hands on me like this. I cursed him for a savage and a Nazi and myself for a novice and a fool. He ripped two buttons off my coat as he tried to strip it off me, bit my neck, then knocked me to my knees on the floor, and when I managed somehow to stand up and start to run, he seized me in a grip that negated my own strength. I screeched, and he stepped back. Seeing my chance, I shoved him as hard as I could, then started up the stairs two at a bound. I was still wearing my coat, with the key in the pocket. He only made it to the second landing. By the time I reached the top, I could hear the downstairs door swing shut.

Sometimes I told Bill about my various failures, which often kept me in black, depressive moods. The near-rape had been my own fault, I reasoned, and I never told a soul. I did recount waking one icy morning to find Arthur/Raskolnikov inside my door, his face half-hidden behind the upturned lapels of his yellow overcoat. He'd sneaked past the concierge and then had told the maid he was bringing me a telegram. "He was dreaming of climbing into bed with me. Just imagine it. I sleep in long underwear, socks, a sweater, and a hat. It was so damn cold, I let him climb in, after he'd taken off his shoes, of course. We sat there for a few minutes, holding hands, and I gave him a little talking-to. Told him he was a sweet boy but we'd both get frostbite if we undressed. I sent him back downstairs, overcoat and all. That was my one chance to find out what he wears under it." In most of the stories I told on myself, I appeared à la Laurel and Hardy, as in this one, but Bill understood that my belief in romantic passion was serious, and that I'd willingly court self-destruction, if not pregnancy, to find it. I think he also understood my humiliation — a predictably Julienesque reaction, in any case.

One afternoon, he put a book into my hands. "You must read this. It's by a man called Choderlos De Laclos. *Les Liaisons dan-*

gereuses. It was written just before the French Revolution. The author never wrote anything else."

"Oh my God. Why must I read it?"

"Because, among other things, it will show you why there was a French Revolution. It's about the abuse of power, about great nobles who behave like shits. The same idea you find in *The Marriage of Figaro,* or in *Don Juan. Le seigneur méchant homme.* The big powerful male who's bad. If those who rule society are evil, then they can't complain when the oppressed rise against them."

"Any other reason? It's awfully fat."

"Because it will educate you in the politics of love. It's odd about women, I never met a one who knew that love is politics. You all think that love is benign. You think you can control it. That's why you're always so astonished when your adventures don't work out. Men teach women that love is benign. Women even teach other women that. Love is war. Love is diplomacy by other means. Sex is a weapon for getting what you want."

"How would you know? Anyway, what a rotten, cynical idea."

"Well, you'll know more after you've read this book. I insist you read it. Also, it's a tour de force. No would-be writer should miss it. Nobody could write this book today." I never knew whether he was trying to rescue me from my folly, to furnish my head with an idea or two, or whether he loved the novels and poetry he recommended more than he loved me, more than he loved himself.

June came, and the Grenoble days ended. Ali Mirza left for Paris and Karachi. He treated me to a delicious dinner, and apologized for not considering me as a prospective bride. We said goodbye at the train station. (Years later, he called me when he came through New York — he'd become a physicist and now held some high government post.) In the heat of late spring,

Arthur/Raskolnikov set off hitchhiking for Bologna in his yellow overcoat, the last I saw or heard of him. My French friend was drafted and sent to Algeria, though he ate two dozen eggs the night before his physical and no doubt had plenty of albumin in his urine. The Communist with the grenades under his bed was also drafted. I never learned what became of his arsenal. Richard Van for some reason did not go to Pamplona that spring, so I was not left behind, disconsolate. My acquaintance with him ended in an angry quarrel over Bill James, of all people. Five or six of us were in a bar, probably drunk, and I don't know how the argument began. But I do remember Richard's diatribe — how Bill James was null and void. "Has no fire. Has probably never fucked a woman. Never shot a gun. Never tied a fly. Never got into a fight. Wouldn't know what pain was. Wouldn't know a damn thing if it wasn't in a book. Wouldn't bleed if he was cut."

I listened in rage and soon burst out, "He damn well would bleed. He would bleed if you cut him. He does know what pain is."

Richard replied — I have always remembered the exact words — "Oh, hey, look how mad she is. Isn't she something when she gets her Irish up? What's the matter, the guy balling you?"

"No, goddammit. Does everybody have to be balling somebody? Bill James does more than you do. He actually knows something. You'll never know what he knows about writing if you live to be 1000. And he does suffer, whether you can see it or not." I struggled out of my chair, stalked out, and have not since encountered Richard Van. My journal entry for that day reads:

Richard Van can wave his wineglass all he likes and say Bill James wouldn't bleed if he was cut, but he's still an ass. Theoretically I could hate Bill James. When you put him into words, he fades from the page. No bloodlust, no flamboyant obses-

sions, for sure. He's not a bit like Hemingway or Richard Van.
But that's exactly why abstractions always miss, why somewhere between words and reality there is a deep and narrow
abyss. Because concretely I could not hate Bill James, not ever.
Richard may be the most brilliant guy in Grenoble, and he'll
probably be a famous writer ten years from now, and I'll be in
some stupid job. But I do hate him and not theoretically. He's
as narrow-minded as a Puritan, except that the things he's doc-
trinaire on are all things relating to sex, or to his so-called
masculinity. Engaged to his own disengagement, he says. The
only way to be an artist is to be ruthless and selfish, he says.
And to have somebody like Nancy to wash your socks. I do
wonder if you can be a decent person and be a writer. I wonder
if you can be a woman and a writer. That's the big question
now.

Whatever I searched for in France remained beyond me, behind
a gate, across a moat. I was simply another American, badly
dressed, struggling to put my thoughts into reasonably correct
French, practicing my uvular *r* in my room at night, never sure
that I had it. During that winter, I had journeyed to Paris as
often as I could, and when there practiced a ritual. As you cross
the Seine from the Left Bank to the *Ile de la Cité*, following the
lovely narrow streets, you come to a certain four-story house,
charming but not remarkable. But at night the topmost windows
were always brilliantly lighted. I could see only the ceiling and a
pair of sconces against the far wall, but the light shone at top
wattage above my head and seemed the essence of whatever it
was I wanted, the very light itself. I was certain that the room
was warm (there was a fireplace) and a meal was on the table:
red wine, a basket of bread, a roast chicken. (I carefully imagined every detail of the meal, student hunger being what it is.
Sometimes there was also a selection of cheeses and pastries.)
Seated on the hearth rug, a faceless but dazzling young man
strummed a guitar and waited — for me, of course. A vision out
of Picasso. I memorized the address. It would be my address one

day. I would live there. My friends would come to visit. I was as yet incapable of any other dream: the man was the center of it. I would pace the street, alone, staring up at the light.

I spent two weeks in Paris before leaving France, and Bill James was there, too, quartered in a cheap hotel not far from mine. Once at nightfall, I decided I must take him to the *Ile de la Cité* and show him my house. The idea took on a sudden urgency — I took him by the arm, pulled him along. What if the building were dark? What if no one were at home? Bad luck, surely. The mist rose from the Seine, couples strolled the *quais*, kissing. Paris always manages to conform to her black and white photographs, to look like a poster or a calendar. When we headed up the right street at last, the house was there, and the topmost windows glowed with light.

"There. That's my secret place. I wouldn't tell this to anybody but you. My lover is up there. With a nice dinner on the table and a guitar. I'm going to own that home one day. With him. You're invited every time you visit Paris. It's the perfect house, the perfect address. I'll have my little typewriter in the corner. It will be the perfect life." I laughed.

If I faced the recollection squarely, I might see his expression through the discoloration of thirty-five years. Surprised? Concerned? Is it only in hindsight, wishful thinking, that Bill James says, "This is not the dream of a writer. The dream of a writer is of an empty room, you know, perfectly empty, except for the table and the chairs, and the light. And maybe the dinner. Even writers have to eat." But of course he said no such thing.

Then we went home — me to New York, he to work on a doctorate at Princeton. Too poor to telephone, we wrote letters, visited back and forth, and sometimes saw plays together from the top balcony. When I went to see my family in Arkansas, or he to his grandmother in Nebraska, our letters were more frequent. We needed to tell one another how it was. "I don't see how it could ever occur to anyone out here that western civilization involves them," he wrote from the prairie. "I don't understand this place but I love it. France I understand but I don't love it. What drives me crazy about that terrible French lucidity is its self-importance. They think the cosmos is contained in them. People who are lucid all the time get in the way of everything. Maybe it's all a little silly at bottom." Once, replying to a letter I'd written of a family reunion in Arkansas with unhappy undertones, he gave me a kind of foundation or guideline for future work:

> I wonder if you would be upset if I said that you have written the essence of a novel. The center of a fiction which could articulate, broaden, and shape the initial intuition but still remain the radiating center. Perhaps this is only to say that I felt the sensation of the complexities and ambiguities of a way of life from this part of your letter. In this sort of situation I would have tried to express my own reaction analytically, tried to understand intellectually what is going on. You speak differently. Your situation adheres more to the reality the *épaisseur* of actuality. This boils down I suppose to saying that there is a decided difference in the way we apprehend the world. But a difference you should make the most of.

On my last visit to Princeton we got drunk on gin in his room and walked around the campus on a heavenly autumn day, giggling and tipsy, eventually collapsing on the grass. Susceptible as ever to clichés — the autumn light, the exquisitely tended lawn, the dying leaves, the liberating effects of gin — I fell momentarily in love with him, and imagined doing that trick Humphrey Bogart and Jimmy Stewart always used on whoever was playing the pretty secretary or schoolteacher. I'd tenderly remove his glasses and say, "See how handsome you are! All you need is some contact lenses and a nice suit. Let's get married." Then he'd kiss me, and wouldn't our friends be surprised?

An hour later, cold sober over hamburgers and coffee, I studied him clinically once more. It's a good guess that he was talking literary criticism as he poured ketchup on his burger — perhaps the evolving concept of reality in Western lit. Increasingly, over the centuries, he probably told me, ordinary people, poor slobs like ourselves, had gradually presented themselves as subjects for Serious Discourse. For example, Beaumarchais had created Figaro, a mere barber, a servant who in every way outclassed his masters. But to create Figaro was the ingenious, the truly inventive thing Beaumarchais had done. His political act. Indeed, as time went on and writers kept writing, a woman knitting a sock, as for example in Virginia Woolf, became as transcendent a subject as all the peers of France.

Or perhaps he spoke of Yeats. "The only poets we really love are those who have confronted the anguish we ourselves know," he had written me the previous week. In any case, I promised sincerely that I would read the books he now placed in my hands. *Mimesis: The Imitation of Reality in Western Literature* by Erich Auerbach. Apollinaire's *Alcools*. Three lesser works from *La Comédie humaine* that simply must not be missed. *The Collected Poems of Yeats.* He cannot have given me all these books on this one occasion, but I did read them because of him. I still read them. I realized, though, that he wouldn't be handsome without his glasses. And that he didn't want to kiss me, and that if I had kissed him, he would have been displeased.

And then we lost track of each other. He got a job teaching advanced French at a small, prestigious college in the midwest (white men only, in the early 1960s), and then vanished. I invited him to my wedding but he sent no reply. I married, raised two daughters, worked as an editor, wrote some articles and books, saw them published. In this interval — a lifetime — two or three letters have come from Bill James, the last several years ago from a small college founded by and for African-Americans.

"This place," he wrote,

unlike my first post so long ago, certainly does not give one the sense of teaching the elite. Perhaps that's why I like it here. I teach English as well as beginning French. The students are not awfully well prepared. Nobody in their families ever came to college before. You wouldn't believe it, but the young women worry a lot about how they look and want to marry doctors. Very Southern in some ways. And alas, the lighter-skinned kids discriminate against the dark. Fortunately there's a lot more going on than that. I have not been a productive scholar. Far from it. My first years of teaching French poetry to upper-class white men almost induced a full-scale nervous breakdown. I stopped teaching, did nothing for a time. This job has saved me. I hope I do some good. As for my personal life, I live alone with an elderly cat. I rise at 4 A.M. and begin work, though I try not to work more than nine hours a day. On reflection, I believe I am reasonably sane, have come to livable terms with myself and am leading — if not a conventionally full — a moderately happy and useful life. For relaxation I have taught myself Latin.

As I reread these words, they burn a hole in my mind. Classical languages, of course, are as good a way as any to scare off existential angst or plain old loneliness. I've actually known two or three other people capable of consoling themselves with a Latin grammar, and the notion that, possibly, they were useful. Perhaps I am one of them. This morning, I tried to phone him. "We show three William Jameses," said the operator in the city I called, and I took down the numbers, rehearsing my opening gambit each time I dialed. ("Is that you? This is me.") The first two numbers produced answering machines — but neither voice was his. (I hung up furtively at the sound of the beep, to avoid explanations.) At the third number a woman answered.

"Is Bill James there? I'm not sure I have the right Bill James."

A pause. "Bill James died six months ago."

"Oh, no. You mean Bill James the teacher?"

"No, honey. Not a teacher. He was a hardware salesman, way up in years, past eighty."

"I'm sorry to bother you." For one moment, I was as happy as if I'd found him.

What I would tell him, if I ever reached him, could only sound lame at this distance. Thank you for seducing my mind rather than my body. ("What?") Thank you for telling me the truth. ("You must be joking.") For giving me something to go on. ("How did I do that?") For not ever acting like a *seigneur méchant homme*. For not attempting to strike the bargain that begins in joy and ends in sorrow — and/or grocery bills, insurance premiums, quarrels, and dirty dishes. If you want to spend an afternoon drinking coffee some time, I'll meet you wherever you say.

🐿 🐿 🐿 🐿 🐿 🐿 🐿 🐿 🐿 🐿 🐿 🐿 🐿

A Friend in Man

THERE'S A PICTURE of my father I've always loved: it was taken around 1965 or so when he was in his twenties; he's wearing a dark suit and dark sunglasses; he's got a serious but smirky expression on his face and for some reason his hand is half-slipped into his vest, à la Napoleon. I remember a friend of mine looking at the photo and observing, "That's not a father, that's Marcello Mastroianni." I had to protest this remark, because firstly, Marcello Mastroianni *is* a father, so therefore the two concepts are not mutually exclusive, and secondly because my father is not a lovable, suave charmer like Mastroianni — my father's charm is rougher around the edges — but her words did make me contemplate what an unusual father I have.

My father and I are friends. I don't know how common that is. People tend to react strangely whenever I mention my friendship with my father — I've had men accuse me of having an Electra complex, I've had men tell me that it's a fatal flaw because I can never take another man seriously — but in general I find that all that is mostly a result of their own emotional baggage being foisted upon me. Women react with equal disbelief: "Oh, you must have had years of therapy to achieve that," or "Your father must be European, American fathers aren't as sensitive as European fathers." I haven't been in therapy and my father is not European, so I can't quite fit into those pigeonholes either. I have no complexes about my father, no need to prove myself, no need to break away and marry somebody completely different, no need to marry somebody exactly the same. I'm good friends with my mother as well — in fact, over the years my parents have ceased to be parents and have become more akin to older colleagues — but my mother and I share so many interests that being her friend is effortless. We can talk about literature or films for hours upon end (much to my father's disgust: "*Who* did *what?*" he'll often interrupt, and then he'll scowl, "Oh, sorry, I thought you were talking about real people"); we both also love art and music, travel, French cooking; we've always been close, and there's very little I won't confide in her. My father and I have almost nothing in common, on the surface. My father hates cities, while I thrive in them; my father has always needed the security of his own house and a plot of land around him in order to function, whereas I see property as a trap and could live in an apartment forever; I've never gone to a play or an exhibit with my father, and I can positively state that in twenty-eight years I've never seen him read a novel. Judging by this it seems that I should have little more than a cordial, obligatory respect for my father as My Father but I don't; I have an utterly incredible rapport with him that only grows stronger with time. He doesn't tell me what to do anymore, he merely listens to my problems or aspirations, or the problems impeding my aspirations; he offers occasional advice; or he rolls his eyes and shrugs his shoulders — he's making a judgment, yes, but he's not imposing it upon me. "Well, you've got to live your own life," he'll say, yet it's not with a stony mock-indifference — there's always the underlying assurance that he'll support me no matter what the outcome. Emotionally, financially, however. That's not so much just a father, that's a friend.

It was not always this way. My father is the beloved despot turned democrat; a definite case of mellowing with age. For the first half of my life, my parents and I were locked in an all-out, intense, daily combat. Because for the first half of my life, I was an all-out rotten kid. And not a boldly rotten kid, but a sullen, moody, sneaky kid whom you'd never expect from her appearance to do anything wrong: small and scrawny, huge-eyed and pale. I remember at the age of seven convincing some sweet, trusting old woman that I was a runaway orphan and having her believe me and give me ten dollars, which I promptly spent on toys. I did horribly in school, my life was a constant reformulation of lies and alibies, and if there was a bad influence to be found I would latch onto it like Bill Sikes's dog Bull's-eye in *Oliver Twist*, forever the faithful little masochist, trotting after thugs. I was an only child, which I resented, and I made sure my parents knew it. My father, who had been a wild kid himself (but not a rotten kid — he'd grown up scratch-poor and had figured out early on that deviant behavior was only going to prolong his misery), generally saw through about eighty percent of my fibs and schemes and generally reacted to them with an explosion of temper. My father's temper was the ultimate boundary for me — if I wasn't afraid of the wrath of God then I was certainly afraid of the wrath of Dad. He was not one to strike or slap (he'd punch a wall instead), but just to have him raging and screaming in the house was as terrifying as the onset of a hurricane. To pull something over on my father was for me the ultimate coup, like outwitting a mastermind. Those occasions, of course, were rare.

I lived in fear of his wrath for fourteen years, always trying to con my way out of it, always cringing at the thought of the next siege, and then I gradually began to settle down. I can't explain why I stopped lying and smoking, shoplifting, getting into fights, taking dares, having detention as regularly as study hall, but I did and therefore I expected never to experience The Wrath again. It was as if I had been put on parole, and my parents and I edged around each other with a tenuous, determined sense of trust. On one occasion, however, perhaps the first time in my life

I had ever been unjustly accused, The Wrath blared through and my father followed me from room to room, roaring, hollering, accusing me of going back to my old ways. In my frustration I picked up a poker from the fireplace and brandished it before him, screaming in reply that I was, for once, innocent and to leave me the hell alone. I expected him to become even more furious over this gesture, this outright disrespectful rebellion — and with a weapon — but I did not care because I was too furious myself. I'll never forget his reaction because it stunned me: he laughed. Hard. He laughed because I had stood up dementedly for my rights and therefore he was proud of me. He walked away, the rage blown over, and then he went and recounted the whole episode to my mother. And to this day, nearly a decade and a half later, it's still one of his favorite stories: The Poker Incident. He narrates it with pride. I personally have always viewed the Poker Incident as that time when my father changed in my eyes from a charismatic tyrant to a good friend. He never doubted my word again. We had finally reached a plateau of trust and could carry on as equals, more or less.

You have to go to the roots of my father in order to understand him. He's a contradictory person. He's a handsome man, yet he has almost no ego; he's a brilliant man, yet he shuns all literary matter; and he's a man of many talents but he keeps them hidden, like cards up his sleeve to be drawn out at just the right moment. I never knew how well my father played the guitar until I was in my late teens — I thought my mother had put on a Segovia record, and then I realized it was him, strumming away. My father came from a background of contradictions as well. His father, born in Italy, was almost ruthlessly domineering, yet sentimental and solicitous at the same time; a man who extolled the concept of the American Dream, yet who did not encourage ambition or the pursuit of "college knowledge." My grandfather was a brilliant man as well; he had had great expectations; he had been crushed by the depression and the demands of a large family; his hopes had been caged, and therefore it was as if he wanted to cage everyone else's hopes as well. His wrath was much worse than my father's, and even though my father incurred that wrath for many years, he rarely speaks of his father with any trace of bitterness. And I don't regard my grandfather in a negative manner, even though my primary childhood memory is of him saying, "You'd make a better door than window" when I blocked his view of the television during a Yankees game. But other family members report that when I was still in the crib, my grandfather used to rush home after work yelling, "Where is that baby? I love that baby!" and pick me up and dance around the room with me in his arms. I feel a certain remorse that my grandfather died before I could truly get to know him. I prefer to think of him not as a bully but as a dapper young man with a pencil moustache and high aspirations, tooling about New York in the 1920s; a self-educated man who quickly mastered English, more or less memorized all the volumes of *Bailey's Horticultural Encyclopedia,* and loved opera with a passion. "He was a victim of his era, of hard times," my father insists. "You would have gotten along with him just as well as you do with me, had he lived long enough." And I probably would have at that. I can empathize with my grandfather now — I understand him much better, but only because my father has told me his story.

My friendship with my father has been mainly an active, outdoors one in which I hand him tools or help him in the garden, accompany him on an errand, or he picks me up or drops me off at train stations or airports. We're always doing something; we don't often sit over coffee and chat. He even likes to shop. This is traditionally a mother-daughter thing, shopping, but in my case all I have to do when I'm home visiting is mention that I need new shoes, a toaster, whatever, and within seconds my father is out the door, warming up the car, ready to roll. You can't get my father to sit still for long — he likes to be out there, all the time. He's forever fixing used cars or cleaning out gutters, running off to garage sales or tilling a plot of earth. He finds a

curative power in physical activity and tends to limit his intellectual intake to books on medicine or history, travelogues or me-
teorological charts. My father is obsessed with the weather, with
nature's elements and the various climates of the world. He's a
product of his background: his father was a landscaper and a
groundsman at Prospect Park in Brooklyn. Even in an urban
environment, nature was always important. My parents now
own a farm in upstate Pennsylvania and, although my father
comes from a nest of city-dwellers, he's utterly at peace there "in
the sticks." It's his retreat. He has about fifty different types of
roses growing in front of the house, and he's contemplating having his own hive of honeybees. His most recent photographic
portrait is on his tractor wearing a straw hat — he's not much
for dark suits and sunglasses anymore.

Because of my father, I find myself able to fix small machines
and pore over maps and almanacs for hours on end; I know
about climate zones and shortwave radios and I read through
history texts like fiction. That's his influence. Data and design.
The concrete and the factual. What's ironic in this is that my
father started out his life as an intellectual. When he and my
mother met, they were both Romance language graduate students preparing for academic careers, but whereas my mother
kept up her passion for foreign literature, my father did not. The
immediate financial necessity of providing for a family forced
him to take a job teaching high school Spanish. He abandoned
his Ph.D. studies and never returned to that world again. And so
my father, who had once read through volumes of Lope de Vega,
Cervantes, and Unamuno, found that literature had little place
in a day-to-day world of teaching basic grammar and vocabu-
lary, drills upon drills, year after year after year. The rules of the
university no longer applied in a school where armed guards
patrolled the halls and brawls erupted as regularly as the seasons
changed. But I believe my father always preferred the mechanics
of a language to its literature because he has a mind that allows
him to dismantle a language just as deftly as he can dismantle a

machine engine or a clock. His life revolves around the immediate and tangible result of one's own labor. A garden, a fixed
motor, a grafted fruit tree mean more to him than any philo-
sophical or intellectual argument. I also majored in Spanish literature in college but we seldom discussed my reading material.
My father always seemed more interested in the weather we'd
had that semester or the details of a course in pharmacology that
I'd taken. I never took this as a personal rebuff. Literature just
wasn't practical to him anymore.

I remember watching Fellini's *8½* on television with my father. He sat through it politely, no doubt enjoying the spoken
Italian more than the plot itself, and when it was over he rolled
his eyes regarding its futility-of-existence ending and remarked,
"Well, I think I'll go jump off the roof now." His favorite Italian
movie is *Seven Beauties*. In that movie, the hero survives. From
the depths of imprisonment and absurdity, he survives. That's
another vital tenet of my father's: life is absurd. Nothing should
ever depress you too much. You should haul yourself out of a
depression forcibly; you should lift up your head and look
around, go outside and observe the greater power of the elements. You should have a good meal and a glass of wine; you
should laugh in the face of it all. Don't be stoic, make a mockery
of bad times. Although for years this attitude puzzled me, I now
find that I share it, and that no matter how morose or bogged
down I become, at the height of a crisis I always assume an almost punch-drunk state of grace and begin to bounce back. It's
a priceless defense mechanism. My father attributes this inherent
attitude to his father, a Neapolitan. Neapolitans have always
maintained a scrappy and sardonic view of life. During the
devastation of World War II, *che onore*, a popular Neapolitan
epithet, stemmed from Mussolini's insistence that any sacrifice
made for the Fascist regime was to be considered an honor, *un
onore*, not a loss. Neapolitans soon began referring snidely to
all misery as honor, such as "I'm starving to death, *che onore*,"
or "My house just burned down, *che onore*." Yet they're also

perversely optimistic people; they live in the shadow of Mount Vesuvius, which for centuries has threatened to erupt at any time, yet they've remained and flourished in their own chaotic way. Neapolitans are often referred to by other Italians as the rabble of the country, and "*va a Nápoli*" is idiomatic for "go to hell." They endure this slur as well, wryly. Make a mockery of it, indeed.

You hear these kinds of things, listening to my father. For all his indifference to literature, he's a consummate storyteller with a vivid memory for detail and a keen wit. I love to prompt him into retelling stories; it's like feeding change into a jukebox. Just a simple drive around the Long Island town where he was raised is a tour of memory, but it's never an overly sentimental or depressive experience. It's more a remembrance of labors past: "I painted that fence when I was ten," or "Your Uncle Jimmy planted those oak trees as saplings in 1936 — see how huge they are now," or "That's Mario so-and-so's house — he built it completely out of scraps, even the foundation." My father can give ordinary fences, rocks, shrubs as much significance as official monuments. That's because of the dimensions he applies — not just who built a house but what he looked like, what his nickname was, what town in Italy he came from, who he was married to, whether the marriage was happy, whether he had any idiosyncracies or shattered dreams — so that you'll remember this years-dead character yourself long after the story is finished. Weddings where my father played the mandolin are recreated as sprawling, day-long affairs with lavish spreads of food and wine; he makes them sound like the great Roman banquets. You always want to hear more.

My father talks in story form, and therefore so do I, and in a sense this was a factor in my desire to be a writer. My father was apprehensive about this idea at first, but he never openly discouraged me because in his forthright treatment of me as a friend, he has fostered a strong sense of competence. Being female was no deterrent, not a handicap — his earlier suggestions for careers for me were oddly progressive, like I should be a cop or a railroad conductor. Nothing was impossible, there were no real limits. That was a generous stance for him to take, since he was hardly offered the same encouragement himself.

As I became more focused on writing, I began to read more in order to contemplate the craft. Without any direct encouragement from my father, I found myself concentrating on Italian literature — not Italian-American literature, because to me it tended to lean too much toward the maudlin and melodramatic — but upon the writings of natives. Alberto Moravia, Ignazio Silone, Domenico Rea, and Cesare Pavese. I loved this literature because it conveyed the same sense of irony and humor as did my father's stories. I particularly loved Pavese, because even though Pavese was a tormented intellectual who ultimately killed himself, many of his novels are concerned with the countryside and the brutality of nature versus the brutality and venal pettiness of man. Plagued by health problems, Pavese confined himself mostly to working behind a desk as a poet and author, translator and critic (he translated Gertrude Stein into Italian: no small feat), but he took great pleasure in the curative powers of the countryside, retreating to it always when things were at their worst. His protagonists, too, are strong, capable Everymen who work in fields or drive trucks and who parallel the characters in my father's stories — that same laboring Everyman, not a stereotype, not a Christ in Concrete or a fool with spaghetti hanging out of his mouth and red sauce stains on his undershirt. Even Pavese's journals, the receptacles of his foulest depressions, maintain a certain reverence for the elements — descriptions of weather and landscapes, the variety of seasons, the restorative heat of the sun, and the mystery of the sea. And even at his most misogynistic and embittered, he kept his mordant sense of humor — "Women are an enemy race, like the Germans," he complained; or how he considered writing poetry to be like making love: one was never sure whether one's pleasure was shared. He had terrible problems with women. He loved them, but he could not communicate well with them. But this was not for lack of understanding, as several of his stories are written from the perspective of women and show acute insight into the female psyche. In Pavese's case one might even say too acute an insight, as he seemed to be unable to distance himself from preoccupation with the motives and mentalities of the women in his life and regard them just as human beings and not objects, like missiles, specifically intent upon his destruction.

In a college class of mine we had to choose our literary soulmate. When I chose Pavese, my professor shrieked: "Pavese was so depressive; why would you ever want to ally yourself with him? Men always identify with Pavese, not women!" I explained my own theory, that it was the brainwork that had destroyed him, made him too internalized and unable to escape himself so that the idea of having what Pavese considered a normal life, with a wife and children, had become a grotesque and distorted grail. Natalia Ginzburg, a close friend of Pavese's, wrote that it was as if his every action were strangled by "some suffocating species of vegetation . . . absurd convolutions of thoughts in which he imprisoned his simple nature." I felt that Pavese had always wanted to be an Everyman, but his social position and his poor health had prevented him. And also I felt that Pavese's incredible mind, with its cameralike perspicacity, had distanced him from an Everyman's life, allowing him to view and analyze yet never to live fully. My professor bought the theory, and even became somewhat misty over Cesare. And I, too, rather liked the thought of having Pavese as my literary soulmate, which was ironically possible because once a respected writer dies, his letters and life all become quite public. A writer is often better understood posthumously by strangers than by friends and acquaintances who knew him while he was alive.

I've come to "know" Pavese extremely well. My friends indulge me in this, regarding him perhaps as my own personal Elvis. If a friend of mine goes to Italy, I always seem to get a Pavese book out of the trip and I remember once how an old boyfriend even broke a strained pocket of silence between us just to call and say, "They're making a movie about your buddy Pavese." To this day, Pavese has remained sort of a patron saint upon the dashboard of my typewriter — whenever I write, he's like a consummate editorial presence inside my mind, reviewing everything I put down, tapping his pen irritably or fiddling with his glasses, telling me to choose a better word or not to be so trite. I told my father all this once and my father looked at me as if my skull and mind together were beginning to crack like an egg right before his very eyes. "Sounds like the type of guy you need to avoid," he advised. "You ought to marry a carpenter instead." Then he added: "I don't know about that type of Italian. He was a Northerner — Northerners are too introspective, too restrained. It's like a whole other nationality — they don't even speak the same dialect. I have nothing in common with him."

I ignored these comments, and then I proceeded to tell him about the fortitude of Pavese's heroes and the influence of nature upon them. My father countered with a story about his father, about how he and his friends used to play cards out under the grape arbor in the yard and it would be so hot on those nights and you could hear the slosh of the wine pouring into glasses and the riffling of the deck, the buzz of the locusts and the music and the half-English, half-Italian conversation. The story initially made no sense to me and seemed to have little to do with what I'd just said about Pavese, but then I realized that in recounting this particular story my father was acknowledging Pavese's existence. My grandfather was precisely the bold, straightforward type that Pavese had written about. He had also been his contemporary, and perhaps he was even the person Pavese always thought he wanted to be. A laborer who had emigrated to the United States and who had had the tenacity and endurance to adapt to a foreign culture; who had married and fathered five children; who had always had direct, if not brutal contact with life and had rarely taken refuge in intellectual pursuit. So in his own oblique way, and through a story, of course, my father had grasped the essence of what I was trying to say. It's always like that with my father, as if we communicate in two different dialects, like Northern and Southern Italian, yet somehow we always manage to understand each other with relative ease.

Of course, we don't always communicate so well, my father and I. We occasionally fight, but it's usually in a humorous vein. A sample disagreement:

My father: Oh, don't be so touchy. You're much too sensitive, you know that?

Me, immediately bristling: I'm not too sensitive. You're overreacting.

My father (immediately beginning to gesture and raise his voice): I'm not overreacting! What are you talking about? I'm overreacting?! You're crazy.

And my father, in his love of nature, sometimes overwhelms me. Like this past summer, I just happened to visit home during the peach harvest. "The trees went wild. I've got all these peaches in baskets," my father complained. "We can't eat them fast enough — they're going to rot. What am I going to do with them all?" I stupidly offered to put them up as preserves, not quite knowing what kind of trap I was stepping into. I began the project with high spirits, but after entire days of boiling peaches, slipping their skins off, slicing them up, my enthusiasm started to flag. The kitchen was close to one hundred degrees, my fingers were stained with peach juice, my fingers were raw with peach juice, I had sliced open my right hand, and there was no end in sight. My father kept bringing in more and more baskets of the things: it was like I had entered Fruit Hell. I recall staring blearily down into perhaps my ninetieth batch of peaches, my eyes blurred with the beautiful yet horrible shades of gold and yellow, pink and red of their flesh, and I thought of a scene from Pavese's *The Moon and Bonfires,* wherein he depicts a character observing a sunrise of the same colors, suffused with "pinkish light . . .

a slice of moon that looked like a knife-cut dripping blood on the plain. I stood watching it for a while. It made me really terrified."

"Come on, don't be so morbid!" my father jeered when I repeated the description to him. "What are you being so morbid for? You're crazy."

I looked again at the slop of skins and fruit in front of me, at the basket of peaches on the floor and the finished jars all around me, and I revised my analogy to how all those colors were like a flashback from an LSD trip I'd never taken. My father laughed with some approval.

"Now *that's* better — *that's* funny . . . sort of," he said, and then he hurried out to haul in yet another bushel of this merciless yield of the earth. "Lighten up!" he yelled from the garage. I nodded to myself, and then I hurled one particularly obscenely lush peach against the wall and watched it splatter. I felt better after that, I truly did. I finished the job quite happily and with enthusiasm, and we ate peaches all winter long.

🐾 🐾 🐾 🐾 🐾 🐾 🐾 🐾 🐾 🐾 🐾 🐾 🐾

The Village Watchman

STORIES CARVED IN CEDAR rise from the deep woods of Sitka. These totem poles are foreign to me, this vertical lineage of clans: Eagle, Raven, Wolf, and Salmon. The Tlingit craftsmen create a genealogy of the Earth, a reminder from mentors that we come into this world as innocents in need of proper instruction. I sit on the soft floor of this Alaskan forest and feel the presence of Other.

The totem before me is called Wolf Pole by locals. The Village Watchman sits on top of Wolf's head with his knees drawn to his chest, his hands holding them tight against his body. He wears a red-and-black-striped hat. His eyes are direct, deep-set, painted blue. The expression on his face reminds me of a man I loved, a man who was born into this world feet first.

"Breech," my mother told me of her brother's birth. "Alan was born feet first. As a result, his brain was denied oxygen. He is special."

This information impressed me as a child. I remember thinking fish live underwater; maybe Alan had gills, maybe he didn't need a face-first gulp of air like the rest of us. His sweet breath of initiation came in time, slowly moving up through the soles of his tiny webbed feet. The amniotic sea he had floated in for nine months delivered him with a fluid memory. He knew something. Other.

Wolf who resides in the center of this totem holds the tail of Salmon with his feet. The tongue of Wolf hangs down, blood-red, as do his front paws, black. Salmon, a sockeye, is poised downriver — a swish of a tail and he could be gone, but the clasp of Wolf is strong.

There is a story of a boy who was kidnapped from his village by the Salmon People. He was taken from his family to learn the ways of water. When he returned many years later to his home, he was recognized by his own as a holy man privy to the mysteries of the unseen world. Twenty years after my uncle's death, I wonder if Alan could have been that boy.

But our culture tells a different story, more alien than those of Tlingit or Haida. My culture calls people of sole-births retarded, handicapped, mentally disabled or challenged. We see them for who they are not, rather than who they are.

My grandmother, Lettie Romney Dixon, wrote in her journal,

It wasn't until Alan was sixteen months old that a busy doctor cruelly broke the news to us. Others may have suspected our son's limitations but to those of us who loved him so unquestionably, lightning struck without warning. I hugged my sorrow to myself. I felt abandoned and lost. I wouldn't accept the verdict. Then we started the trips to a multitude of doctors. Most of them were kind and explained that our child was like a car without brakes, like an electric wire without insulation. They gave us no hope for a normal life.

Normal. Latin, *normalis; norma*, a rule; conforming with or constituting an accepted standard, model, or pattern, especially corresponding to the median or average of a large group in type, appearance, achievement, function, or development.

Alan was not normal. He was unique; one and only; single; sole; unusual; extraordinary; rare. His emotions were not measured, his curiosity was not bridled. In a sense, he was wild like a mustang in the desert; and like most wild horses, he was eventually rounded up.

He was unpredictable. He created his own rules and they changed from moment to moment. Alan was twelve years old, hyperactive, mischievous, easily frustrated, and unable to learn in traditional ways. The situation was intensified by his seizures. Suddenly, without warning, he would stiffen like a rake, fall forward, and crash to the ground, hitting his head. My grandparents could not keep him home any longer. They needed professional guidance and help. In 1957, they reluctantly placed their youngest child in an institution for handicapped children called the American Fork Training School. My grandmother's heart broke for the second time.

Once again, from her journal,

> Many a night my pillow is wet from tears of sorrow and senseless dreamings of "if things had only been different," or wondering if he is tucked in snug and warm, if he is well and happy, if the wind still bothers him.

The wind may have continued to bother Alan, certainly the conditions he was living under were less than ideal, but as a family there was much about his private life we never knew. What we did know was that Alan had an enormous capacity for adaptation. We had no choice but to follow him.

I followed him for years.

Alan was ten years my senior. In my mind, growing up, he was mythic. Everything I was taught not to do, Alan did. We were taught to be polite, not to express displeasure or anger in public. Alan was sheer physical expression. Whatever was on his mind was vocalized and usually punctuated with colorful speech. We would go bowling as a family on Sundays. Each of us would take our turn, hold the black ball up, take a few steps, swing an arm back, forward, glide, and release — the ball would roll down the alley, hit a few pins, we would wait for it to return, and then take our second turn. Little emotion was shown. When it was Alan's turn, it was an event. Nothing subtle. His style was Herculean. Big man. Big ball. Big roll. Big bang. Whether it was a strike or a gutter, he clapped his hands, spun around on the floor, slapped his thighs and cried, "Goddamn! Did you see that one? Send me another ball, sweet Jesus!" And the ball was always returned.

I could always count on my uncle for a straight answer. He was my mentor in understanding that one of the remarkable aspects of being human was to hold opposing views in our minds at once.

"How are you doing?" I would ask.

"Ask me how I am feeling," he answered.

"Okay, how are you feeling?"

"Today? Right now?"

"Yes."

"I am very happy and very sad."

"How can you be both at the same time?" I asked in all seriousness, a girl of nine or ten.

"Because both require each other's company. They live in the same house. Didn't you know?"

We would laugh and then go on to another topic. Talking to my uncle was always like entering a maze of riddles. Ask a question. Answer with a question and see where it leads you.

My younger brother Steve and I spent a lot of time with Alan. He offered us shelter from the conventionality of a Mormon family. At our home during Christmas he would direct us in his own nativity plays. "More —" he would say to us, making wide gestures with his hands. "Give me more of yourself." He was not like anyone we knew. In a culture where we were taught socially to be seen and not heard, Alan was our mirror. We could be different, too. His unquestioning belief in us as children, as human beings, was in startling contrast to the way we watched the public react to him. It hurt us. What we could never tell was if it hurt him.

Each week, Steve and I would accompany our grandparents south to visit Alan. It was an hour drive to the training school from Salt Lake City, mostly through farmlands. We would enter the grounds, pull into the parking lot to a playground filled with huge papier-mâché storybook figures (a twenty-foot pied piper, a pumpkin carriage with Cinderella inside, the old woman who lived in a shoe), and nine out of ten times, Alan was standing outside his dormitory waiting for us. We would get out of the car and he would run toward us, throwing his powerful arms around us. His hugs cracked my back and at times I had to fight for my breath. My grandfather would calm him down by simply saying, "We're here, son. You can relax now."

Alan was a formidable man, now in his early twenties, stocky and strong. His head was large with a protruding forehead that bore many scars, a line-by-line history of seizures. He always had on someone else's clothes — a tweed jacket too small, brown pants too big, a striped golf shirt that didn't match. He showed us appearances didn't matter, personality did. If you didn't know him, he could look frightening. It was an unspoken rule in our family that the character of others was gauged in how they treated Alan. The only consistent item in his attire was a silver football helmet from Olympus High School where my grandfather was the coach. It was a loving, practical solution to protect Alan when he fell. The helmet cradled his head and absorbed the shock of the seizures.

"Part of the team," my grandfather Sanky would say as he slapped him affectionately on the back. "You're a Titan, son, and I love you —"

The windows to the dormitory were dark, reflecting Mount Timpanogos to the east. It was hard to see inside but I knew what the interior held. It looked like an abandoned gymnasium without bleachers, filled with hospital beds. The stained white walls and yellow-waxed floors offered no warmth to its residents. The stench was nauseating, sweat and urine trapped in the oppression of stale air. I recall the dirty sheets, the lack of privacy, and the almond-eyed children who never rose from their beds. And then I would turn around and face Alan's cheerfulness, the open and loving manner in which he would introduce me to his friends, the pride he exhibited as he showed me around his home. He demanded no judgment. I kept thinking "Doesn't he see how bad this is, how poorly they are being treated?" His words would return to me, "I am very happy and I am very sad."

For my brother and me, Alan was our guide, our elder. He was fearless. But neither one of us will ever be able to escape the image of Alan kissing his parents goodbye after an afternoon visit and slowly walking back to his dormitory. Before we drove away, he would turn toward us, take off his silver helmet, and wave. The look on his face haunts me still. Alan walked point for all of us.

Alan liked to talk about God. Perhaps it was in these private conversations that our real friendship was forged.

"I know Him," he would say when all the adults were gone.

"You do?" I asked.

"I talk to Him every day."

"How so?"

"I talk to Him in my prayers. I listen and then I hear His voice."

"What does He tell you?"

"He tells me to be patient. He tells me to be kind. He tells me that He loves me."

In Mormon culture, children are baptized as members of the Church of Jesus Christ of Latter-day Saints when they turn eight years old. Alan had never been baptized because my grandparents believed it should be his choice, not something simply taken for granted. When he turned twenty-two, he expressed a sincere desire to join the Church. A date was set immediately.

The entire Dixon clan convened in the Lehi chapel, a few miles north of the group home where Alan was then living. We were there to support and witness his conversion. As we walked toward the meeting house where this sacred rite was to be performed, Alan had a violent seizure. My grandfather and uncle Don, Alan's elder brother, dropped down with him, holding his head and body as every muscle thrashed on the pavement like a school of netted fish brought on deck. I didn't want to look but to walk away would have been worse. We stayed with him, all of us.

"Talk to God —" I heard myself saying under my breath. "I love you, Alan."

"Can you hear me, darling?" It was my grandmother's voice, her hand holding her son's hand.

By now, many of us were gathered on our knees around him, our trembling hands on his rigid body.

> And we, who have always thought
> of happiness as rising, would feel
> the emotion that almost overwhelms us
> whenever a happy thing falls.
> — Rainer Maria Rilke

Alan opened his eyes. "I want to be baptized," he said. The men helped him to his feet. The gash on his left temple was deep. Blood dripped down the side of his face. He would forgo stitches once again. My mother had her arm around my grandmother's waist. Shaken, we all followed him inside. Alan's father and brother ministered to him, stopped the bleeding and bandaged the wound, then helped him change into the designated white garments for baptism. He entered the room with great dignity and sat in the front pew with a dozen or more eight-year-old children seated on either side. Row after row of family sat behind him.

"Alan Romney Dixon." His name was called by the presiding bishop. Alan rose from the pew and met his brother Don, also dressed in white, who took his hand and led him down the blue-tiled stairs into the baptismal font filled with water. They faced the congregation. Don raised his right arm to the square in the gesture of a holy oath as Alan placed his hands on his brother's left forearm. The sacred prayer was offered in the name of the Father, the Son, and the Holy Ghost, after which my uncle put his right hand behind Alan's head and gently lowered him into the water for a baptism by immersion.

Alan emerged from the holy water like an angel.

> The breaking away of childhood
> left you intact. In a moment,
> you stood there, as if completed
> in a miracle, all at once.
> — Rainer Maria Rilke

Six years later I found myself sitting across from my uncle at the University Hospital where he was being treated for a severe ear infection. I was eighteen. He was twenty-eight.

"Alan," I asked. "What is it really like to be inside your body?"

He crossed his leg and placed both hands on the arms of the chair. His brown eyes were piercing.

"I can't tell you what it's like except to say I feel pain for not being seen as the person I am."

A few days later, Alan died alone; unique; one and only; single; in American Fork, Utah.

The Village Watchman sits on top of his totem with Wolf and Salmon — it is beginning to rain in the forest. I find it curious that this spot in southeast Alaska has brought me back into relation with my uncle, this man of sole-birth, this man who came into the world feet first. He reminds me of what it means to live and love with a broken heart; how nothing is sacred, how everything is sacred. He was a weathervane; a storm and a clearing at once.

Shortly after his death, Alan appeared to me in a dream. We

were standing in my grandmother's kitchen. He was leaning against the white stove with his arms folded.

"Look at me now, Terry," he said smiling. "I'm normal — perfectly normal." And then he laughed. We both laughed.

He handed me his silver football helmet that was resting on the counter, kissed me, and opened the back door.

"Do you recognize who I am?"

On this day in Sitka, I remember.

𝕏 𝕏 𝕏 𝕏 𝕏 𝕏 𝕏 𝕏 𝕏 𝕏 𝕏 𝕏 𝕏

Stripes

IN PRAIRIE VILLAGE, Kansas, on Tuesday, May 29, 1962, Shawnee Mission East High School loosed five hundred and fifty-three of us on the world. Whether with distinction or by the skin of our teeth, we had graduated. Even Bob and Julie, who *had* to get married during senior year, made it.

Thirty years later, on Saturday, July 13, the class of '62 rediscovered each other. Baby boomers pushing fifty, we came to our reunion like peeping toms to spy on our past and catch a peek at what changes three decades had wrought in us.

And, lo, Susan had gone gray. Peg had gone blonde. Ted had gone bald. Anne had gone blind. Larry had gone to lard. Nick's acne was gone. And Luke, a suicide, was gone from the face of the earth. But Rick was still a good dancer. Joan was still so pretty. Katie still loved horses. Paul still talked about that winning touchdown against Rockhurst. Rhonda still needed dressing lessons.

What had lain ahead of us on that May night of mortarboards was now behind us, or beyond reach biologically or otherwise, or turning out more or less as we had hoped. As for Bob and Julie, the class of '62's first married couple and first parents, not only did they not attend the reunion, but no one could even supply a last known address for them. By now, though, almost all of us were married — or had been — and some of us were even grandparents.

Over the thirty years since we had last laid eyes on one another we had accounted for Lord knows how many garage sales, bake sales, going-out-of-business sales, golden retrievers, goldfish, and generic cats. We had lost untold numbers of sunglasses, umbrellas, and hopes, and had acquired Visa cards, mortgages, bald spots, and revised dreams. We had gone through Lamaze, C-sections, psychotherapy, consciousness-raising, hot flashes, divorces, mastectomies, vasectomies, infant car seats, and countless rolls of film to capture our lives at their photogenic best. Our cars had lower mileage than our bodies.

As someone who pitches alumni mail right along with schlocky catalogs, it's odd that I so obediently opened the envelope that said, "Here's information about your High School Reunion! Open immediately!" But what's even odder is, I went to it. Having passed up my tenth and twentieth reunions without a backward glance, I fell for it this time.

The main event was to be held at Arrowhead Stadium Club at the Truman Sports Complex. Casual dress. Cash bar. Buffet dinner. Entertainment. Directions were given. A good thing, too. There *was* no I-70 when I was growing up in Kansas City and, back then, it would have been assumed that a sports complex was a male psychological problem.

When I zip into K.C. once a year to visit family, I always stick to the beaten paths of familiar childhood streets and only go to places I've gone forever, like Winstead's Drive-In, Bennett Schneider's Bookstore, and Watkins' Drugstore. Until driving around town that reunion weekend, I had not realized — *fathomed* is more like it — just how accurate that old song is about everything being up-to-date in Kansas City. Residential developments and high-rise business parks sprawled clear out past where I used to go riding at Indian Valley Stables in what was then wooded and creeked countryside. The drastic changes I saw in the landscape of my youth put me on full alert to expect similar great changes in my classmates, as if they might have become the human equivalents of malls, fancy hotels, fast-food franchises, and interstates.

When I graduated from high school, there were no such things as pantyhose, seat belts, blow dryers, waterbeds, velcro, digital watches, microwaves, The Establishment, The Silent Majority, The Moral Majority, miniskirts, afros, PC's, VCR's, IRA's, Perrier, Pop Tarts, or pasta salad. No human had trod the moon, gas was 29.9 cents per gallon, a movie cost 75 cents, and that status symbol, the Cadillac, set you back about six grand. Elvis was king, and JFK was president.

I arranged to go to the reunion events with Katie, whom I've adored since second grade and who, like me, now lives in California. I say arranged, but it was more like two scared kids making a pact: I'll go if you will. It does take a certain amount of bravery to attend a reunion. Lingering memories of adolescent angst make the thought of walking into some banquet room stuffed to the rafters with your classmates a daunting prospect. You know for certain that you will be putting your person and your life story on the line from the minute you check in at the reception table and pin on your name badge.

Nothing spurs self-improvement like the goal of a reunion. Fifteen pounds overweight? Drinking too much? Still smoking? Haven't jogged in a blue moon? Hate those gray hairs? Still wearing those glasses with the safety pin through the hinge? Get cracking! When I complimented one of my classmates on her appearance, she said, "God, you don't know what I *went* through getting ready for this. I've been in training for it for *months*."

Whether in their looks, careers, or overall lives, the people who came to the reunion felt presentable. Those whose lives have not panned out or whose immediate circumstances were rocky sent their regrets. They said wild horses couldn't drag them there, said they wouldn't go if you paid them a million dollars.

What you cannot know until you get there is that it does not matter if the years have been kind to you, your classmates will be. The courageous part is only in deciding to go; once there, everything takes care of itself. A reunion unclogs a wellspring of goodheartedness and brings out a capacity for friendliness in people like nothing I've ever seen. A reunion reminds us that we humans are by nature friendly creatures. No matter how stunted someone's capacity for friendship has become in the course of life, the warmth of a reunion makes it bloom, even if it is only a fragile, hothouse, one-night-stand blossom.

The mood of a reunion is fond. That's what it is: *fond.* Like a strawberry dipped to the stem in warm chocolate, you will be immersed in kindness and come away coated with it.

"Why, this is *wonderful!* I'm having such a good time! And I hate big parties. Just despise them. But this one's different. This one's *fun!*" We exclaimed over and over in amazement, as if some dreaded potluck dish had turned out to be simply delicious.

No longer young but not yet old, we savored our thirtieth reunion as one of the perks of maturity. "I like everything about being an adult except the paperwork," writer Anne Tyler has said. Most of us would agree that, despite the paperwork, it is a better thing by far to be a middle-aged adult than a teenager in high school. If nothing else, we can now laugh at the things that were once so serious, like Steve, who said he remembers high school as "nothing but a big haze of being constantly horny and obsessed by girls' butts."

Of all the people I talked to at the reunion, surely no one has been happier to age than Vicky. Every year she lives lengthens her future, and in two years, when she reaches fifty, the ticking time bomb of Huntington's chorea, a hereditary disease which ends in dementia, will finally be defused: Vicky will have outlived the odds and will be safe from it.

Knowing Vicky in school and relishing her bountiful trademark laugh, I never suspected she bore a dark secret, never knew she was living in dread of the disease which had befallen both her mother and grandmother, never knew why she was so certain so young that she didn't ever want to have kids. In one brief, rich conversation with her at the reunion I came to know her better than I had over years of slumber parties, double dates, and knocking around together in a group.

Really, though, it's not surprising that none of us knew one another as well and truly as friends made later in life do. With the solipsism of adolescence compounded by the distractions of estrogen, testosterone, zits, tits, and driver's licenses, speaking with eloquence straight from the heart does not come easily to adolescents. Witness our fumbling attempts to express our heartfelt feelings when it came to signing each other's yearbooks. And, too, there's the problem of shyness, a form of egotism which comes on like gangbusters in adolescence, because never is one more self-conscious, more I-mindful, of how one looks, of the impression one makes, and of what others think.

Now, at forty-eight, reunited with people I had not seen for thirty years, the feelings poured forth as pure and articulate as if distilled and fermented in oaken barrels all those years. The human heart, over time, not only becomes less tongue-tied but learns to speak in a kind of shorthand which is tailor-made for just such an intense but brief occasion as a reunion. Forthright but not unkind in its honesty, it is communication stripped of nervous frills, unhampered by bashful qualifiers, and informed by a sense of the brevity of life itself.

There was also a kind of wonderfully androgynous humanity operative in us. It was as if, for the space of that evening, we had suspended or transcended gender. Although many of our reminiscences were semisexual or romantic in nature — adolescence is, after all, such a juicy time of life — the passage of time had nostalgically neutered them.

At our reunion we were simultaneously two people: who we had been and who we had become. Before-and-after analogies are what lie at the heart of reunions. The past self is the template overlaid on the present self to measure how much someone has changed. Clearly, Leo had traded in his luxury nose for a compact model. Paula had come into her beauty. Anne had lost her eyesight but gained radiance (she came to the reunion with her handsome guide dog, whom she introduced as her significant other).

The makings — and unmakings — of ourselves must have been germinating way back then, but who would have guessed that klutzy Tom would have wound up becoming a topflight East Coast brain surgeon? Or that timid Jim had, for a time, been a porn filmmaker? Or that quiet, sweet Ed would now be a homicide sergeant and head of the hostage negotiation team for the KCPD?

Others had stayed absolutely true to form. In high school, Jennifer had been a compulsive perfectionist, an extra-credit-seeking, A+ student who moaned if she got ninety-nine percent on a pop quiz the rest of us were relieved just to have passed. Proof that Jennifer hadn't changed one bit came from a friend on the reunion committee who told me that Jennifer had pleaded with them to get hold of a copy of the reunion book beforehand so that she could bone up on her classmates' biographies and know what to talk to them about. Cramming for a *reunion?* That's *summa cum laude* Jennifer.

And Greg, the erstwhile varsity-everything star and cheerleaders' darling, showed he still thinks he's God's gift to women. I saw him flash a grin and squinch a wink at two women in the buffet line, which they had been inching along for a good twenty minutes, and cut in front of them just as they reached for plates. And the two women, exchanging wouldn't-you-know-it looks, lapsed into '50s demureness and let him get away with it.

Memory was the spark that let us bridge the thirty-year gap. Memory was what lent meaning to each encounter. Reunions, like marriages, funerals, and births, are occasions which jog the memory and call forth dormant remembrance. "The memory be green," says Hamlet, and indeed memories that had lain in such

deep hibernation as to seem beyond rousing sprang up as fresh
and untrampled as spring grass.

The outsider spouses who braved the reunion brought home,
by default, the starring role that memory played. Fifth wheels at
a huge party where they didn't know a soul and where, worse
still, no one was particularly interested in getting to know them,
classmates' mates who were not from S.M. East got short shrift
because, having played no part in our collective past, they were
out of the loop. Despite polite efforts to make them feel included, they were excluded *de facto* from the animated reminis-
cence, in-jokes, and "incontinent nostalgia" (to borrow psy-
chiatrist Oliver Sacks's phrase) in which we wantonly indulged
ourselves. Once-removed from the fun, they stood apart like
chaperones, jumping back with gritted smiles from the splashes
their spouses sent geysering as they cannonballed into their private pool of memories.

The people at my reunion were my memory of myself embod-
ied in others. They were touchstones of my history, the living,
breathing souvenirs of my youth. *Souvenir,* after all, is French
for memory. In greeting a long-forgotten someone with a hug,
what you are embracing is your own memory of that person.

The experience of being at a reunion with two hundred and
fifty of your classmates present and the spirits of two hundred
and fifty absent ones hovering about is akin to trying to take in
the Louvre in an afternoon. Naturally, I kept my eye out for
certain classmates who were the most memory-laden and therefore meaningful to me. A reunion is not only a vast museum
containing priceless treasures of your past, it is also a souvenir
shop where you browse for those faces that best rekindle the
known universe of your youth.

There were people at my reunion who had known my family,
my house, my dog Lucy, my life plans, and my don't-tell-a-soul
secrets. And I had known theirs. Mindful of thirty years' passage, our inquiries about parents and the outcome of our hopes
were phrased with gentle open-endedness. Instead of asking,

"How are your mom and dad?", we said, "And your folks
are . . . ?" We knew that, by now, the answer might well be
something like, "Well, Dad passed away in '87, but Mom's doing okay, keeps herself real busy." And the boy who had yearned
to be an architect had had to leave K.U.'s School of Architecture
to shoulder the family store after his dad had a heart attack.

In high school everyone who lay beyond the bounds of whatever group I belonged to — or *longed* to belong to — had been
like scenery whizzing by a daydreamer's window at 60 mph. But
the blurry background figures of my life had been others' fore-
ground friends. Everyone at the reunion was historically central
to someone, and even classmates who, to me, had been like
painted sky and plaster of Paris mountains in the backdrop of a
diorama suddenly took on a dearness of familiarity: I recognize
you; I register you; I remember you.

There was a thrilling jolt in simply catching an across-the-
crowded-room glimpse of classmates I had known only in the
scantiest way and whose very existence had not crossed my mind
once in thirty years. On one level or another, there was no face
I didn't welcome the sight of. "My God, that's Andy Yellin over
there! Hasn't changed a bit. That goofy grin!"

I realized how much common ground I shared even with classmates I had rubbed shoulders with only by virtue of an alpha-
betical seating plan. Had we not breathed the same drowsy
classroom air? Had we not suited up together in those godawful
P.E. uniforms? Had we not all gone through the Great Cranberry Scare and had cranberries dished out to us in one thinly
disguised form or another for months on end after the federal
government, finding them safe after all, bought up the whole
damn crop and designated our school district one of the dump-
ing grounds?

If I didn't immediately recognize a face, a quick glance at the
nametag clicked the synapse. The adult mind sorts out names
that lose their importance and knows that, failing all else, a
membership directory, a roster, or a business card in the Ro-

lodex can supply it if need for it arises again. But the names from childhood are fixed in memory permanently. The names remain. The names alone summon the past.

What's more, at a reunion you find yourself spontaneously greeting classmates with names they haven't been called by in a thousand years — nicknames and diminutives they started kindergarten with and couldn't get rid of until they went away to college: Jimbo, Parky, Big Al. Billy, Babs, Woodsy, Tad, Tootle. As Beryl Markham says in *West with the Night,* "This is remembrance — revisitation; and names are keys that open corridors no longer fresh in the mind, but nonetheless familiar in the heart."

Twenty-odd years ago, *Rolling Stone* had a cover photo of singer Janis Joplin performing in Port Arthur, Texas, at her tenth high school reunion. Bottle of Southern Comfort dangling from one hand and the other raised in a fist, Janis clearly had come to her reunion not to see old friends but to thumb her nose at them. Spite and gloat had brought her there.

Had Janis lived long enough to make it to her thirtieth reunion, she might have found that her rage and pain had mellowed into near nostalgia for such mundane miseries as a bad complexion, small tits, and lonesome Saturday nights. By the time a thirtieth reunion rolls around, you find that bygones really are bygones. Old grievances and grudges are fondly laid to rest, and all bitterness is past.

It is a wonderful thing to reach the point in life where you can kid someone about having broken your heart. When I spotted Mike over by the *hors d'oeuvre* table, I bore down, grinning and shaking my finger at him. "Mike McLean! You heartbreaker! You stinker! The *nerve* of you!" I said by way of greeting.

On February 14, 1956, Mike had given my best friend, Katie, and me candy for Valentine's Day: fancy, red, heart-shaped boxes of Russell Stover candy with two tiers of assorted chocolates. I was in sixth grade and madly in love with Mike McLean. Katie was playing the field and had not settled on a favorite.

Mike was a definite contender, though. The boxes of candy were identical, but when Katie and I compared enclosure cards it became clear who the runner-up in Mike's affection was. My card was signed, "From, Mike"; Katie's, "Love, Mike." My heart hit my shoes with a thud that echoed for years.

My reunion lent a kind of retrospective coherence to a world I had long since left behind. I felt as if I had been caught at the outermost edge, the farthest reach of a far-flung net, and been gently hauled in hand over hand, to the very anchor of my being, to that place I had floated far away from, carried out by currents I had swum out to ride. And, like any salmon, I knew my home waters when I got there.

I felt somehow *clarified*. My vivid recollections of my classmates and theirs of me — how I was remembered and how I remembered them — combined to create a refracted clarity like sunlight jiggling off translucent seawater in a grotto. Even contradictory views of me made perfect sense in a crazy, kaleidoscopic way.

On one hand there was Nancy, who said, "God, Popham, you were always such a *prude!*" On the other hand, there was Laura, who said I was the ballsiest person she'd ever known. She thought so because of the time I'd given a false name to Sally Powell's mother when she caught a bunch of us sneaking back into the house at five A.M. after toilet-papering half the trees in Prairie Village. Flattered though I was by her appraisal, I had to set the record straight: "I hate to tell you, Laura. That wasn't balls, that was bare-naked *terror* that Mrs. Powell would call my mother."

A reunion, like travel, is a digestive experience. By midnight I had taken in all I could absorb. I was so stuffed I could not swallow another morsel of memory, another tidbit of personal history. Saying my goodbyes, I knew better than to make rash promises about staying in touch and getting together again soon. We had long since outgrown the type of overwrought, grandiose vows we had penned aslant entire pages in one another's yearbooks. Our ongoing lives lay elsewhere and would resume on our return from this reunion which we nonlocals had flown in from all over the country to attend.

I took one last look around the room at my reunited class-mates. They would come with me, encased in the glowing moment, preserved and perfect as the Cenozoic fish fossil back home on my desk. The ending of Edward Abbey's "Drunk in the Afternoon" comes to mind.

My friends, he said, my good comrades, buddies, pals, *compañeros de mi vida*, let me tell you something. I want to tell you guys something you will always remember, never forget. I want you to remember this glorious moment, this radiant goddam hour, this splendid shining immortal day, for the rest of your miserable lives.

We got home that night, some way. We graduated from that New Mexico cow college a month later. We wandered off in various directions. For a few years we exchanged letters, then postcards, then Christmas cards, then nothing. That was thirty-seven years ago. I don't know anything about any of them now.

I returned to my father's house and went to bed. I could not get to sleep. I turned on the light, began leafing through the reunion book, and got caught up all over again.

I looked up suddenly remembered classmates I hadn't seen that night. I looked up some I had seen and wanted to know more about. I studied then-and-now pictures of my classmates and read thirty-year autobiographies nutshelled into three hundred words or less. Some were as tautly factual as a résumé; some were hilarious; some were tragic. I read the four columns of names on the "Missing Persons" page. I looked at the ten faces on the "In Memoriam" page. One of them was the first boy I ever danced cheek to cheek with. At three A.M. I turned off the light.

Several months later, the videotape arrived. I invited my husband and children to watch it with me, glad that they could now see this event from which I had come home afterglowing like a desert sunset. My husband and son lasted about ten minutes. My daughter Lilly, ever the diplomat, tried to go the distance, but about the time all two hundred and fifty of us got called out to the dance floor to sing the school song, she said she really hated to leave but her rabbit urgently needed brushing.

I didn't blame them. I nearly threw in the towel myself. What I was seeing shocked me. Mortified me. Threw me for a loop. I couldn't understand it. How could we look so ridiculous, so farcical? How was it possible that the reunion evening, this grand and glorious event, looked like the sort of boisterous gathering I'd find laughably stereotypical and sneer at if I glanced in at it while passing a Holiday Inn banquet room? How had we been reduced to a bunch of flabby, gabby, middle-aged, silly nincompoops?

I knew — I *knew* — how moving and soul-satisfying my reunion had been. I didn't make it up. I wasn't faking it. I wasn't drunk. Dammit, it was wonderful — it *was*. Then I remembered Barry Lopez's horse.

At a reading I attended, Lopez had read a passage about an immense and fantastic intaglio horse way, *way* out in the desert. The archaeologist who had stumbled across it revealed its location to Lopez, who, after hiking out to the middle of nowhere, found the horse inlaid in a stretch of so-called desert pavement. To form the horse's shape, its creator had removed thousands upon thousands of the flat, black volcanic rocks which cobblestoned the desert floor. Lopez sat beside the horse for several hours and observed it. He walked around it, studied it from every angle, became intimate with its every detail. He made himself at home with it. He had what he calls "a fully dilated experience."

As he was leaving, Lopez remembered that in addition to the hand-drawn map the archaeologist had given him an aerial photo of the horse. He pulled it out of his pocket and unfolded it. What he saw was something so puny, trivial, and unworthy of the hellish hike he had undertaken that he quickly refolded the photograph and jammed it back into his pocket.

I well understood Lopez's desire to keep his own experience of the horse alive within himself and not have it demeaned by the photograph. A pulled-back, cold-eyed, impersonal, on-high perspective is not the way to view a quiet masterpiece — or a reunion. What it fails to convey, does not even hint at, is the spirit within the participant, the same way that a wallet-size school photo of your child fake-smiling *cheeeese* is a "bad" picture because of how ordinary, how *typical* it makes your own beloved, extraordinary child appear.

The gaping discrepancy between what I had experienced at the time and what I later saw on the video is mercifully summed up by psychoanalyst Erik Erikson's term "psychological reality versus historical actuality." The video may have accurately documented a sequence of events over the course of an evening, but memories are not captured on videotape any more than in aerial photos; they are captured in the heart.

In Hal Borland's *When the Legends Die*, a Ute man returns to the mountains of his boyhood to find the way back to himself:

He sighed, knowing why he had come back. And he remembered a chipmunk he had as a small boy, a pet that came when he called and sat in his hand. He had asked his mother the meaning of the stripes on the chipmunk's back. Those stripes, she said, were the paths from its eyes, with which it sees now and tomorrow, to its tail, which is always behind it and a part of yesterday. He had laughed at that and said he wished he, too, had a tail. His mother had said, "When you are a man you will have a tail, though you will never see it. You will have something always behind you."

Now he understood. Now he knew that time lays scars on a man like the chipmunk's stripes, paths that lead from where he is now back to where he came from, from the eyes of his knowing to the tail of his remembering. . . . [Nothing can] erase the simple truth of the chipmunk's stripes, the ties that bind a man to the truth of his own being, his small part of the enduring roundness.

Beyond the backslapping, the squeals of greeting, and the jokes about girth, wrinkles, and hairlines, something profound and worthwhile takes place at a reunion: you experience the length and width of your own stripes. A reunion enables you to see the stripes from eye to tail, from now to way back then.

A reunion is a reminding experience. It touches a core, uplifts like singing — never mind how off-key — an old song whose lyrics and melody, although unsung for decades, are so ingrained as to seem inborn. A reunion is something which, to borrow a word from Dr. Seuss, *biggers* you. I came away from my reunion feeling biggered through and through. When all is said and done, that is the true and enduring value of a reunion: becoming reunited with yourself.

CHRISTINE O'HAGAN

Ⓧ Ⓧ Ⓧ Ⓧ Ⓧ Ⓧ Ⓧ Ⓧ Ⓧ Ⓧ Ⓧ Ⓧ Ⓧ Ⓧ

Friendship's Gift

> You can close your eyes to reality but
> not to memories.
>
> — Stanislaw Lee

IF THE FIRST PLACE one learns friendship is in the home, one's first friend, it seems to me, is a mother, although my mother, now seventy-four, would vehemently disagree.

She still thinks it a terrible mistake to make one's child a friend, warning me of the dangers for the entire twenty-one years of what she still sees as my own maternal apprenticeship. Such friendly familiarity, she insists, soon earns a child's contempt, and then discipline flies out the window. But I can remember a dreadfully rainy afternoon in our top-floor apartment that looked down on rusty fire escapes and on an empty courtyard so bleak that only the alley cats might notice the Christmas lights.

On this rainy day, my young mother has planned for us to have a picnic, my very first. I am around three. Together we spread an ancient, unraveling, white damask tablecloth and two equally worn napkins (all liberally stained pink with cranberry sauce) on the gray living room carpet. We carry a plateful of cream cheese and jelly sandwiches from the kitchen for lunch, and big red apples (with soft brown spots that we won't notice until it is too late) for dessert. We bite into the apples at the same time, screw our faces in giggling horror, hold the old napkins over our mouths, the dangling strings tickling our cheeks, then we fall on the floor laughing.

My mother's hair is long and copper-shiny; when she falls on her back, her hair fans out around her head like a peacock's tail. When I climb on top of her, I am struck by how much smaller she seems than the mountain of my father.

For the rest of my life, apple pieces make me think of that rainy-day picnic and of my mother, despite her protests, my (first) friend.

The friends one's mother chooses for herself, though, let her daughter see what grown-up female life is like: to see, to paraphrase Simone de Beauvoir, how one becomes a woman.

My mother's friends were once our apartment house neighbors and they seemed beautiful to me, lush. Some had ebony hair curled around their shoulders, there were the redheads with poodle cuts, and the blondes in towering beehives or Debbie Reynolds–style ponytails pulled back by headbands that matched their heavy cotton bathing suits. Their full breasts as they bent over the coolers packed with cola on ice made me squeeze my arms over my own freckled flat chest in giddy anticipation.

On hot summer mornings, these women packed all fifteen of us, their collective children, into one old beige Rambler and brought us from Jackson Heights, Queens, to Rockaway Beach. They wore white rubber bathing caps strapped underneath their chins to keep their hair dry, and they bounced the children atop the waves. Their shiny wet arms were as strong and firm as their devotion.

They made all the novenas (especially the somewhat more intense ones to the Sacred Heart, who seemed to be their favorite), bringing us to confession on Saturday afternoons, watching us kneel in the quiet pews to say our penance prayers. They grew angry when they realized that we were stealing their Jayne Mansfield—style chiffon scarves and wrapping them tightly around our Miss Tonied heads pretending to be a peculiar group of repenting nuns. Lying prostrate on the building's cold vestibule floor (and courting polio) we prayed to the imaginary remains of some imaginary saint atop the very real mahogany lobby table that someone later stole.

They hemmed their daughters' stiff pastel dresses and starched their husbands' and sons' shirts and made sure that everyone went off to Sunday Mass. Standing at the altar rail with their heads bowed after their babies had been born, they waited to be churched, or blessed. Afterward, they stopped in one another's kitchens to borrow the often-borrowed christening gowns and the tiny matching caps.

Most voted first for Ike and then for Nixon, but only if their husbands said they should, ignoring the fury of their own Irish Democratic pasts (their old fathers coming to visit looked aghast when they found out, climbing up to the roof to brood). Feeling rebellious and excited they secretly swooned before handsome Kennedy, although they laughed when they saw that same ardor in the parish nuns, the real ones, leading our classes through the schoolyard with their starched habits covered in Democratic campaign buttons.

They went to the movies together once a week — usually on a Tuesday night, when men tried to be home for the children — unless of course there was a Fuller Brush party which was outing enough. Sometimes in the dead of winter they traded ironing baskets, stiff cotton pants and shirts piled on top of one another like kindling, just for fun.

After everyone had grown up and gone away, the neighborhood a nightmare of graffiti and broken glass, one of the women in whose bed I had slept, her sheets smelling of roof-dried Oxydol, was found murdered in the exact spot where the mahogany table had stood. All that penance in our bones, in the very air, and not a suspect in sight.

·   ·   ·

It seemed to me then that becoming a woman had much to do with keeping my hair not only curly but dry, and going to church — doing as I was told and working like a horse, like my mother and the others did. I'd see them dragging shopping carts bulging with A&P food up four flights in our creaking walk-up building, and when mice began slipping out of the painted-over dumbwaiters, the women carried the leaking bags of garbage down to the cellar, closing their eyes when the mice scampered around their feet.

Sometimes, while they sat on folding chairs underneath the big tree out front, watching the children play, the mothers argued with each other, screaming and shaking, while we children stood up and stared at them, but we never knew what had happened. Sometimes there were the whispers of an affair, one of the women alone with one of the men, but the truth was denied us. A day or two later, one of the mothers sent one of the girls through the hallways with flowery, Scotch-taped notes of apology. These were delivered into the tiny hot kitchens where blazing ovens held turkeys, rib roasts, legs of lamb, the boiling vegetables sending tears rushing down the windows' glass. Often, the tears belonged to the woman setting the table, the quickly read note dropped on the dishes, we daughters overwhelmed by someone else's mother crushing us in her arms, her wet cheek stuck to our foreheads.

They cut and dyed one another's hair and lent each other clothes, milk, slipcovers, curtains, and a ton of cigarettes. They ran back and forth over the roof from one apartment to the next when the children were sick, carrying alcohol for fever rubdowns, cod liver oil, Ace bandages and squares of flannel to press Musterole to our chests. Sometimes they delivered the big red encyclopedia everyone borrowed for school reports, or baby food jars filled with whiskey that they mixed in our milk to ease our coughs.

They lent each other the table money even if it meant hocking their wedding rings at the pawnbroker's, and if they met one another on the roof at dusk, looking for their husbands who were late again, they never made mention of it to each other, although they were terrified that the men had fallen fast asleep in their seats and were at that moment snoring in the railroad yard. In a way, that might have been something of a relief, for many of the men were what was called "hard drinkers," subject to raging senseless tantrums, throwing ottomans and toasters through the windows, or the carefully prepared dinners and the schoolbooks out onto the street, the homework floating softly to someone else's fire escape.

Last summer, before the first reading from my first novel, my heroine a bit of all of them, I waited across the street from Brentano's on Fifth Avenue, watching my mother and these same friends (save one) slowly making their way down the street in soft pastel dresses like the ones their daughters wore long ago. My mother wore a light pink dress much too big for her; she looked delicate and pale, as if she were made of rice paper. (Such clarity, I thought, in what can be seen from a distance.)

They were all in their seventies now, their men tucked safely in their graves (they finally know where they are at night), no longer neighbors but still friends. Their faces are softly lined and worn, thin cheeks surrounded now by pillows of soft gray hair, carefully arranged yet thin at the crown, like a baby's. They laughed when I read the scene where one of my male characters pitches his Copacabana ashtray through his darkened living room, and they were silent hearing the part where he beats his daughter, although they seemed glad somehow that I'd remembered. After it was over they came up to the podium and hugged me, one after another, with faces more strange than familiar, like faces in a dream.

Their eyes were gleaming and they fluttered around me like little girls at a birthday party, dressed up in shiny flat shoes and party dresses.

I watched them through the bookstore window, surprised at

how they grabbed for one another's hands crossing the busy street.

I thought of Emily Dickinson: "We don't get older with the years, just newer."

There was an awful silence at the end of writing this first book, after it was actually gone from my life, leaving me furiously angry at my characters for their sudden silence, as if they were shunning me after I had learned to trust them, after we had become — in the deepest sense of the word — friends, and I was stunned by their cold-hearted indifference.

It was autumn when I finished, the sudden black nights crashing down on my head. The afternoon the manuscript was mailed, I stood in the yard, pulling stiff towels from the clothesline and shuddering at the chill in the air, almost as if the summer had passed before I'd had a chance to notice. I cried, dropping laundry into the wicker basket, wiping my eyes on the hem of my shirt. At least, I thought bitterly, at least you'd think they'd have the decency to *write* and let me know how they are. I realized that such concentrated work in such peculiar isolation has to be temporary or else lunacy settles itself around your feet like a cat.

Someone once wrote that one of the hardest things in the world is looking at the backs of the people you love, that it makes you sting.

When my mother and her friends left Brentano's the minute the applause died down (for none of them wanted to be out in the dark) they took the soul of my first book along.

I realized, watching the party dresses melt into the crowd, that Delia Delaney, my heroine, was no longer with me but with them, for her story began just like theirs did; it was never mine at all, except maybe around the edges where children tend to live. In life, Delia would be an old lady now, just like the others.

Delia Delaney, as you might have already guessed, was born from my mother's missing friend who had died fairly young, her decline begun by the death of her third daughter, stillborn, the cord wrapped around her neck.

It happened in the Kennedy years, when everyone in the world it seemed was Irish and proud, enraptured with the president whether they'd voted for him or not. His picture was everywhere in the Heights, like Orwell's Big Brother, hanging in the hallways of St. Joan of Arc School, on the walls of all the dusty bars where we were sent to find our fathers, and even in the window of the Chinese hand laundry. It was summertime, a broiling August when this woman was too uncomfortable to go to the beach and sit wedged in the sand, dabbing zinc oxide on her fair-skinned daughters' noses.

Like the other men, her husband was a hard drinker but unlike them he was a traveling salesman and so she was twice as accustomed to being without him. She sat by herself that month of August, on the roof where it was cooler, staring in the direction of New York. If any of the other women climbed the stairs to the roof to hang their clothes, she'd ask each of them in turn if their babies had moved near the end, and though they whispered among themselves they assured her that their babies were always quiet.

Everyone went to the same doctor, a compassionate general practitioner who spent most of every August on vacation, sending his patients to doctors in the area. He tried to send the woman to an obstetrician but she trusted nobody else — none of us did — and so she waited, sitting on the roof, staring into the air. Her friends were worried and so they gave her some presents for the child, not a shower but more like a show of faith, and she piled them into the newly painted crib which stood in the corner of the girls' bedroom. We girls hung over the crib that entire summer, shuffling the baby's things.

By the end of the month it was over, a day or two after the

doctor returned. For the rest of his life, for some twenty years, the doctor told everyone who knew her (and some who didn't) of her courage and her strength.

When she came home she never spoke of the child, nor the experience, and neither did anyone else, as if she might have forgotten. Her husband was home long enough to clean the apartment, disassembling the crib and giving back the unopened things, and then he was gone again. By September she was back in her old clothes, the neatly ironed skirts, the primly buttoned blouses.

And then she began to drink. With her husband, people said, something they did together when he was home as if they were playing bridge. And then when he was gone again, they said she drank out of her loneliness.

She went without him to the church dances with the other couples, something she had never done before. The other women urged her to come along, bright-eyed and smiling eagerly, but she soon began to drink more than the men who were weaving on their feet anyway, having to half-carry her up the stairs, unfolding her from their shoulders onto her bed, telling her daughters she was feeling sick. When her husband came home, the terrible fights began. He blackened her eye and she stabbed him in the hand with a steak knife while the furniture splintered all around them and their daughters' screams filtered through the courtyard.

Everyone said that another baby would "cure" her, but when she gave birth to a son it seemed to be too late. She continued to drink. She left the child alone. Her daughters left her when they were teenagers, renting a tiny apartment nearby where their mother regularly appeared, smashing on the door for drinking money when she had run out.

In time, *bodegas* sprouted up around the shamrock-studded doors of the gin mills, the pictures of President Kennedy grew dusty or disappeared altogether from the walls, and the woman's daughters left the area altogether, tired of crying their hearts out in the other mothers' kitchens, tired of picking her up from the street.

While we children were peering in the gin mill windows looking for our fathers, she smiled and waved at us from her perch near the back and eventually one father or another felt obligated to wait for her and walk her home, her blonde ponytail resting limply on his shoulder. The wife watching from the roof, keeping dinner on the stove, was fit to be tied, but she or one of the others brought the woman to the priests anyway, caring for her son and consoling her daughters. They made her pay her bills on time, putting her on a budget, forcing her to ask them for extra cash. They visited her in the city hospital's psychiatric ward where she delighted in the young doctors' gullibility at her made-up stories — she told them she thought she was a bag of peanuts — then she signed herself out, and friendship began to show its limitations.

When many of the Irish bars became discotheques she took to wearing false eyelashes and white go-go boots, dancing with younger men, strangers who would buy her a drink. By then her son was a street urchin, a modern-day Oliver Twist. Some of the bolder youngsters from the street seemed to forget all about Rockaway and the zinc oxide and the way things used to be and they smirked when they saw her and called her by her first name.

She tried hard to have good days, desperate to redeem herself, walking her young son to school, pulling on her tan raincoat and trotting off to the A&P with a shopping list.

Every St. Patrick's Day, she appeared in all of the women's kitchens with freshly baked loaves of soda bread that none of us dared to eat, for we had seen the roaches climbing out of her washing machine.

When the neighborhood became unsafe and the other families were forced to leave, she'd laughed and said the only way she could afford to go would be feet first, and that was exactly how it had happened.

On a cold and rainy April night, she'd left one of the old places with the wrong dancing partner, a dark-skinned stranger, or so the rumor went, and she was found early the next morning strangled like that baby daughter of long ago, the one that the Church had buried as quickly as possible with a name the woman hadn't chosen for her child at all: Mary.

It was in all the newspapers. At her wake in the funeral home underneath the el, her elderly mother passed around a scrapbook filled with newspaper clippings of the crime, as if her daughter were someone important at last.

But Delia Delaney, my heroine, faced with the same circumstances, survives.

For in the end, I gave this woman the only gift of friendship a novelist has to offer, the chance at another sort of life.

The Friendship Tarot

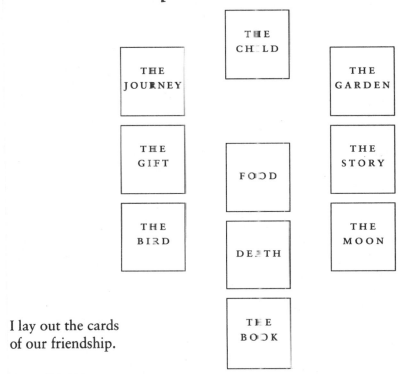

THE
CHILD

THE
JOURNEY

THE
GARDEN

THE
GIFT

FOOD

THE
STORY

THE
BIRD

DEATH

THE
MOON

I lay out the cards
of our friendship.

THE
BOOK

THE CHILD
The card shows a child with chocolate on his face wandering through an art gallery in downtown Poughkeepsie devoted — for two weeks — to illustrations from children's books. Ilse Vogel and I have not met, but we both have work in this show. In one room stands the six-foot doll's house I made when I was writing

A Visit to William Blake's Inn. In the next room hang Ilse's meticulous pen-and-ink drawings for her book *Dodo Every Day*.

What I saw: an elegant woman with white hair, a knitted cloche, and eyes that missed nothing.

What she saw: a woman with a seven-year-old boy whose face was smeared with chocolate.

What I thought: Who is this remarkable person?

What Ilse thought: Her child has a dirty face, but does she worry about it? No. And neither does the child.

THE GARDEN

The card shows two married couples eating dinner in a garden: Eric and me, Howard and Ilse. Four artists: one painter (Howard), one photographer (Eric), one writer (me), and Ilse, who can't be pinned down to one category since she illustrates her own stories. The dinner Ilse has prepared is exquisite. Butter blooms in a little pot; Ilse has sculpted it into the face of a sunflower. Howard helps her carry dishes from the tiny kitchen into the Francesa, a shelter shingled in nasturtiums and morning glories. The front is entirely open to view; over the edge of the second story dangle the tails of four sleeping cats. Once it was a rickety outbuilding for storing tools. Now it is paved with round river stones chosen and put into place years ago by Ilse. Shortly after she'd laid the last stone, she felt chest pains. The day she came home from the hospital, Howard filled the house with anemones.

Ilse heaps seconds on our plates without asking us and tells us they bought this small yellow house in the country because they loved the apple tree blooming outside the kitchen window. The soil is rocky but the garden is full of flowers; Ilse has put out one hundred and four pots of flowers. When a large tabby springs from behind one of them, Ilse explains that they are down to ten cats.

"Ten cats!" exclaims Eric.

"We have only two," I add apologetically.

Is this the first step into friendship? Ilse knows right away she can discuss the excellence of cats without boring me: Velvet Paws, Parsley, Comedy Cat, Mr. Goldie, Chives. Summer and winter the ten cats that live with Howard and Ilse sleep in the garage at night.

Winter and summer the two cats that live with Eric and me sleep at the foot of our bed so they can watch over us.

THE JOURNEY

The card shows three people in a car headed for New York. Ilse wears the same knitted cloche she wore at the gallery, and Howard's hat is the identical shade of oatmeal. When I remark on this, Ilse explains that she knitted them both.

We three are traveling to New York to see *The Tin Drum*. On the way, Ilse explains that she lived in Berlin all during the war, so naturally she's curious to see this film.

Of the movie I remember only a few scenes, not because the film was forgettable but because of what happened on the trip back.

THE STORY

The card shows a woman talking and a woman listening.

I am riding in the back seat of the car and I lean forward and ask, "Ilse, was it really like that in Germany?"

Ilse answers by telling me about the day the Russians marched into Berlin.

"When the Russians came so close to the house, you could hear them talking and shouting. And all the inhabitants of the house were sitting in the bunkers except me, because I hated to be down there with the Nazis. I was in my apartment with a friend of mine. And then we heard shooting and voices, and then we heard a sound as if masses and masses of water would come rushing in, and then my friend said, 'Oh, something has hit the canister of gasoline,' and within seconds I saw the flames and the gasoline floating in under the doorway of my apartment, and everything was in flames. There was just one window where we could get out. We crossed the yard to the door of the bunker and went inside and then the house did burn with tremendous speed. Smoke came and people started to pray and to sing, and others cursed and screamed. I sat with my friend and we held hands and I said, 'This is the end, there's no way out.' And my friend had a little flute with him which he always carried. I'll show it to you tomorrow — I still have it. He pulled it out and played a little Bach sonata for us, to comfort us."

She tells me how she worked in the Resistance against Hitler, hiding Jews in her apartment and printing passports to smuggle them out of Germany. Two hours later we are back in Poughkeepsie.

"Ilse," I say, "have you written this down?"

"It's not a story for children," she says. "And I can't find the right voice to tell it."

"You must tell it," I say, "so people don't forget." Ilse asks to use the bathroom. When she emerges she says with a smile, "I'm so glad your house isn't neat all the time."

THE GIFT

The card shows a restaurant strung with red and green lights.

The week before Christmas, Ilse and Howard and Eric and I meet for lunch at Dickens. Ilse calls ahead so that we can have the same table we had last year — a table intended for six. She tells the waitress we are expecting another person, a man, and during the meal she laments his bad manners — why couldn't he have phoned? She brings the snapshots we took of each other last year. In the snapshots we are always opening presents. Here I am, opening the present Ilse made for me: a muff, to keep my hands warm. It is made of brown corduroy, lined with synthetic lamb's wool, and decorated in orange and turquoise and lavender: braid, felt hearts, pyramids, and silver beads, each bead no bigger than a mustard seed. It has a corduroy strap and a pocket, into which Ilse has tucked a bright red handkerchief.

Since I ride a bicycle to class and my arms are usually full of books, I seldom have the leisure to use a muff unless I decide to take a muff-walk: a walk with no other purpose than exercise and pleasure. Which is probably why Ilse gave it to me.

This year Howard gives Eric a book of Vuillard's paintings and Ilse gives me a Waring hand-held blender which, she assures me, will make cooking much easier.

Eric gives Howard a photograph he took inside the conservatory of the New York Botanical Gardens and I give Ilse a set of flannel sheets and pillowcases printed with cats.

FOOD

The card shows dinner tables, side by side.

When we eat dinner at their house, they serve hors d'oeuvres and drinks in the living room or the garden, just for the four of us. Ilse makes the salad dressing. The courses arrive in succession at the proper time.

When they eat dinner at ours, I am famished from having skipped lunch to meet with students, and I rush everything to the table at once. The salad dressing is Paul Newman's finest, the cake is the handiwork of the Aurora Café Bakery. The last time I baked a cake, it collapsed like an old hat and I filled in the holes and cracks with frosting, which made it astonishingly heavy but quite tasty. Howard warned Ilse not to eat it.

"All that chocolate is bad for your heart," he said softly.

She smiled and took another bite.

THE MOON

The card shows four people perched on top of the world.

Ilse phones us in great excitement. Tonight, if we stand on a certain hill a mile from their house, we can watch the sun go down and the moon come up, all at the same time. She has checked the weather; the sky will be clear.

The road to the hill runs past stables and pastures broken by white fencing into parcels that give expensive horses enough room to run free by keeping them apart from each other. Howard regrets that the landscape feels so owned.

When we climb out of the car and look east and west from the crest of the windy hill, the valley sweeps broadly around us; could we see the Hudson if we knew where to find it?

As the sun slides into its nest of light behind the Catskills, the moon rises silently, secretly. She is so pale and thin that she might be the shed carapace of some large round animal. As darkness gathers, she grows solider, more golden.

"In German, the moon is masculine," says Ilse. "And the sun is feminine."

I can't think of another language in which those genders are assigned to my old friends in the sky.

Ilse says she is trying to write about those last days before the fall of Berlin, but she is not yet ready to read me what she has written.

THE BIRD

The card shows an empty cage in a garden.

Ilse phones us — can we come over and see the dove? It seems that the postmistress in their little town of Bangall runs an animal adoption service on the side, and she has presented Ilse with a dove.

When we arrive, Ilse has put its cage on a pile of stones in the garden, like an altar to flight. The cage is made of the sticks that Ilse gathered in the yard, but it is very small, and when Eric and I approach, the dove beats her wings against the bars. All during dinner she makes endearing noises.

"You can't imagine how we enjoy hearing that wonderful sound," says Ilse. "And the cats don't seem to notice her."

We sit outside and watch the singular stars arrive, one by one, like notes in a music box winding down to silence.

The next day I telephone Joanne, a friend of mine who does excellent carpentry, and ask her to make a catproof cage for Ilse's dove. I tell her it should be made of sticks gathered in a

forest and it should be huge. Ilse's birthday is two weeks away —
could she possibly have it finished by then?

Two weeks later, Joanne drives up with a cage nearly as tall
as herself on her truck. It is a gazebo, a minaret, a chapel, it
is the mother of all birdcages. I phone Howard and tell him
we want to deliver it as a surprise to Ilse, who likes surprises
but does not like unexpected visitors. Howard can tell her whatever he likes; we will arrive with the cage at eleven o'clock on
Thursday.

When we appear, the two of them are sitting in the garden,
attended by Velvet Paws. Joanne and I carry the cage across the
lawn. Ilse is speechless with astonishment. That is just the way I
hoped she would be.

"You've given me exactly what I wanted!" she exclaims.

The dove takes to the cage at once. Soon it no longer feels like
a cage; Ilse adds branches and leaves and nasturtiums and she
removes the bottom so that the dove sits directly on the grass.
How good the grass feels on her little coral feet! All night long
she enjoys dewfall and moonrise and starshine. When the sun
warms the dark world, Howard arrives with her breakfast.

One morning Howard goes to feed the dove and finds a dash
of bloody feathers. There is a snake in Eden; nothing but a snake
could insinuate itself into so stout a cage.

Ilse mourns her dove. All winter the cage is filled only with
cream-colored twigs and the curious seedpods that catch her eye
in the garden. One day the postmistress telephones her. A relative of the slain dove has recently laid a clutch of eggs; two of
them hatched. Would Ilse like two doves? Howard snakeproofs
the cage. It is spring again and the voices of Ilse's doves are heard
in the land.

DEATH

The card shows a shelf on which Ilse has arranged the skulls of
their cats. After their deaths, she digs them up. The skulls are
light and beautiful as parchment.

"Some people think it's a strange thing to do," she says, "but see how beautiful their bones are!"

When I cook chicken, I save not only the wishbone but the breastbone. Scrubbed clean and dried, the breastbone looks like a mask or a saddle intended for an animal unaccustomed to carrying passengers. On the apple tree in our back yard hang the shells of half a dozen horseshoe crabs I found on Cape Cod. Anyone passing the tree would take it for the site of a secret ceremony devoted to saving what holds us up but is never seen under the living flesh.

THE BOOK

The card shows pages falling and gathering like snow.

Ilse is now seriously at work on her stories about life in Germany under Hitler. Howard is typing them for her. The stories arrive in the mail, one by one, in white envelopes bordered with a green stripe.

Without telling her, I am sending them to my editor at Harcourt Brace.

Velvet Paws has had her kittens behind a canvas of Howard's which he imprudently left leaning against an upstairs wall. Ilse invites us to view the kittens. Eric and I sit in the living room of the little white house and wait for the great moment. We wait and wait. And suddenly here is Ilse, presenting them to us in a basket lined with violets and strawberry leaves, as if she had just picked them in the garden.

Later, as we are leafing through a box of old photographs, I pull out a picture of two blond girls standing side by side: Ilse and her twin sister, Erika, who died of diphtheria when they were nine.

"Which one is you?" I ask.

Ilse is not sure.

"Perhaps that one, with the knees bent a little. Erika was born first and she always was the more courageous one."

·   ·   ·

Eight years ago, when I published my first novel, *Things Invisible to See,* I dedicated it to Ilse and Howard.

Today I open the book of Ilse's stories, *Bad Times, Good Friends,* and find it is dedicated to Eric and me. Over the dedication is Ilse's pen-and-ink drawing of a dove turning into a woman. She is flying over a bed of pansies, carrying three tulips in one hand and pointing to our names with the other.

"They didn't want a dove-woman on the dedication page," says Ilse. "I had to fight for it."

PHYLLIS ROSE

X X X X X X X X X X X X X

Shall We Dance?
Confessions of a Fag Hag

MANY YEARS AGO, when I was thirty-one and in the tenth year of a marriage that was not going to last, my discontent with my husband and my despair over my private life expressed themselves as an interest in, then an enthusiasm for, then a passionate infatuation with another man — a man in almost every way the opposite of my husband. His name was David. He was three years my junior and looked like Pushkin, or Pan, with brown eyes, curly black hair, and a beard.

David was in the art department of the university at which I was in the English department, and between classes, meetings, office hours, and lunches we had plenty of time to play. We went to the army-navy store and tried on fatigues, spats, and goggles. We went to a greenhouse and enjoyed the flowers in winter. We put on Motown records and danced in the afternoon, just for the pleasure of dancing. It was his capacity for play, above all, that set him apart from my husband, who seemed to me at that time grimly bent on advancing his career.

At first David told me that he was bisexual, but as we spent more and more time together, as we fell in love, he changed that to homosexual. He had had sexual relationships with women in the past, but always felt put upon, as though he were being asked to service them. However keenly he appreciated certain women — and he really did like women — his sexual excitement was aroused only by men. He wanted to be quite clear that he had no intention ever of making love to me, and that, whatever happened between us, sex was not a possibility. He needed me to reassure him that that didn't matter.

It didn't matter. Perhaps unusually naive, I was not accustomed to expressing my attraction to people through sexual activity. My husband was the only man I'd been to bed with, and sex with him had moved onto the battleground of late-stage marriage: my refusal to be aroused, my greatest weapon against him, provoked from him a fierce determination to arouse me — which utterly turned me off. It had come to seem that whenever he was especially nice to me he intended seduction. I wanted affection. I wanted diversion. I wanted a secret life, perhaps, and excitement. But I didn't especially want sex. Affectionate gestures and moments of intimacy which were not merely preludes to sex seemed a great luxury, and a homosexual lover was from many points of view a perfection I could not have thought up for myself.

What David and I shared seemed to me more fun than sex. We shared music, poetry, art, clothing, antiques, jokes, and gossip. Sometimes, on the pretext of one piece of business or another, we went from our homes an hour and a half away to New York, where the city served as a grander playground than our usual one. On the streets, he noticed everything. "That man was attracted to you," he'd say, or "That man noticed us both." In the stores, he tore through racks of clothes saying, "This is good for you" or "That's impossible" with a decisiveness I found appealing and a vision of my style I found flattering.

He enjoyed dressing me and seeing me play different roles. It was part of the theatricality of his approach to life. Whatever we did, we not only did it, we observed ourselves doing it, so that having a hamburger and a bloody mary for lunch, running into an old friend from college, became the stuff of Noel Coward comedy in the instant replay that was our conversation. All this contrasted favorably with the mode of discourse I engaged in with my poor at-a-disadvantage husband in our discussions of our daily life, which tended to be analytic, drearily searching for motives and assessing effects, hopelessly bound to reality and the problems of everyday life. On one hand I had someone who rebuked me for failing to record checks in the checkbook or for spending $50 on cosmetics; on the other I had someone who would calculate delightedly that his printing press cost the same as corned beef, $3.50 a pound.

We loved to sing while driving. We specialized in lyrics from Broadway musicals of the 1950s and got a particular pleasure from recalling all the words to introductions, like that of "Shall We Dance?" The recitative of the intro, a kind of pathless waste we had to negotiate, prepared for the grand, melodic outburst of the song itself, fulfillment after suspense. In the duets, we had a kind of communion: the words in our minds overlapped exquisitely. In the car, we had intimacy without the possibility of sexual demand.

One trip to New York stands out in my mind because after we got back to New Haven, after David, my husband, and I had had dinner, David seemed unusually anxious to be on his way again. He did not tell me until days later that he had a party — for men only — to go to in New York that night. He had not left me in the city and let me drive back to New Haven alone — the sensible thing to do — because the day would have seemed incomplete. He had not even told me about the party because he did not want to spoil a day of perfect intimacy by mentioning something that did not include me. For that delicacy he did an extra roundtrip from New Haven to New York, three hours of driving.

Details of the party, when they came, were fascinating and even exciting to me and my husband. At midnight, about the time that we were going to sleep, the party became an orgy. Many people left, but the rest began coupling up and retiring to bedrooms. They would make love, emerge, find a new partner, make love some more. The host wandered from bedroom to bedroom offering orange juice. At three o'clock he rang a bell and summoned everyone from the bedrooms to partake of masses of Chinese food which had been brought in. David had gone to the party with Jim, but no, he said, of course they didn't make love with each other at a party like that. They can do that any time. And what would they have had to talk about on the drive home?

From my point of view, David changed my relationship with my husband in good ways. For one thing, David, a connoisseur of men, enjoyed my husband's company and admired his looks: I found him more attractive by seeing him through David's eyes. For another, my demands on him eased as David provided more and more of the laughter and joy in my life. I was no longer so resentful and disappointed.

But my husband had not signed on for a ménage à trois. Although at first he had liked David well enough, he came increasingly to resent his presence in our lives and household. What made me feel free to introduce David into our daily routine — the fact that we were not sleeping together — made it from my husband's point of view so much the worse. It was only too clear that I preferred David's company to his, even *without* sex.

David, too, had needs and desires I found not entirely convenient or comfortably triangular. I suspected him of wanting to make people think that we were having an affair when we were not. He came into my office too often, too ostentatiously. He touched me in public, although he never did in private.

Things became uncomfortable. When he treated me seductively in public, I was seduced. I thought he finally meant to make love to me. I became obsessed with making love with him in a way I had not before. I was in the grip of the rescue fantasy:

I thought if only the circumstances were right, if it was easy enough, relaxed enough, we would fall into bed together and I would save him for women. That nothing about our situation was easy or relaxed did not occur to me. In my fantasy, only ideal circumstances prevailed. I pondered obsessively the nature of homosexuality. Before I'd met David, I had thought homosexuality was a choice you made, like the choice of whether or not to take up golf. Now I saw it was not so simple. He liked to think he was free to choose, but I wasn't convinced. Often he seemed to want to make love to me but was more afraid of failing at it than he was desirous of trying. He told me that his relationship with me had made him see how delicious it would be to live with a woman and raise a family. He said he intended to do just that, when he was forty, after the pleasures of sex had waned. He said this as a politician might talk about the joys of raising begonias in the country — after he was no longer electable.

At about this time — it was the early 1970s — Carolyn Heilbrun published a book about something she called "the ideal of androgyny." Lytton Strachey, the flamboyantly homosexual author of *Eminent Victorians* who had asked Virginia Woolf to marry him one day and took it back the next, was an example of the androgynous ideal. I was in the middle of writing a book about Virginia Woolf and had my own thoughts about Lytton Strachey. When I discussed Heilbrun's book with my colleagues in the English department, I pooh-poohed the idea of Strachey as androgynous. "He was a queer maintaining a fiction of heterosexuality," I said with some feeling. "Carrington was in love with him, he was in love with Carrington's husband, Carrington's husband was in love with Carrington. It was a situation in which no one was satisfied. Androgynous ideal, my foot!"

And yet, it sometimes seemed to me that David represented something new — not just in my life, but within the range of possibilities for masculine life in America. It seemed to me that he was an antidote, not just to my husband, but to an ideal of masculinity in America that had become unsatisfying, both to the men who lived it and to the women who lived with those men. In those heady years of hippy culture, communes, sexual experiment, new forms of marriage, and breakthroughs for women, it seemed possible that a new kind of man could come into being, one less focused on the classic success track, more open to emotional experience and expressing emotion, clinging less to the traditional division between work (male) and family (female), defining himself less by aggressiveness and domination than the classic patriarchal male, and willing to cede some of what had been male turf to women. A bending of masculine and feminine, a new womanly man for the new manly woman.

It was hard for me in those years — and I suspect for others — to separate what was happening to me from what was happening to my generation, how to know what was personal experience and what was historical. We were so aware of living at a time of change. My marriage was a mess. But it also seemed Marriage as an institution was in crisis. There was a new man in my life, very different from my husband. Was there a New Man evolving, different from the traditional patriarchal male? It seemed possible.

The new man, of course, could be exasperating. Sometimes his theatricality seemed no more than narcissism. One day we had a date to play tennis. It turned out that he didn't play tennis, but he'd always wanted to arrive at the tennis court in a sports car and emerge in whites twirling his racket. So we played that scene. But it bothered me. It's interesting to me in retrospect that it bothered me more to play at playing tennis than it did to play at having an affair. Maybe because I knew that I knew what tennis was, but I wasn't so sure about love.

Afterward, back at his house, when he changed from his tennis clothes into regular clothes, he came from his bedroom into the living room to display himself at every stage: first with blue jeans and no shirt, then jeans and unbuttoned shirt, then with his shirt neatly tucked in, all ready to go. He wanted, I felt, to make me desire him. He also wanted me to make no move, to accept his unavailability. I complied. I admired. I told him he looked good. I made no move.

I had assured him that sex didn't matter. At first, it didn't. When sex came to matter, the first, passionate stage of our relationship had to end. I had to sort out in my own mind whether David had alienated me from my husband, or whether my alienation from my husband made me receptive to David. When I decided that the latter was true, that David was, in effect, an embodiment of a need, it was only a matter of time and gathering courage before the marriage ended.

David and I have been friends for twenty years now. We're fossilized, in many senses. I could not describe the whole of our friendship or even define how much and exactly what his presence in my life has meant. We have taken and ignored each other's advice, we have solved and complicated each other's problems, we have done each other favors, given each other gifts, and provided each other with new friends. We have traveled together, entertained together, subscribed to the opera together, had Thanksgiving dinner together, found babysitters for my son together, exchanged clothes, and fantasized about sharing our declining years. My husband, whom I married sixteen years after my first marriage ended, has had to assert his rights in the face of so long-standing a friendship. He has had to establish that our house is *our* house, that David can't come into it any time he wants. He has had to establish that we are a pair, not two parts of a triangle.

I say that he has had to assert his rights but that isn't accurate enough. My husband has not felt the need to make a similar assertion of his primacy in my life to my female friends, no matter how long-standing our friendships. If I spend two hours a

day on the phone with Wendy, for example, my husband thinks
that is my business entirely. If I spent that much time on the
phone with David, he would resent it. David is a man, after all.
Old patterns of jealousy and suspicion die hard, and perhaps it
is also true that David presumes on a privileged position. At
times he has managed to give the impression — as unwelcome
to me as to my husband — that the real and enduring tie is between me and David, my marriage merely an episode, a temporary entertainment.

Now a friendship between women, now a friendship between
men, now a friendship between a man and a woman with seduc-
tive undercurrents, now a straightforward friendship between a
man and a woman with no undercurrents of sex at all, the
friendship between a man like David and a woman like me is
perhaps especially rewarding to the people involved and especially threatening to others because its nature is so protean, so
shifting, so unclear. The man and the woman get to play out
many parts of themselves within the friendship. Observers can't
be sure what it is they're witnessing. During the most intense
time of my relationship with David, the Restoration comedy *The
Country Wife* was being performed at a local theater. I thought
it would be fun for David, my then-husband, and me to see it
together until I remembered the plot: a man pretends to be a
eunuch in order to gain access to the wives.

Between a gay man and a straight woman the bond is special
for many reasons, not the least of which is that the possibility
of *some kind* of marriage — whether consummated or not —
underlies it, and marriage, trailing as it does its legal implica-
tions, is still the most socially serious of voluntary ties. For
people to ally themselves so conspicuously for other reasons
than procreation and sexual companionship is subversive. It in-
tensifies the insidious suggestion implicit in this kind of friendship — a suggestion in no way undermined by the enthusiastic
promiscuity of pre-AIDS gay bathhouse activity — that sex is

not as important as we're told it is, and certainly not as important as play, fantasy, mutual support, and affection. One way of defining the difference between homosexual men and heterosexual men of my generation is that the gay men I know have more friends and dedicate a whole lot more time to friendship.

Not long ago my eighty-six-year-old mother went to a reception at the Metropolitan Museum of Art in New York. For various reasons, none of her three children could go with her. She very much wanted to go and could not manage it alone, so I asked David if he would take her. He kindly agreed. He is fond of my mother and he misses his own mother, who died a few years ago.

Their outing was a success and, in the telling, sounded much like a date. Mother, taking David's arm, had no trouble negotiating steps, turns, and obstacles that would have impeded or intimidated her alone. She felt, she said, like she had wings. To people she knew, she introduced David ceremoniously, "This is my friend," and she gave his name. "He is a professor of art," and she named the university. Even second hand, I could feel the wonder in Mother's acquaintances and sense how suddenly more glamorous she must have seemed to them. What was she doing with this younger man who looked like a gypsy and was certainly not her son? Could it be? Could Minnie — though hampered by a heart condition, winded, half blind, shrunken with age, and bent from osteoporosis — have been visited by Venus? That old magic had cast its spell again, spreading the glitter of uncertainty and possibility.

For David, the loveliest moment came when my mother turned to him and said, "You know, I introduce you as my friend, but you're not my friend. You're my stepson." He took it as she meant it, as a badge of honor, an acknowledgment of ties she considered closer than those of friendship. David was one of the family. At the highest reaches of friendship, these are often the metaphors that come to mind: you are my sister; you are my brother; we are married for life; I consider you my son. But I confess that I was taken aback when my mother used the word stepson for David, perhaps because I find it an ugly-sounding word and perhaps because the relationship between child and stepmother is so fraught with fairy-tale suggestions of malevolence. For me, for him, there is no better word than friend.

JANETTE TURNER HOSPITAL

𝔛 𝔛 𝔛 𝔛 𝔛 𝔛 𝔛 𝔛 𝔛 𝔛 𝔛 𝔛 𝔛

Old Friends Are Best

> Old friends are best; King James used
> to call for his old shoes; they were
> easiest for his feet.
>
> —John Selden,
> seventeenth century

IN A NOMADIC LIFE, easy-come easy-go friendships are as common as mail-forwarding cards, a pleasant convenience. They make no demands of us once we have moved on. We couldn't live without them, but they expire. They leave no trace and no regrets. Other friendships linger, who knows why? We stay in touch, write letters, make phone calls, and will gladly pull out the sofa bed on one another's behalf at any time.

Then there are the friendships that are part of muscle and blood. These are of a different order altogether, usually, but not always, going back to childhood, high school, college, the young parenting years; and tattoos are easier to erase than the grooves these leave in a life. You go to school with someone, you work alongside another, you share dull chores and perfectly ordinary days until *whoosh,* some moment of fission occurs when the two of you step out of the cordial shallows and give off a different light, and you feel, as it were, the scorch marks on your skin.

Tattoos, scorch marks, does this sound oddly like anguish?

Adieu, adieu, kind friend, adieu, a friend in need, etcetera, but the best of friends must part, faithful are the wounds of a friend, friends, Romans, countrymen, *et tu, Brute?*, he makes no friend who never made a foe, some great misfortune to portend / no enemy can match a friend.

Ah, yes, friends of the ten-year, twenty-year, thirty-year-or-more club, *cost.* When I bleed, they bleed. And vice versa. Aye, *there's* the rub. For me, at any rate, the durable bonds, arising out of shared history, seem to have been forged out of a volatile mix of shared joy and shared pain.

I am soldered to such friends, joined from memory to hip. Siamesed. I tell them like beads. Our bonding has nothing to do with geographic proximity (unless, perhaps, *inversely*), nor even with any diligent "staying in touch." Here is their litmus test and sign: whether we make contact after two months, two years, five years, ten, it always seems as though we last spoke yesterday. We have intimate knowledge of each other's vulnerabilities, so there is never any pretense, any façade, any face-saving, any need for it. Metaphorically, we always see each other naked, but without sentimentality, condemnation, or risk. Anger might be present from time to time, we may flex the capacity to give and receive pain (and who is more expert than the close friend?), and yet trust is absolute, reconciliation is swift, love (*caritas,* not *eros*) endures. For these bonds, "friendship" seems a pallid, inaccurate word. I think of such people as blood kin.

In a lifetime, if we're lucky, we might be blooded and bonded in this way a dozen times. Some of my blood kin are lost, some are dead, some dead by their own hand, though none is any less present in my life for all that. In this essay I will speak only of Patrick — Australian, my age, my schooldays twin, my fellow head prefect in high school, fellow competitor for all the high school prizes, mirror of my own subtropical past. Of Patrick, who now moves between Australia and North America; of Patrick, whom I've known for nearly forty years.

I choose to speak of Patrick in particular because true friendships between a man and a woman are so rare; because it is so tricky (for us heterosexuals) to keep walking the fine line of intimate friendship without ever sliding into a love affair; and because it is to me so remarkable to lose someone for twenty years and then find him again, and so reassuring to be still such frantic rivals and such good friends.

Picture the high school students of Brisbane, Australia, in the year 1957, on the twenty-seventh of January, a slow, steamy scorcher of a day, the day after Australia Day, the first day of the new school year. Picture in particular the fourteen-year-olds, still wet behind the ears from grade eight and the state scholarship examination, that feared entrance ritual for high school. All over the city, they stand at tram stops and bus stops, waiting, or they cluster on platforms, watching for their trains.

The boys are self-conscious in socks and shoes (most of them went barefoot for the eight years of primary school), uneasy in their first pair of long trousers (gray flannel), in their uniform shirts and school ties, their hats banded with the colors of their new tribe.

The girls wear thick stockings (murder in the wet heat) and heavy black lace-up shoes. They wear regulation tunics and blouses, felt gloves to match, banded hats. They crane their necks about like awkward chickens, unaccustomed to wearing ties, disliking the damp heat rash at the throat. From time to time, surreptitiously, they nudge at a suspender belt that is cutting into buttock or thigh.

No one dares to loosen a tie, leave a button undone, a glove off. Such laxities would bring down a range of arcane punishments. High school is archaic tribal culture in Brisbane. Everyone is known by cut of uniform, school colors, the design on a blazer pocket. Unseemly behavior in uniform is a sin.

On Newmarket Railway Station, all the uniforms are burgundy and blue. They are all waiting for the train that will move on through a catchment area of six more stations before depositing them, a multiheaded burgundy-blue monster, at Mitchelton Station, from which they will walk another mile to Mitchelton High.

On Newmarket Railway Station, I am quaking with fear. I don't know a soul. Just about everyone from my primary school, at the edge of a different catchment area, is going — by tram and bus — to Kedron High. Not that this is without advantages. At primary school, for one reason and another, I was marked, and I am hopeful of shedding a contaminated past. No one knows me here. No one knows anything about me. My uniform, hot and new and prickly, offers blessed anonymity. I don't look different from anyone else, a state which has been my notion of hitherto unattainable bliss.

Just the same, I'm terrified. I don't know a soul. I am certain I am the only person on this platform, at this high school, who doesn't know anyone else, who has no defender, no friend. What if it all happens again?

There is a boy I recognize by sight because he lives a few blocks away from me. I've never spoken to him. He went to a different primary school. He bounces his briefcase against his knee and looks about him disdainfully, chin tilted up, nose in the air. I recognize the type. He thinks he knows everything, he despises girls, he is never troubled by the shadow of self-doubt. I hate him.

"But I was *ill* with nerves," Patrick tells me thirty years later. "I was *vomiting* before I left home. And as for you, what a stuck-up little smarty-pants you were. You always got everything right, what a show-off, I couldn't stand you."

1957–1960

For four years, we waited together on Newmarket Station every morning, we rode the train together every day, walked up the Mitchelton hill together, sat in the same classes, rode the train home, and then stood on the corner of Patrick's block, which came before mine, for anything from fifteen minutes to two hours, arguing. We argued physics and chemistry and math. We argued Shakespeare. Patrick said Wordsworth was a sook. I said it was outrageous to call Wordsworth a crybaby. I said Patrick didn't know what he was talking about. Patrick said like all girls I was stupid. I told Patrick he made me sick.

"I'm going," I would say, turning on my heel. We had hours and hours of homework ahead of us. There were, in those days, rigorous expectations by teachers of at least four hours' work per night. I might get ten feet closer to home. "But I will admit," Patrick might say, "that in *Tintern Abbey*, at least . . ." And I'd turn back, and we'd talk for another half hour. "Well, I've got to go," he'd say, panicked about the work to be done. And I'd say: "I still think you're wrong about that condensation experiment, I still think . . ." And he'd turn back and we'd argue some more.

Those two, our mothers said, will argue till the cows come home.

We were always neck and neck at exam time, both at the top of the class. Patrick beat me in the sciences and math, I beat him in English, Latin, French. I suppose everyone else thought life was an academic breeze for us, but we even got ill with anxiety together. Exams were hell for both of us; on the nights before, we were sleepless, vomiting wrecks. I never thought of myself as studying to beat Patrick; I thought of my frenzy as studying to survive. We both constantly expected and dreaded failure (not that we admitted this to anyone else; we did our damnedest to be nonchalant on the surface). But I don't think there was any disguising our terror to ourselves. It was genuine. We competed for everything, even intensity levels of the fear of public disgrace. We both thought of exams that way — as occasions for potential public disgrace — though once the exams were behind us, we watched like hawks the marks being posted. We were always neck and neck. We always sparred. If I'd ever analyzed then what I felt about Patrick (I don't think I did; there wasn't any reason to), I believe I would have said he was one of my best friends and that I hated his guts.

Once I had a poem published in the *Telegraph,* the evening paper, and earned five shillings for it. I was immensely, but very secretively, proud of this. I wasn't expecting anyone at school to notice it. My poem was called (oh, so typically colonial a title!) "The Scottish Burn." (Poetry still happened *over there.*) Patrick clipped it out, brought it to school, and never said a word to me on the train or on the way up the hill, though he seemed to be buzzing with some sort of suppressed inner mirth. Between classes, he stood and read my poem out loud, unctuously, satirically, with a plum in his mouth. A plum? With a mouthful of treacle.

I'll kill him, I vowed privately — though, from this distance, I have to admit his critical judgment was way ahead of mine.

Anyway, I had sweet revenge. Patrick was in love with a girl a year ahead of us who got on the train at Alderley, the station after ours. Her name was Margaret Starr, and Patrick used to stare at her, lovelorn. She was indeed beautiful and also, as the boys used to say, she was stacked. One day I found, scored with a ballpoint on the underside of his desk, this cryptogram: AMO SIDUS.

I wrote a quadratic equation, anonymously of course, on the board between classes:

AMO SIDUS = I love a star
Patrick X + Margaret Guess Who? = LOVE

I took enormous pleasure in Patrick's discomfort, for thereafter boys in the class used to chant the phrase softly whenever Margaret Starr happened by. "*Amo sidus, amo sidus, amo sidus,*" they would murmur with sibilant glee. Patrick would color up like a sunburn casualty, and I would raise innocent eyebrows and give him my most beatific smile. *I'll kill you,* his eyes would promise. Privately, I was in fact deeply impressed by the witty cross-linguistic pun, though I would sooner have died than tell him so.

In our third year, we both, alone from our school, made it

into the statewide public speaking finals of a contest sponsored by Shell Petroleum. We both won certificates of merit and a modest cash prize. Neither knew the other had even entered the contest until we met at the awards night in the city hall. We had to listen to each other's presentation speeches. I was impressed with Patrick's; Patrick, I recall, mocked mine on the train the next day, mimicking my gestures. For some reason, I don't recall minding, I think because the adjudicator had commented favorably and I felt immune.

The awards night was the first time, and I think maybe the only time, that I met Patrick's father close up — to speak to, I mean — and I suppose it was the only time he met mine. Everyone knew everyone else's mother, but fathers were foreign turf. They were never around. They were always away at work — though, when I thought about it, Patrick's father *was* around when I dropped by Patrick's place. Sort of around. Around in the distance. He would be mowing the lawn, or tinkering with something. He didn't pay any attention to us, and we didn't to him, but this didn't seem out of the ordinary. I don't recall thinking about it particularly. I suppose I thought his dad was shy, but most people's fathers were inarticulate. Apart from the decidedly odd fact that Patrick always called his parents by their first names — Bessie says this, he would say; Joe says that — I didn't register anything out of the ordinary.

I did ask him why he called them by name, which struck me as bizarre, rude, sacrilegious even. I'd never heard of anyone who did such a thing. Patrick's older brother and only sibling did so, too. *Why?* I demanded. *Because,* Patrick said.

Thirty years later, Patrick tells me: "I lived in a sweat of embarrassment about my parents. I lived in *dread* of other kids meeting them."

"Why?" I ask, startled.

"*Why?* They were so much older than anyone else's parents, that's why. My father was as old as everyone else's *grandfather*."

"He was?"

"Janette," he says, impatient, exasperated, "it was *obvious* he was."

"Was it? It wasn't obvious to me."

"And my father had a wooden leg."

"He did?"

"He was a TPI from the war."

Totally and Permanently Incapacitated: it was not too uncommon among the fathers of kids I knew at school. Just about everyone had TPIs in the family somewhere, a father or an uncle, casualties of Japanese prisoner-of-war camps in New Guinea, on the Burma railway at Changi. We were all war babies. I close my eyes and summon up the shadowy figure pushing the lawnmower at Patrick's place. I cannot recall being aware of any sign of disability.

"He was an old man when I was born," Patrick says. "He had shell shock. They never went anywhere, they never saw anyone, they lived totally inside our house. So he never did anything with us that other fathers did with their sons. I used to have to watch other families all the time, to find out what was normal."

"Yeah," I sigh. I know what that is like. "That's the way *primary* school was for me. But I stopped having to do it in high school. I felt so safe in a uniform."

In our senior year we were appointed school captains, and also, respectively, Head Prefect of Boys, Head Prefect of Girls. There were in fact six of us, riders in the train, all school prefects, who had become a close group. It was in our senior year that we began cycling up into the rain forest which sent tentacles down from the mountain range toward our school. We went hiking, and some weekends we camped at Cedar Creek Falls, swimming together in the rock pools, and climbing.

There were things the group did without me. They all went to "the pictures" on Friday nights; Saturdays, they went to the record hops; they went to school dances. These activities were forbidden to me, but the best thing of all about my high school friends was that they accepted my restricted social life as something apart from me, a curious affliction I was saddled with. They never made fun of me on this score. I loved them for it.

Patrick and I graduated from the statewide matriculation exam with distinction and went on to the University of Queensland. There our paths forked into science and arts and I didn't see him, other than fleetingly in the cloisters or the refectory, for several years. Nor did I think about him.

1965

We bumped into each other in the university cloisters. There was mutual delight and excitement. Having already spent a year teaching in the equatorial far north of the state, I was still finishing off my degree at night. I was very recently married, and the prospect of going overseas for my husband's Ph.D. was dazzlingly close.

Patrick had embarked on his master's degree in physics, and was planning to go to Melbourne for his Ph.D. He was engaged to be married.

There was something prickly about this quickfire exchange of news. You certainly couldn't say we were jealous, though Patrick remarked tartly that Australians shouldn't think they had to go off to America for a doctorate. And I thought, startled: Patrick getting *married?* A romantic thought about Patrick had never crossed my mind; and vice versa, I'm sure. We'd both mooned about other loves in high school. Patrick was more or less an extension of myself, not boyfriend material. It struck me now, with some surprise, that he was a very attractive man. Not *my* kind, of course, but still . . .

I think it was just primitive childhood possessiveness that I felt (*What's she like then? Bet she doesn't know him as well as I do!*), and an extension of old academic rivalry that he felt

(*Trust Janette to marry someone going to do a Ph.D. at Harvard. Showoff!*). As much out of curiosity to see his girl, I think, and out of a desire to show off my husband, I invited Patrick and his fiancée to our place for coffee and dessert. It was a cordial but slightly strained evening.

Patrick's fiancée looked expensive and immaculate, as though she had stepped out of *Vogue* magazine. She was studying law. She was, I thought, politely bored with us and with our nest. I felt totally intimidated by her, suddenly gauche and clumsy.

I was also astonished. I thought of Patrick's house and of my parents' house. We'd both come from very modest working-class backgrounds. Our high school was working class. We all bought our clothes at discount stores or wore hand-me-downs. But Patrick's fiancée came from a wealthy sugarcane-farming family, she had gone to private school, she clearly did not buy her stunning clothes at discount stores. She was landed aristocracy.

I thought of the times we had stood on Patrick's corner and vied to say scathing things about the private-school kids. But if I felt that he had let down the side, I didn't hold it against him. What I felt was awe. I felt the way I had, I think, when I discovered the Latin pun on his desk. How did he do it? How did he manage this?

I felt he had gone through some door that was locked to me, and up some staircase, and would henceforth live on a different plane. It wasn't that I wanted to follow. I was in love, and happy, and excited about going overseas. I just felt some vague sadness that I couldn't quite name, and I thought Patrick and I would probably never see each other again.

1985
I am returning to Brisbane with husband and children and — *mirabile dictu* — a literary reputation. My third novel is being

published in Australia, and my Australian publisher has done some advance publicity. There has been an article in the Brisbane paper. I've won overseas literary awards. I'm the local kid made good in the Big Wide World and I'm coming home. People come out of the woodwork of my past and phone my parents. A high school reunion of our senior class has been organized. (This is not at all an Australian thing to do. There are no alumni societies, no records of addresses or career moves have been kept. I've stayed in touch with no one. The whole thing has been possible only because everyone's parents are still living at the same addresses as back then.)

But there's been a catch, the organizer tells me. Patrick's father has died. His mother has given the organizer two Melbourne phone numbers: one for the research laboratories where Patrick works, and the other his home number. Patrick's mother has warned, however, that he keeps his home phone unplugged all the time, except for dialing out. One has to call his laboratory and leave a message with a secretary. If one is very lucky, he may call back.

Many attempts have been made to speak with Patrick. Many messages, and full details of the reunion and of my return, have been left. Patrick has not called back.

The reunion takes place, a glorious evening, one of the great nights of my life. It happens to be the twenty-fifth anniversary of our graduation, but that is a pure fluke. Even some of our teachers are here, people I worshipped and admired from afar in those distant years (and thereby hangs another tale for another time, of teachers who, a quarter of a century later, become very dear friends). The night begins sedately at seven, and doesn't end till the wee hours of morning. People have flown in from around the country. If only Patrick were here. . . .

If only he had at least sent regrets.

The next night, at some godawful hour after midnight, the phone rings at my parents' house. My father, half-awake and incredulous, taps on the guest room door. "It's for you, Janette. It's long distance from Melbourne. It's *Patrick!*"

I stumble to the phone. "Bloody typical, Patrick," I tell him, as though I last saw him yesterday on Newmarket Station.

"Well, sorry," he laughs. "But I never get home from the lab till this late."

"I can't believe you'd phone after midnight. You nearly gave us all a heart attack."

"You sound like a bloody Yank," he says, disgusted. "I hate the way you talk."

We talked, I think, for two hours. We argued, we laughed, we got maudlin with nostalgia, we argued, we had fun, we argued. Patrick's marriage had long since gone down the drain of his workaholic habits, he confessed. There had been no children. He was publishing madly, he was frequently invited to give lectures in Europe and Japan, he'd made some breakthroughs in his particular area of physics, he'd won international citations and awards. He was manic with excitement over what he was working on at present. A scientist's life, he said, is ninety-eight percent disappointment and failure. You have a hypothesis, you spend months, years, tracking it, only to find out you were wrong, you were going nowhere. That's simply the way it is, he said. Those are the facts of a scientist's life. But every morning, he said — and I could feel blue sparks and high voltage on the line — every morning I wake up with this furnace inside me. I think: maybe today will be one of the two-percent days. Maybe today will be the day when the breakthrough comes. Every morning, he said, I feel this wild hope. I know I'm a lucky man.

And finally, he said, it's not the careful calculations that matter. It's imagination, intuition, dreams. That's how the breakthroughs come.

But that's what writing a novel is like, I said.

I could hardly bear it that Patrick was 1,200 miles away. "Oh I wish you were here," I said. "My God, look at the time! You're going to have one hell of a phone bill. It would have been cheaper to fly up for the party. Oh, couldn't you come up for the weekend?"

"I can't afford the time," he said. "I can't bear interruptions in my work."

"It's so terrific to talk to you again. Well, at least we can write now."

"I *never* write letters, Janette. I don't have the time."

"Well, I'll write to you then."

"No, don't," he said. "I hate that sort of emotional pressure. It interferes with my work."

"Damn you, Patrick. Well, I'll send you a copy of my book."

"I won't have time to read it," he said. "Listen, I've got to get a few hours' sleep. I have to get back to the lab at six in the morning. I'm proud of you, Janette. I've read the reviews. Keep up the good work. Bye."

1988
I'm heading for Australia again for a book promotion tour, and I've written to Patrick to let him know that I'll be in Melbourne for a week.

He calls my hotel, and we arrange to meet at a pub for afternoon drinks. "But I can only afford half an hour," he warns. "Maximum. I'll have to get back to the lab."

The half hour becomes an hour, becomes two. We are absorbed in each other's life and work. We reminisce and argue and laugh until Patrick says with panic: "My God, the time! I have to get back to the lab. I'll walk you back to your hotel."

For another hour, we stand just outside the front doors of the Hyatt, driving the doorman nuts. Every couple of minutes, one of us, absorbed in discussion, gesticulating, manages to step on the pressure pad that opens the doors. Dimly aware of this, we step off again. The doors open and shut, open and shut.

The doorman suggests we move into the lounge. I second this

suggestion. Patrick, urgently, says *no*, he's just going, he has to go.

He starts to go. But don't you think . . . ? I say. But I just want to add . . . he adds, turning back. This circus goes on and on, much as it used to thirty years earlier on the way home from Mitchelton High.

"Patrick," I ask, concerned for him. "Isn't it appallingly lonely living on your own, working these eighty-hour weeks?"

"Sometimes," he says. "Yes, sometimes loneliness is a problem." He looks away. "Sometimes it's fairly awful. Anyway, I have to go."

"Patrick, wait. Surely there must be some . . . Why don't you . . . ?"

"It's not as big a problem as trying to manage a relationship that interferes with my work," he says firmly.

"I know you won't write," I say. "But how about an international phone call from time to time?"

"I never take incoming calls direct," he says. "You'd have to leave a message with my secretary."

"And would you call back?"

"Maybe," he says. "I can't promise anything, Janette."

1989

I'm in Melbourne, teaching at La Trobe University. Patrick is director of a research institute at the University of Melbourne. I've written, I've phoned his secretary numerous times, I've faxed the institute. No response.

I begin sending wittily rude faxes, warning that I will reveal embarrassing details from his past on the fax machine unless he returns my calls. AMO SIDUS, I fax. To no avail.

I take a cab to the address I have for Patrick, which is close to the university. He lives in an elegant little terrace house, very common in inner Melbourne, and very desirable real estate. They are row houses, two story, with cast-iron lace balconies on the upper floor. They have pocket-handkerchief-size front yards with high pickets of cast-iron fencing in front of them, like a row of black spears on the street.

The gate in Patrick's fence is chained and padlocked. At the risk of impaling myself, I climb over the spiked gate. (I was a notorious tomboy in school days.) The bell on Patrick's front door is disconnected, and the letter slot is nailed shut. The front window is sealed shut with the blind drawn. There's a tree in front of the balcony. I climb it and manage to reach across and clamber over the iron railing onto the second level. There's no way of seeing through the window off the balcony, since it is sealed and shuttered. I bang on the shutters with my fists.

Getting back to the tree is trickier. I begin to fear the upper-crust neighbors will be calling the police any minute. I begin to fear I will break my neck. *Serve you bloody well right,* I imagine Patrick grinning. I have an infuriating suspicion that he is watching me from a crack in the blind. I also have a melodramatic fear that he has worked himself into a coronary collapse.

I tear a page out of my checkbook and scribble a note on the back of it.

PATRICK, WHAT IS THIS ARROGANT SHIT?
ANSWER MY PHONE CALLS, DAMMIT.
ARE YOU OKAY? I MISS YOU. JANETTE.

I twist the note around his doorknob. There is no response the whole time I'm in Melbourne.

I fly out of Australia via Brisbane, and go to see Patrick's mother, taking some flowers with me. She peers out through the veranda louvers before she opens the door nervously, and I remember Patrick telling me at the Melbourne pub that she never leaves the house. She gapes when she sees me. "Janette Turner!" she says as though she's seeing a ghost. She lets me in. "You don't look a day different," she says.

"Mrs. X, is Patrick okay?"

"Yes," she says worriedly, forlornly. "I think so. I never see him, you know. He phones me once a week, but sometimes he forgets. If you get in touch with him, Janette, will you ask him to phone me?"

1990 and 1991
Same routine as for 1989, above. I'm teaching in Melbourne for part of each year, I inundate Patrick with messages, he fails to respond.

1992
Ever hopeful, I've written the standard letter, I've given my current phone number. *I miss you,* I've written. *Dammit, Patrick, this isn't fair. Please call. I promise not to interfere with your work.*

For weeks and weeks I hear nothing, then there's a phone call. I can hear the phone ringing as I come up the stairs to my flat, and I think: it'll stop before I get my door unlocked. It's still ringing as I fumble for my keys, and drop them. Amazing, I think. Must have rung twenty times by now, must be Canada. Must be my son or my daughter. It's still ringing when I get to the phone.

"Janette, listen, I'm giving a lecture out at La Trobe tomorrow at four. I thought you might be interested."

My mind, expecting the far side of the Pacific, is blank. "Who is this?" I demand.

"It's Patrick," he says impatiently. "Who'd you *think* it was? The lecture's at four in the physics building."

Patrick?

"Patrick! My God! *Wait!* What? At four? Oh, heck, that's my office hours. I teach a class myself from five to seven."

"Oh, well," he says. "That's that then. It would have been nice to see you. Gotta rush now. Bye, Janette."

"Patrick, wait! *Wait!*" I'm shouting into the phone for fear he'll hang up on me. "I'll *be* there. I'll *be* there. I'll make arrangements with my students . . . But I'll have to leave at five for my own class . . . now tell me where?"

We have about five minutes in the corridor outside the lecture theater before he begins. We hug like cousins, like siblings. There is (or so it seems to me, anyway) this electric current of pure pleasure zapping around us. I note the way graduate students and other professors treat Patrick with considerable deference. By now I have read articles by and about Patrick. I know that he works in a research area so arcane that there are only about a dozen physicists in the world in this field. I know that they all hunt a specific elusive goal, and that the first team to reach this goal will probably win a Nobel Prize.

I sit near the door, since I will have to leave early, and the lecture begins. I am dazzled. Patrick has a rare quality among experts: he is articulate and lucid; he is able to make the most abstruse material understandable to interested lay persons. He is charming, polished, self-confident, witty. He talks about his work and the nature of his quest and he makes it seem *simple*. He shows slides, he draws quick diagrams on the board. He talks about the need for more graduate students to enter this field. Above all, what he conveys is his passionate excitement about his work. I can see tongues of fire hovering above the heads of enthralled students. Dazed, I think: There are a dozen people in the world in this field. I am so full of awe and admiration that I think: For four years, I sat next to a god on the Mitchelton train and didn't know it.

I hate to slip out to teach my own class. I am furious that I didn't think, while we were in the corridor beforehand, to make some arrangement to meet again. I call the lab the next day and, wonder of wonders, Patrick returns my call.

"You were out-of-this-world fantastic," I rave.

"Did you really think so?" And I can tell by the tone of voice it's a serious question, not *pro forma*.

"I really did. I felt proud just to know you. You were so wonderfully *polished*, so confident —"

"*Confident*," he says sardonically. "You know when you saw me coming out of the men's room in the corridor? I'd been vomiting. I usually vomit for two days before a public lecture."

"Oh Patrick," I sigh. "I thought at least one of us was through with all that. And your pleasure in your work was so *palpable*."

"What's that got to do with it?" he demands. "Of *course* I love what I do."

We arrange to meet for dinner later in the week, and right up until the last minute, I fear Patrick won't show up, but he does. He has, of course, explained that this has to be a short evening, very short, that he only has time for a quick meal then he'll have to rush back to the lab.

It is not a short evening. (I suppose this is why Patrick avoids so assiduously subjecting himself to temptation.) It is a wildly hilarious evening. Over pasta and copious wine, Patrick explains the ghastly complications of funding huge research projects, the sordid politics of it, the academic jockeying for the research pie, the backstabbing, the huge, wearying, time-consuming hassle of having to interrupt the *real* work to secure enough money to keep doing it. It is all dreadfully depressing stuff, but he tells me about it with manic energy and black hilarity, acting out scenes between himself and grants committees, oblivious to the goggle-eyed listeners at other tables in the restaurant, playing both roles in his scenes, jumping up and changing chairs, doing different voices. He discusses his colleague in Tokyo, the problems and advantages of scientific teamwork in Japan, again the money crunch, the Japanese pressure to pull international prizes and prestige from the hat, the terror of failing to do this. I begin to see how his passion and his terror go hand in hand, inextricable. We drink a great deal and laugh a great deal and commiserate.

It doesn't sound so different from the literary world, I tell him. I confess that I love being hermited away writing, but that when a book comes out is my least favorite time. "That is putting it mildly. I *dread* publication," I tell him. "It's like signing up for a stint in the village stocks. My most cherished fantasy is to be out of the country the book is coming out in."

"I wonder what it would be like," Patrick says, "not to feel anxious." We sip our wine, pondering this. "Well, we've survived so far," he says.

"*Survived!*" I say. "In your case, moving among the gods is more like it. Patrick, when you think of our backgrounds, when you think of Mitchelton High, could you possibly have believed . . . ?"

I trail off, and we think of our backgrounds. Patrick's parents had a sixth-grade education; mine, because of the depression, didn't finish high school. Mitchelton High was blue collar. Almost no one's mother had a washing machine; everyone's mother spent Monday pounding with scrub brush and washing board. Some families had cars; most didn't. (Patrick's didn't; we had an ancient Bedford van.) Some families had TV sets; most didn't. (We didn't.)

"How do you account for how we got from there to here?" I ask him, bemused.

"Terror," he says. "That's the simple explanation. Being made fun of when I was a kid. Not just other kids. Teachers would say stuff too."

"Yes. But by now it should mean nothing to us."

"I felt naked," he says. "It was intolerable. I lived in terror that more shameful things — things I didn't even know about — would be revealed. So I made up my mind to be perfect. I made up my mind I would be so good at everything I did that no one would ever make fun of me again. I always think that if I can just achieve the goal ahead, I'll be safe. I'll have reached a point where public disgrace is impossible. But as soon as I get there, I realize I'm not there yet. The stage just gets higher, the audience waiting to make fun of me just gets bigger and bigger. I'm running like crazy to stay in place, and I'm still terrified of making a fool of myself."

"Yes," I sigh. "But we should be able to turn it off. I'm looking for a safe retreat and for *explanations*. I reinvent the world over and over, trying to get it to make sense, and trying to make it safe. But the more I seclude myself to write, and the more I grope for answers, the more public my explorations seem to become, and the more they risk public attack and ridicule. So I often think I will end up mute, and that silence is the only safe place and the only explanation that makes sense."

"Do you know," he says abruptly, intensely, "I sometimes hated you so much for your English marks, I wanted to tear your stupid essays to shreds."

I'm rather shaken by the vehemence of this confession.

"You would dash them off without thinking," he says angrily, "and English teachers would gush over them and give you 19 out of 20. And I'd slave over mine for days and get a 14, with some snide remark written across the bottom. I've never forgiven our English teachers."

He's glaring at me. "Patrick," I say, incredulous, "if you want me to acknowledge that you're brighter than me, no contest. I concede. I've never thought otherwise, for God's sake. *Never*. I fought you tooth and nail in high school because you were like bloody Everest."

Anger leaves him like air from a punctured balloon, and he gulps his wine, sheepish. "Yeah?" He grins at me. "The trouble is, *I'm* never sure. To be beaten by a *girl*, it's so humiliating, it's the ultimate humiliation."

"What?! I don't believe you *said* that. Bloody sexist Neanderthal Australian men!" I fume, exasperated. "You are the limit. You are beyond the pale. You are truly, genuinely *stupid*, Patrick."

It was a rich time, 1992. We had numerous long dinners, long walks, long talks, much serious discussion and much shared hilarity. Patrick actually came to my book launch, though he loathes social occasions. In the last week of term, the day before he was flying out to Japan and I was flying back briefly to Canada and then on to England, he called. We were both frantically busy, marking papers, getting ready to leave. We agreed there was time only for my husband and me to meet him for morning coffee.

The two of us — Patrick and I — talked in great rushes, as though all possible past and future news had to be exchanged instantly in case there wasn't a next time. My husband, affectionate, complained: "It's exhausting just sitting at the same table as you two. You've got to be the two most driven people in Melbourne."

"What?" I said. "Me? *I'm* not driven. It's Patrick who's driven."

"Hah," my husband said.

"Hah," Patrick said.

Anyway, Patrick *was* manic, and also ill. He'd had angina pains and various other extreme symptoms of stress. He said he'd begun to be afraid he'd die before he found — in scientific terms — what he was looking for, and he couldn't bear it. He couldn't *bear* it, he'd have to speed up, he was exhausted. He said he'd been so frantic at the volume of work demanded by the department, paperwork he simply couldn't get done, that in an act of flamboyant despair, he'd burned several years' worth of research notes the night before.

I was horrified. I felt frightened for him.

"It felt wonderful for about five minutes," he said, laughing manically. "Then I thought about what I'd done and was afraid I was cracking up."

"Are you?" I asked nervously.

He laughed. "Probably no more than usual. Anyway, gotta go. Take care of yourself, Janette."

"*You*. You take care of yourself," I said. We hugged fiercely, and he felt as comfortable to me as slippers or an old pair of shoes. "*Please,* Patrick, slow down a bit. You're frightening me."

"It's been good," he said. "It's been good seeing you. It's been good for me."

"See you next year."

"Yeah," he said. "Maybe."

"*Promise.*"

"Can't promise anything," he said.

SUSAN KENNEY

X X X X X X X X X X X X X

Ringing the Net

ONE OF MY HUSBAND'S favorite books was Norman Maclean's *A River Runs Through It*. Perhaps because he had at one
time been an avid fly fisherman himself, the title story held particular interest for him, and he often used the book in one or
another of his classes at the college where he was a professor of
English. We looked forward to seeing the movie together, but
when it finally came out, Ed was gravely ill in the hospital and
couldn't go. So I went to see it with one of our oldest friends —
appropriately enough, the man who had actually recommended
the book to us in the first place. The movie was beautifully pho-
tographed and well-acted, but we agreed that as fine a movie as
it was, the story was still finer. So when I got home, still under
the spell of the atmosphere and the splendid landscape delivered
so clearly by the screen images, I picked our copy out of the
bookshelf and sat right down to reread it. I had always been
particularly moved by the ending — which to this day I cannot
read without weeping — but in going back over the story this
time, I was struck as well by something the narrator's father says
earlier that seems to lead into it.

> "Help," he said, "is giving part of yourself to somebody who
> comes to accept it willingly and needs it badly.

"So it is . . . that we can seldom help anybody. Either we don't know what part to give or maybe we don't like to give any part of ourselves. Then more often than not, the part that is needed is not wanted. And even more often, we do not have the part that is needed."

Maclean ends his story with these words:

Now nearly all those I loved and did not understand when I was young are dead, but I still reach out to them.

Of course now I am too old to be much of a fisherman, and now of course I usually fish the big waters alone although some friends think I shouldn't. Like many fly fishermen in western Montana where the summer days are almost Arctic in length, I often do not start fishing until the cool of the evening. Then in the Arctic half-light of the canyon, all existence fades to a being with my soul and memories and the sounds of the Big Blackfoot River and a four-count rhythm and the hope that a fish will rise.

Eventually all things merge into one, and a river runs through it. The river was cut by the world's great flood and runs over rocks from the basement of time. On some of the rocks are timeless raindrops. Under the rocks are the words, and some of them are theirs.

I am haunted by waters.

Ed died not long after this, in December 1992 at the age of fifty, from a rare form of cancer. The course of his disease was long and, despite extended periods of apparent good health, both physically and psychically difficult to sustain, for unlike most cancers, which, if not cured outright through various combinations of surgery, chemotherapy, or radiation, either progress rapidly to a fatal conclusion or go into periods of remission, his did none of these, remaining a capricious and sinister shadow figure in our lives for well over fifteen years. Yet through it all we were able to raise our two children; continue to work at careers in college teaching we both found rewarding; travel;

write books; hike and ski and sail; lovingly fix up an old house and then happily trade it for a new one; to live a good, full life together, so that in the end Ed's leaving of it, though profoundly sad, was not bitter or clouded by regret.

This is where I come to the part about friendship, for I am convinced that we could not have lived this life together as well as we did for as long as we did, nor seen it come to its peaceful and dignified conclusion, without the help of our friends. In *Sailing*, the novel I based on the first nine years of our experience with Ed's illness, Sara Boyd meditates on the nature of help and friendship, and on the instinctive ability some people have to know exactly the right thing to do at any given moment. On the way to see her husband in the hospital, Sara characterizes these friends as "a narrow fringe of upturned faces ringing the net under this fragile balancing act [the two of them] call their life, and as she heads over toward the hospital to check on Phil, thanks them; thanks too (just in case) a God she still can't quite believe in — but how else to explain the relentless, seemingly vindictive quality of it all? — for giving them such friends." And so in our lives too: it was the love of friends that allowed us to carry on. Friends who with incredible persistence, dedication, creativity, and yes, even humor, surrounded and sustained us through the dark times, and laughed and played with us in the lighter moments, of which there were, I continue to believe, at least an equal share.

Friends. So many times over the years, particularly in the last months, I heard them say the words, "I feel so helpless. I don't know what to do." I even said them myself. Yet when I look back over all these years and months and days, I see them coming in ripples, in waves, a creative tide of helping hands and hearts, reaching out, supporting, caring for us and about us, not always the same people, some going out of our ken for one reason or another and others coming in to take their place, still a constant, steadying presence in our lives, so manifest in what they did and said and gave to us over so many years.

These friends became our extended family throughout these years; often acting invisibly or behind the scenes, and almost always unasked, but even in our saddest and most frenzied moments we noticed their reaching out with countless acts of kindness and support, so that we never lost the feeling that, as the father in *A River Runs Through It* says, there was always someone there with the part that was needed. Thus it was that for us both help and understanding were enacted cooperatively, through the love of many friends acting singly and together, caring and taking care, to create a very special friendship that was the sum of many parts that were given freely, and — though Ed was a proud and independent man — in the fullness of time, accepted willingly.

When I brought Ed's Dopp kit home from the hospital, along with the toothpaste and dental floss, this is what I found inside: a water-stained green scapular; a worn moonshell and a branch of coral; a dollhouse-size plaster Christmas pudding; three silver English threepenny bits, dated 1911, 1912, 1916; three pieces of sea-washed glass, aquamarine, rose pink, and yellow-green; three smooth, palm-size stones, one tan with the likeness of an antelope inked on it, one gray and striated with igneous intrusions (one of Ed's favorite phrases, smacking as it does of paleolithic outrage), one maroon, tumbled wafer-thin by water and polished to a sheen from being rubbed between his fingers. In his desk I found a tiny troll with Day-Glo red hair, a quarter taped to an index card, half of a broken baby rattle, two silver tinkling Chinese balls in a brocade case, and more — tokens that he carried with him or kept nearby, for luck. Never a saver of useless objects, if asked he would have said he didn't really believe in luck, or magic, or kharma, or destiny, or sin and guilt, or even tokens, but these were things that meant something to his friends, and thus to him, and so he kept them always, because they gave them to him and — who knows?

Friends gave us these lucky tokens, and more. They also gave us food — sometimes both together. Twelve years running, as

guests at Christmas dinner, we watched those threepenny bits
that meant luck and good health for the whole year turn up, if
not in Ed's plate of plum pudding, then in mine or one of our
children's, thus keeping it in the family, though to this day our
hosts continue steadfastly to deny they had a thing to do with
this strange run of fortune. Still, not taking any chances, these
same friends sent from Ireland one Christmas the special 1916
coin taped to the bottom of the miniature dessert. Finally, embarrassed, the next year Ed gave all but two back to those who
had sat so long, luckless, at the table — and still ended up with
another to take home. Others made gallons of chicken soup and
lentil soup, scores of matzo balls and blueberry muffins, enough
trays of lasagna to cover the Colby College football field up to
the 50-yard line (I don't want to exaggerate here). They fed us
breakfast, lunch, and dinner; included us in their family meals
not just at Christmas, but at Thanksgiving, New Year's, St. Patrick's Day, Easter, or any old day they thought we might be
hungry, or lonely, or in need of talk or company. They took care
of our children when they were little and when they were big;
our pets when they were hungry or needed walking; our houses
when they needed fixing, even our cars when they needed to go
to the garage.

They wrote us cards and letters, poems and stories, and papers.
Lots of papers. Our students gave us the opportunity to write
glowing recommendations on their behalf to graduate schools,
overseas programs, Japan, Nepal, and Disneyworld, and they
sent us back picture postcards, sometimes even T-shirts, when
they got there. Long-distance friends called from Amherst, Boston, Cambridge, Cherry Hill, Ithaca, Los Angeles, New Orleans,
Bonn, Brussels, Cork, Dublin, Jaca, Paris, Connecticut, Florida,
Indiana, Michigan, New Hampshire, North Carolina, Pennsylvania, Tennessee, Vermont — everywhere it seems but South
Dakota — to offer news, advice, encouragement, tell us stupid
jokes and make us laugh, or just keep in touch. They came many

miles by land, by sea, by air to visit, and we had good times, as well as good food and talk, together.

Of course there was the sailing. After I chickened out, they sailed with Ed in races and for fun, and as he grew more casual in his expertise, one of them both flabbergasted and chastened him by tipping over his supposedly untippable boat. They signed him on as crew and took him sailing in blue water to magical places, the islands of Roque and Damariscove, and Isle au Haut, and helped him gain the confidence to sail alone, which he did often, as well as with good friends. When the time came that he could no longer sail alone, one of his sailing companions made it his mission to go with him at least once a week, and when he became too weak to get himself on board *Metaphor,* he steadied the dinghy Ed still insisted on rowing out, and lifted up his legs, so that he could have that one last summer of sailing his own boat on the ocean he loved so much. At the end of the summer, this same friend sailed Ed and *Metaphor* back to port and sat in the stern while he rowed the dinghy in that one last time.

When the time came that Ed could no longer go on with his work at the college, our colleagues picked up his classes where he left off, met with his students, graded his papers, chaired his committees, ran the department, stood in for him on the dreaded promotion and tenure deliberations. When he had to give up the distinguished teaching chair he'd been awarded and of which he was so proud, the president and the dean of the college brought him an actual chair that he could sit in, with a seal and a plaque that held the honor forever etched in brass — all accomplished virtually overnight.

When there was no longer any hope of further treatment, his doctors gave us enough hope to keep on going as we were, and so we did. Friends rubbed our backs and soothed our psyches; they fed our stomachs and our spirits; they produced pickles, chili, cigars, smoked salmon, lobsters, beer, and bourbon on the rocks, martinis so dry the word vermouth was merely whispered over the glass, hot rice packs for our headaches and cranberry juice for our stomachaches from all of these. When he could no longer go outside to do the yard work, neighbors raked our leaves and cut the grass and clipped the trees. As the days grew short and the fall turned to winter, they got up early to shovel the snow and chip the ice from our driveway, our sidewalk, and our hearts.

When it became clear he would not be leaving his hospital bed, they brought him pumpkins and gourds and Indian corn, and finally a Christmas wreath to hang in the window of his room. They sent flowers and wrote cards and hand-delivered so many daily bulletins from the department that the hospital wondered if we should install a fax. The hospital did install a VCR, only to find the medical staff (and our friends) profoundly shocked by the revelation that Professor Kenney's taste in movies ran to Clint Eastwood, Bruce Lee, and the martial arts. One friend fell off a ladder and broke his back, just so he could keep Ed company for a week. They brought him books and magazines, tapes and movies, Ben and Jerry's ice cream, red Popsicles and yellow Jell-O. His nurses gave him their full attention and their patient, loving care. His doctor stopped by the hospital long past midnight, just to make sure Ed wasn't kidding when he told him he wasn't having *that* much trouble breathing, and of course he'd make it comfortably through the night.

When word got out that I was going to start spending the nights in his room, magically our friends showed up, singly and in pairs, spontaneously, a whole platoon of them, so that, always the good host, Ed sat up one more time and we cracked jokes and sang songs and told stories, and his room was filled with laughter, even though the hallway outside was drenched with tears. His greatest fear was not of death itself, but that he would die choking or fighting for breath, suffering, undignified, alone. So when it came down to those last few days, they logged themselves in shifts, friends and nurses and doctors alike, took turns with our son James and me, so that Ed was never left alone. At literally a moment's notice, a priest whom he had never met came and prayed with him, comforted him and blessed him with the rites of his church, so that he felt at peace.

When the days dwindled down to hours, even minutes, and it seemed there was nothing more to do or say, not even enough time for his daughter, Anne, to drive the long miles home from school to be there when he died, once again, unasked, they came, singly and in pairs, and took turns sitting by his bed, one on either side, and held his cooling hands and kept them warm, and talked to him, not even knowing if he could still hear, and kept him connected to this life for eight more hours until Anne could get there to take one of his hands in hers. Then, unasked, they went quietly away, leaving us alone with him until the last breath came. But the warmth of their love stayed behind, and filled the room, and surrounded us and comforted us all. And so he died just as he had wished, peacefully, with dignity, and not alone.

So all this time, these long years and months and days, these friends were never in fact helpless; they did know what to do. They were there, and we remember. They were our doctors and our nurses, our students and our colleagues, our neighbors, and our friends. They were our family, and they helped us to remember what we were: human, mortal, and alive.

And now, months later, once again recalling Norman Maclean's words about help and understanding, and rocks and rivers and time, what I want to say to all our friends, both near and far, is this:

If, as I believe, our tears are the timeless raindrops, then the river is our laughter, and they all run together to form the current of our lives. You are the rocks by which we held our course, and all of these words are yours.

Thank you.

BIOGRAPHICAL NOTES

SHIRLEY ABBOTT, born and raised in Arkansas, has lived in New York for more than thirty years. *Womenfolks: Growing Up Down South*, a memoir inspired by her mother's death from cancer, is about her maternal heritage. Abbott's latest work, *The Bookmaker's Daughter*, is an exploration of her life with her father who, for many years, "made book" at the notorious Southern Club in Hot Springs. Abbott is currently a medical writer for the *University of California at Berkeley Wellness Letter*.

ROSELLEN BROWN's *Before and After* is a highly acclaimed literary novel that uses a murder to question the nature of violence in society. Brown is also the author of *The Autobiography of My Mother*, *Tender Mercies*, and *Civil Wars*, and of two collections of short stories: *Street Games* and *Banquet: Five Short Stories*. Her poetry is collected in *Some Deaths in the Delta and Other Poems* and *Cora Fry*. She lives with her husband in Houston, Texas.

MICHELLE CLIFF, the Allan K. Smith Professor of English Language and Literature at Trinity College, grew up in Jamaica and the United States and now lives in Santa Cruz, California. She is the author of three novels, *Abeng, No Telephone to Heaven,* and *Free Enterprise;* a collection of short stories, *Bodies of Water;* and two poetry collections, *Claiming an Identity They Taught Me to Despise* and *The Land of Look Behind.* Cliff, who was educated at the University of London, is internationally known for her essays, articles, lectures, and workshops on the issues of racism and feminism.

ANGELA DAVIS-GARDNER is a Charlotte native who teaches at North Carolina State University in Raleigh. She is the author of *Felice,* the story of an orphan who grows up in the 1920s among the nuns at L'Academie du Sacre Sang in Nova Scotia, and *Forms of Shelter,* a novel about abandonment, family secrets, and religious and secular obsessions. Her short fiction has appeared in *Carolina Quarterly, Kansas Quarterly,* and *Greensboro Review.*

JANETTE TURNER HOSPITAL was born in Melbourne, Australia, in 1942, but grew up and was educated in the tropical state of Queensland. She has lived for many years in the United States and Canada, as well as, for briefer periods, in India and England. She now divides her year between Australia and North America, and has taught at the University of Sydney, La Trobe University in Melbourne, M.I.T., and Boston University. Hospital's novels include *The Ivory Swing,* winner of Canada's Seal Award, *The Tiger in the Tiger Pit, Borderline, Charades,* and *The Last Magician.* Her short story collections include *Isobars* and *Dislocations,* winner of the fiction award of the Fellowship of Australian Writers.

SUSAN KENNEY lives in Waterville, Maine, where she is the Dana professor of creative writing at Colby College. She is the author of *In Another Country,* which won the Quality Paperback Book Club New Voices Award for best first novel of 1984, and the novel *Sailing,* based on her husband's battle with cancer. She has also written a series of mystery novels: *Garden of Malice, Graves in Academe,* and *One Fell Sloop.*

MARGOT LIVESEY grew up fifty miles north of Edinburgh, Scotland. She has taught for several years at American universities and colleges including Carnegie Mellon, Williams College, and the Iowa Writers' Workshop. Her first published work was a collection of short stories, *Learning By Heart,* which was followed by a novel, *Homework,* featuring a difficult relationship between stepmother and stepdaughter. Livesey lives in Cambridge, Massachusetts, between teaching assignments.

JILL MCCORKLE, a native of Lumberton, North Carolina, graduated from the University of North Carolina at Chapel Hill and earned an M.A. from Hollins College. She now lives near Boston with her husband and two young children and teaches in the creative writing program at Harvard. Her first two novels, *The Cheer Leader* and *July 7th,* were issued simultaneously in 1984 when she was just twenty-five years old. They were followed by *Tending to Virginia, Ferris Beach,* and a collection of short stories, *Crash Diet.*

JOYCE CAROL OATES, one of America's most acclaimed and prolific writers, is the Roger S. Berlind Distinguished Professor in the Humanities at Princeton University. She is the author of many novels, including *Black Water, Because It Is Bitter, and Because It Is My Heart, Foxfire,* and *American Appetites,* and short story collections, among them *Where Are You Going, Where Have You Been, Heat: And Other Stories,* and *Where Is Here?* Her plays include *Twelve Plays* and *In Darkest America: Two Plays.* Oates is also a poet, with fourteen collections in print, and she is the author of many works of nonfiction, including *On Boxing* and *(Woman) Writer: Occasions and Opportunities.*

CHRISTINE O'HAGAN's first novel, *Benediction at the Savoia*, takes place in the early sixties in the Irish-American neighborhood of Jackson Heights, Queens, a few subway stops but many worlds away from Manhattan. This is the home of her character Delia Delaney, a pregnant thirty-two-year-old whose father and husband are both alcoholics. O'Hagan now lives on Long Island with her husband and two sons where she is at work on her second novel.

MICKEY PEARLMAN is the editor of *America*␣*Women Writing Fiction: Memory, Identity, Family, S*␣␣␣␣*␣er Puzzles: Daughters and Mothers in Conte*␣␣␣␣*␣n Literature; The Anna Book: Searchi*␣␣␣␣␣␣*History;* and *Canadian Women W*␣␣␣␣␣␣*␣hor of A Voice of One's *␣␣␣␣␣␣␣␣*uthor of *Listen to T*␣␣␣␣␣␣␣␣*␣␣en Who W*␣␣␣␣␣␣␣␣␣␣*␣␣r R*␣

Lives. She is a professor of English at Wesleyan University, where she has been on the faculty for more than twenty years.

CAROLYN SEE lives in Topanga Canyon, north of Los Angeles. Her latest work is *Dreaming: Fifty Years of Drugs and Drink in One American Family.* Her novels, *Making History, The Rest Is Done with Mirrors, Golden Days, Rhine Maidens,* and *Mothers, Daughters,* all speak to her long-standing interest in the lifestyles of California and the Pacific Rim. Together with John Espey and her daughter Lisa, See has written — under the collective pseudonym of Monica Highland — *Lotus Land* and *110 Shanghai Road.*

JANE SMILEY's novel *A Thousand Acres* won both the 1992 New York Book Critics Circle Award and the Pulitzer Prize. She is the author of, among others, *Barn Blind, The Greenlanders, The Age of Grief,* and *Ordinary Love and Good Will.* Smiley, who is from St. Louis, has a Ph.D. from the University of Iowa. She lives with her husband and three children in Ames and teaches at Iowa State University.

WENDY WASSER␣␣␣␣␣

for the Arts, and in 1991 the O. Henry Award. Several of Watanabe's stories have appeared in anthologies and literary journals. Her first collection, *Talking to the Dead,* published in 1992, was nominated for the PEN/Faulkner Award.

NANCY WILLARD, who teaches at Vassar and lives in Poughkeepsie, New York, is from Ann Arbor, Michigan. She is best known as a poet — her 1989 collection, *Water Walker,* was nominated for the National Book Critics Circle Award, and her collection of poems for children, *A Visit to William Blake's Inn: Poems for Innocent and Experienced Travelers,* won the Newbery Medal. Willard is also a playwright, the author of the novels *Things Invisible to See* and *Sister Water,* and of a collection of essays, *Telling Time.*

TERRY TEMPEST WILLIAMS has been called one of the new voices of the West. A fifth-generation Mormon, Williams is the naturalist-in-residence at the Utah Museum of Natural History. She is the author of *Pieces of White Shell: A Journey to Navajoland* and the coauthor of *Coyote's Canyon. Refuge: An Unnatural History of Family and Place,* her most recent work, is a memoir. She lives with her husband, Brooke, in Salt Lake City and serves on the governing council of The Wilderness Society. Ms. Williams is a recipient of a nonfiction fellowship from the Lannan Foundation.